A Traveller's Wine Guide to
FRANCE

A Traveller's Wine Guide to

FRANCE

by Christopher Fielden
Additional material by Jim Budd

Interlink Books

An imprint of Interlink Publishing Group, Inc.
Northampton, Massachusetts

First published in 2007 by

INTERLINK BOOKS
An imprint of Interlink Publishing Group, Inc.
46 Crosby Street, Northampton, Massachusetts 01060
www.interlinkbooks.com

Library of Congress Cataloging-in-Publication Data
Fielden, Christopher.
A traveller's wine guide to France/
Christopher Fielden, Jim Budd.—3rd ed.
     p. cm.—(Traveller's wine guides)
Includes bibliographical references and
index.
ISBN 1-56656-624-X (pbk.)
ISBN 13: 978-1-56656-624-7

Printed and bound in China

1. Wine and wine making—France—
Guidebooks. 2. France—Guidebooks.
I. Budd, Jim. II. Title. III. Series.
TP553.F5 2005
641.2'2'0944—dc22

                              2005019330

*Images kindly provided by Sopexa unless otherwise
noted in the text.*

To the grapes, the sun, the soil, and the spirit of France.

CONTENTS

HOW TO USE THIS BOOK

This book is designed for the visitor to France who wants to see how wine is made, to taste it and, possibly, to buy it. While wine can be bought in shops, buying direct from the producer is both more edifying and more enjoyable.

In some towns—Beaune is a notable example—there are a number of shops specializing in the sale of local wines. For the most part, however, French people buy their wine in supermarkets or direct from the grower. They do so by going to a producer's winery or to one of the many regional fairs, where you can taste and buy a range of producers' wines.

Visiting vineyards

This book is about vineyard visiting, though a number of local wine fairs are listed. These are wonderful events for tasting and comparing, though the chances of purchasing more than the odd bottle or two on the spot are small; most of the orders taken are for subsequent delivery. I would not recommend this method of buying wine, however. Direct importation is best left to the professionals.

As you travel through France, you can dip into this book to find basic information about the local wines, the names and addresses of some of the local growers and merchants, and places of interest.

For most areas, too, I give contact details of the organization that promotes the local wines, where they will usually have complete lists of local growers and detailed wine maps of the region.

Tourist offices

I can also recommend a visit to the local tourist office. They are invariably helpful and they can usually come up with some individual or topical advice.

In addition, if you wish to know about the basic driving regulations in France, how many gallons a grower produces when he talks in liters, or the best way of buying wine to bring home, it is all here in this book.

Wine touring

This book is structured around the French motorway system. The French have a marvellous system of roads that are generally very well maintained. Please remember that the French have strict drinking and driving laws, which are now rigorously enforced.

While this book is designed to be as self-contained as possible, it cannot take the place of a road atlas. For detailed maps showing short cuts or scenic routes, the spiral-bound *Michelin Motoring Atlas of France* is essential. It is updated annually. For details of Michelin maps and guides as well as a route planning service, see www.viamichelin.com; further details on page 272.

One of the pleasures of wine touring is the limitless interest of the subject. Each year the wine is different; each season the scenery changes. Around every corner there is a new grower or merchant waiting to be visited.

SYMBOLS

AN	*Appointment necessary*
TF	*Tastings free*
TP	*Tastings cost*
WS	*Wine for sale*
D	*Dutch spoken*
E	*English spoken*
G	*German spoken*
I	*Italian spoken*
H	*Hotel*
H/R	*Hotel/Restaurant*
J	*Japanese spoken*
R	*Restaurant*
S	*Spanish spoken*
T	*Tasting*

There can be few more enjoyable ways of passing time in France than talking to a grower about his or her wine, with a glass of it in your hand. I hope that this book will help you to achieve this satisfaction.

Introduction

A hillside of carefully tended vines with the hut of a vigneron *(wine grower) on the crest. Many of these huts are now disappearing—made redundant by cars and tractors.*

France is no longer regularly the world's largest producer of wine, nor does it have the largest area under vines. Those distinctions belong to Italy and Spain respectively. Nevertheless, it is to France that the consumer tends to look for quality. Although wine is now being made throughout the world, French wines still provide the benchmark against which many producers in other countries assess their output.

France makes the broadest variety of wines. You can find every style of wine there if you are prepared to look for it: not just the classic wines of Bordeaux and Burgundy, but also such rarities as Château Chalon from the Jura, which rivals the finest Fino sherry.

This book should be particularly helpful to motorists who are interested in visiting some of the vineyards of France while they are driving through, because it is based on the motorway system. Although Paris remains the center of the motorway system, this is much less oriented toward the capital than it was. For readers approaching France from the UK, there are now several all-motorway options for travelling south. The A26 will take you from Calais to the Rhône Valley without going near Paris.

The A20 now connects Paris with Montauban by way of Cahors, and the A75 that connects Paris with Béziers and Montpellier was complete with the opening of the viaduct at Millau in January 2005.

Many of the most important wine regions lie close to major roads—who can forget the first sight of the vineyards of Burgundy when the A6 swoops down on the town of Beaune?

Visiting Producers

There are many thousands of wine producers in France; this book can only give a small selection. Some are individual growers who might perhaps work the soil and make the wine with only the help of their immediate families. Others are multinational companies whose brands are household names around the world and whose cellars welcome hundreds of thousands of visitors each year.

Faced with fierce competition abroad, the French are becoming increasingly equipped for wine tourism, making sure that their welcome is more professional, with better facilities for tasting, and that visits are as interesting as possible.

Throughout France there are many roadside signs to tempt you to stop to visit and taste producers' wines, and it is often not essential to make an appointment. However, if there is a particular producer you want to see, it is best to phone in advance, especially if the winery is just a small family affair. They will not have someone always on hand to welcome you—the vines need almost constant attention. If you are unable to make an appointment, do let the producer know. Cellular phones now make that easy to do.

Visiting hours

Most producers are open six days a week from around 9AM to midday and from 2PM to around 6PM. It is still rare for producers to be available on Sunday. It is important to realize that you need a reasonable amount of time for your visit, so don't arrive just before the last time shown.

Don't visit at lunchtime!

Remember that the French take their lunch seriously, so do not arrive too soon before—or after—the lunchtime closing.

At many of the smaller companies, there may well be no one who speaks English. In general, speak French if you can, even if it's rusty. The effort will certainly be appreciated. This book does, however, include a number of firms that are used to receiving tourists and employ multilingual guides to look after the visitor.

Vignerons are hospitable people, but both their time and their stock are precious. Most growers are happy to offer you wine to taste free of charge, particularly if they think that you might buy some.

To spit or not to spit?

It is best to spit out the tasting sample. A few glasses can soon persuade you that the wine is better than it is. Spitting is acceptable in all parts of France. If there is a spittoon (*un crachoir*) provided, make use of it; otherwise spit on the floor—if you are in a cellar, that is!

There are two further things to remember about tasting: first, wine on an empty stomach can have a noticeable effect, so it is wise to take some ballast on board first. Secondly, drinking and driving is as serious an offense in France as elsewhere and your car can be impounded.

To buy or not to buy?

You are not obliged to buy any wine, but no grower can make a living by pouring limitless numbers of free glasses. If you do buy wine, you will pay French VAT (sales tax) of 19.6 percent.

Remember that wine is heavy, and a few cases add considerably to the weight of your car. Try to spread the load, and make sure that your tires have sufficient pressure.

The System of Classification

Vins de table

All the wines of France are classified according to a rigid hierarchy, depending on the potential quality of the wine. At the bottom comes the simple *vin de table*. This may come from anywhere in France and is generally blended from a variety of sources, mainly from within France itself, though other wines made in the European Union can be added if the fact is mentioned on the label.

This is the wine for everyday drinking, sold in plastic bottles or the ubiquitous, returnable, six-star liter bottles. It will have no vintage, and the label will generally give no more than a brand name and the alcoholic degree of the wine. Sales of *vin de table* have been falling for 30 years.

Vins de pays

One step up the ladder come the increasingly important *vins de pays*. There are strictly defined quality controls on these wines—production per hectare, the grapes used, and their source. The region of production may be quite small, for example, the Vin de Pays des Coteaux de Peyriac; from one *département*, such as a Vin de Pays de l'Aude; or from a much wider area such as a Vin de Pays du Pays d'Oc. Up to two grape varieties can now be mentioned on the label.

This category was formally established in 1979 and there are now 11 million liters of *vin de pays* produced. Eighty-five percent of the production comes from the Midi. Some of France's most interesting and best value wines are in this category.

Superior quality wines

Higher up the scale come VDQS wines. The letters stand for *Vin Délimité de Qualité Supérieure* (superior quality wine). These are sometimes traditional regional wines, such as the acid rosé wines of Lorraine called Côtes de Toul, and sometimes wines that are progressing up the ranks. Here the controls on production are more strict—and the prices higher.

At the top of the ladder come the *appellation contrôlée* wines. I say at the top of the ladder, but there one finds a broad platform, which will include wines that have recently been promoted from VDQS status, such as the Coteaux de Giennois, and some of the greatest and most expensive wines in the world, such as the Romanée-Conti from Burgundy.

The label

Whatever the French wine, its classification will appear on the label. Thus you can tell easily where it stands in the classification scale. A word of warning, however: the rating is not necessarily related to quality, but more to the controls that have been made on the production. It is possible to find excellent, and expensive, *vins de table*. Equally, it is regrettably easy to find poor-quality *appellation contrôlée* wines. Perhaps the vineyard is in the wrong place, perhaps the vines are too young, or the grape variety is not accepted in the region. The producer's name is the best guarantee of quality. Here lies one of the real attractions of visiting the growers—the opportunity of discovering a wine that belies its status. Happy hunting!

Château Lagrange: *the name of the vineyard*
2003: *the vintage*
Saint-Julien: *the name of the village where the vineyard is situated*
Appellation Saint-Julien Contrôlée: *the guarantee of the origin of the wine*
Propriétaire a Saint-Julien Beychevelle (Girond): *the name of the company producing the wine*
Mis en bouteille au Château: *bottled at the château that made the wine*
750 ml: *the contents of a normal bottle of quality wine*
13% vol.: *alcoholic strength; thirteen percent alcohol is slightly above the average for French appellation contrôlée wines*

Travelling in France

Highways

For the most part, driving in France is not difficult. There is a remarkable network of roads with an increasingly comprehensive highway system. On the highways, there are frequent rest areas and numerous restaurants where one can eat and drink at reasonable prices. The sign *Aire* means an open-air stopping place or picnic site, usually with restroom facilities. Speed cameras are now installed on highways and main roads.

The cost of highway tolls can mount up, however; if speed is not a priority, there are generally main roads that run parallel. These can, however, be crowded with heavy vehicles also intent on avoiding the tolls.

In any case, all main roads are to be avoided at the beginning and end of holiday periods, even holiday weekends, as traffic jams appear to be endemic. Alternative long-distance routes are marked with green signs. You can keep up to date with traffic conditions through the Bison Futé website (www.bisonfute.equipement.gouv.fr) and also on the radio on channel 107.7 FM.

Gasoline

Gasoline is expensive in France. At the pumps you will find *Super 98 sans plomb* (unleaded), 95 octane unleaded, and *Gazole* (Diesel), which is significantly cheaper than Super. Hypermarkets are the cheapest places to buy gas. Credit cards are almost universally accepted, but a warning—many non-French credit cards do not work in automated 24-hour gas stations.

Car rental

With offices at airports and mainline stations, rentals are easy to arrange. French railways have special combined train ticket and rental deals. The cheapest option is to choose a car with a diesel engine.

France by rail

Travel between Britain and France has been transformed

The quiet charm of Burgundy: nearly empty roads and gently undulating countryside. Image © Nadia Ivanova/Dreamstime

by the Channel Tunnel, which provides a link between the two countries both for motorists and rail travellers.

Paris is now 2 hours and 35 minutes from London by train. The other main Eurostar terminus in France is Lille, on the Franco-Belgian border, with easy connections to high-speed trains going to many parts of France. It is now possible to travel from Britain to France's wine-producing regions by Eurostar and TGV (high-speed train) without passing through Paris.

Travelling at speeds of up to 300 km/hr (186 mph), the TGV from Lille takes about four hours to reach Avignon, the center of the southern Rhône. The Loire Valley is about six hours from London by rail and Bordeaux about eight hours. Paris is, however, still the hub of the French rail system.

France by air

Paris's two airports—Charles de Gaulle and Orly—are the main points for international arrivals. From here there are frequent regional flights, which may be an attractive option if you are headed to the south of France, for example. There is also an extensive network of budget flights from the UK to such destinations as Bergerac, Bordeaux, and Lyon. The two best-known British budget airlines are easyJet (www.easyjet.com) and Ryanair (ryanair.com). Most budget flights depart from Stansted airport, north of London.

Hotels

Hotels are for the most part not expensive, though the bedrooms can be somewhat spartan. The Logis de France is a chain of independent, family-run hotels. They are generally reasonably priced, clean, and comfortable. Bed and breakfasts (*chambre d'hôte*) are another option. They range from simple homes to grand châteaux. Internet sites such as www.likhom.com and www.pour-les-vacances.com carry listings.

There are also a number of hotel chains, found generally on the outskirts of the town, with all rooms having private baths and television, which can be ideal for one-night stopovers. They also have clean, friendly restaurants. Three such middle-market chains with hotels all over France are Ibis, Campanile, and Climat de France. More basic are chains like Formule 1 and Etap. These are very cheap and can be ideal if you need a brief overnight stop, especially if you are travelling late.

Finally, it is always wise to book your hotels in advance. It is increasingly possible to do this on the internet, especially with hotel chains.

Driving in France

Here are a few simple rules about driving in France. Driving is on the right and priority is on the right. In the open countryside, main roads always have priority, but beware of cars leaping out from the right in towns.

Until recently, cars coming into a rotary always had priority, therefore often leading to a position of stalemate. This has now changed and there will be clear signs saying if you now do not have priority. The sign *Giratoire* before a rotary indicates priority on the left.

Carry a valid driving license, vehicle registration document, and proof of insurance; consult your insurer to be sure you have full coverage.

> **SPEED LIMITS**
> _____
>
> **Urban areas:**
> 50 km/hr (31 mph)
> **Normal roads:**
> 90 km/hr (56 mph):
> (when wet)
> 80 km/hr (49 mph)
> **Dual carriageway:**
> 110 km/hr (68 mph):
> (when wet)
> 100 km/hr (62 mph)
> **Motorway:**
> 130 km/hr (80 mph):
> (when wet)
> 110 km/hr (68 mph)

Seat belts must be worn in both the front and rear seats of a car. Children under ten must not travel in the front, except in a two-seater.

Even if no one else was involved, an accident causing injury must be reported to the police, and you should file an accident report form.

In order to reduce the high death rate on French roads, the French government has recently cracked down on speeding and drinking and driving. Fines for speeding and other traffic offenses are heavy. Fines range from 137

Euros for exceeding the limit by less than 20 km/hr (91 if paid immediately) to 1,524 Euros for exceeding the speed limit by more than 50 km/hr, as well as the possibility of losing your license for up to three years. These are levied in cash.

In the case of drunk-driving offenses, the car can also be impounded, as it can for excessive speeding. The blood alcohol limit in France is now 0.5 grams of alcohol per liter of blood. Random breath tests are now common, so do not consider driving after serious cellar visits!

Eating in France

O ne of the greatest pleasures of travelling in France is tasting the wide range of foods that are available. The French are interested in what they eat and drink, and this shows at all levels. Children are welcome in restaurants and most have special menus for children.

Shopping for food

If you want to picnic, you can probably buy everything you need in a supermarket, but if you want to buy everything at the specialist shops, these are the ones to look for:

Boulangerie: the baker's. The traditional French loaf is a baguette; a *ficelle* is a long thin one; and a *miche* is a round one, often made of less-refined flour. A roll is a *petit pain*.

Charcuterie: the pork-butcher's. Here you can buy a broad range of pâtés and sausages. Pâtés can be bought by the slice. Often there is also a range of prepared dishes such as pizzas and *coq au vin*, which can be useful if you are doing your own cooking. If you want take-out food, the phrase to look out for is *plats à emporter*.

Bars and restaurants

As in other countries, there is a broad range of places at which you can eat. The word for snack is *casse-croute*, and these are available in most bars. Most frequently offered are sandwiches, comprising a large slice of French bread with cheese, pâté, or ham. Unless you ask for it there will

not be any butter. Also widely available is the *croque-monsieur*, a welsh rarebit, with a slice of ham.

Moving up a stage, there is the brasserie. Here you can eat a complete meal or just one dish. Normally, there is one set meal and a large choice à la carte.

Restaurants come in a broad variety of styles and prices. Serving hours are generally from noon until 2PM and 7:30PM to 9:30PM, although many brasseries serve food throughout the day. Outside big towns it can be difficult to find places open on a Sunday night and Monday.

The menu

Confusingly, the French word for menu is *carte*. *Le menu* means a set meal (as opposed to the *à la carte* selection). It is compulsory for restaurants in France to display their

menus outside, which gives you a chance to check them out before going in.

There will normally be a selection of menus at a variety of prices. Often there will be a "tourist" menu (*menu touristique*) for a basic price. There may be four or five differently priced menus. There may be a *menu dégustation*, which will include several dishes, but only small quantities of each with the opportunity of tasting a wide range of the restaurant's specialties.

Eating à la carte

In addition to the variety of set menus, there will be an à la carte selection. This can be useful if you do not want to eat too many courses, but it is normally a more expensive way of eating, and, if you do your sums carefully, you may find that you get an extra course free of charge if you take one of the set menus.

By law, restaurant prices now must include any service charge and sales tax.

Champagne

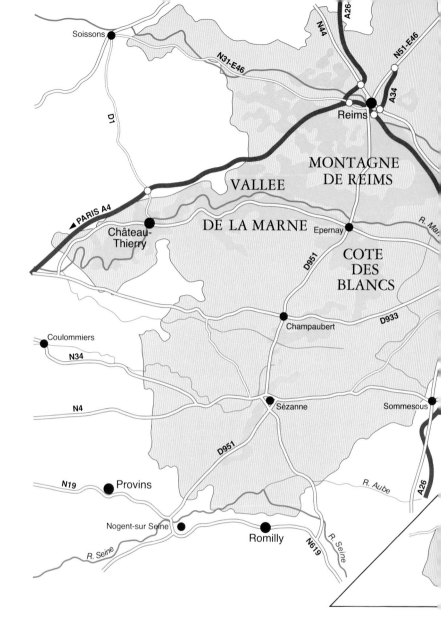

CHAMPAGNE

Of all the wine regions of France, Champagne is for many people the most readily accessible. Its center, the ancient city of Reims, is an easy 90-minute drive along the highway from Paris, and, for motorists from Britain, under three hours from the Channel Tunnel and ports.

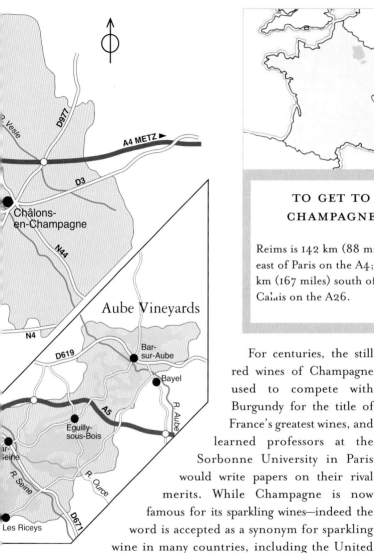

TO GET TO CHAMPAGNE

Reims is 142 km (88 miles) east of Paris on the A4; 268 km (167 miles) south of Calais on the A26.

For centuries, the still red wines of Champagne used to compete with Burgundy for the title of France's greatest wines, and learned professors at the Sorbonne University in Paris would write papers on their rival merits. While Champagne is now famous for its sparkling wines—indeed the word is accepted as a synonym for sparkling wine in many countries, including the United States—it was not until the beginning of the 18th century that the bubbling wine we know today was first made in the region. Though Champagne is for the most part a white wine, it is made largely from a blend of red (Pinot Meunier/Pinot Noir) and white grapes (Chardonnay). The red grapes come mainly from the valley of the Marne and the Montagne de Reims; the white from the Côte des Blancs.

Champagne—How It Is Made

The high reputation, and the price, of Champagne is due to a number of factors. First, the vineyards are among the northernmost in the world and, as a result, it is not easy to make wine every year.

Second, because red grapes are largely used for making a white wine—and a delicate wine at that—particular care has to be taken at the time of picking and pressing. Only Champagne, among the major vineyard regions of France, insists that the grapes be pressed whole as near to the vineyards as possible, rather than at the winery. Each village has one or more press houses.

Pressing

The pressing, too, is tightly controlled, with the grapes being pressed up to five times. The finest wines are made from the first two or three light, rapid pressings. This is known as the *cuvée*. From every four metric tonnes (4.5 US tons) comes the equivalent of thirteen casks of juice. Ten of these are *cuvée*.

The second, a harder pressing, gives two casks of *première taille* juice, with the final cask coming from the *deuxième taille*. These last pressings cannot be made into Champagne.

Fermentation

The juice, or *must*, from all the different villages is then brought to the cellars of the merchant for the first fermentation. When this has taken place, all the distinct wines will be blended together to produce a wine typical of the particular brand. This is also the time when some reserve wines will be added to non-vintage Champagne to maintain the house style.

Champagne bottles have to be especially strong and the cork well-fastened to resist the five atmospheres of pressure inside. Always take care when opening sparkling wine—hold on to the cork and never point the bottle at yourself or anyone else.
© Tom Schmucker/Dreamstime.com

Bottling

The wine is then bottled, with a little sugar and wine yeast added to induce a second fermentation and give the wine its sparkle. This fermentation leaves a deposit in the wine. Removing the deposit was traditionally one of the most time-consuming stages.

Traditionally, bottles were put in sloping racks called *pupitre*. Every day, a specialist workman would give each bottle a quick twist and leave it in a slightly more vertical position. This involved considerable labor and took several weeks. Now most companies have computer-programmed machines that do the job in a few days, though they keep a few *pupitres* for the tourists.

When the deposit has settled on the cork, the neck of the bottle is frozen and the cork removed; the pressure in the bottle forces out the ice pellet with the sediment in it. The bottle is then topped up with wine and a syrup of old wine and cane sugar.

Aging and blending

Most bottles of Champagne remain in the cellars for at least three years before being sold, adding to the price. Champagne is generally made from a blend of wines from different parts of the region and from different years. This enables each company to maintain a house style.

In the best years, companies make a "vintage" wine, with a date on the label.

Other styles

—Rosé Champagne is usually made by blending red and white wines before bottling.
—Blanc de Blancs is made exclusively from Chardonnay.
—Prestige *cuvées* have special bottles and prices.
—The still wines of Champagne are called Coteaux Champenois.

The Champagne Vineyards

There are 33,000 hectares (81,545 acres) of vines planted in Champagne. On a map, the main vineyards of Champagne take the form of a double hook, with the shank lying along the valley of the river Marne. Here is the town of Epernay, where many of the great Champagne companies are based. To the north, sweeping back in a loop, are the vineyards of the Montagne de Reims, above them the town of Reims itself, its massive cathedral dominating the rolling countryside. Most of the other important names of Champagne have their cellars here.

Visitors to the house of Pommery at Reims (see page 24) complete their tour of the cellars near this vast barrel, magnificently carved by Gallé.

The southern barb of the hook is known as the Côte des Blancs. There are also two other areas where champagne is produced. To the north of Reims lies la Petite Montagne; many miles to the southeast are the remnants of what used to be the important vineyard area of the Aube. Because they are from further south, the base wines from the Aube tend to be rounder and less acidic, and so are very useful for rounding out and mellowing those from the classic vineyards close to Epernay and Reims. There is now a renaissance of Champagne production here, but also a specialized rosé wine, Les Riceys, made in very small quantities from the Pinot Noir grape.

The skill in creating one of the great wines of Champagne lies in taking wines from a number of sources and styles and putting them together to make a glorious whole. Unlike the large brands, the small growers do not have the same range of choice. However, growers' Champagne can be very good and distinctive.

REIMS

Champagne Piper Heidsieck

51, blvd Henri Vasnier,
51100 Reims
Tel: 03 26 84 43 44.
Email: visit@
piper-heidsieck.com
Fax: 03 26 84 43 84.
www.piper-heidsieck.com
AN for groups of 15+.
Cellar open daily Mar 1–Dec
31, 9:30–11:45AM and
2–6PM. Boutique open daily
Mar 1–Dec 31,
9:30AM–12:30PM and
2–6PM; open Mon–Fri in
Jan and Feb. Tour by car.
E, S, G, I, D, J.

Champagne
Pommery & Greno

5, place du Général Gouraud,
51100 Reims
Tel: 03 26 61 62 56.
Customer service tel:
03 26 61 62 56.
Fax: 03 26 61 62 99.
www.pommery.fr
TP; reception rooms, cellar.

Champagne Ruinart

4, rue des Crayères,
51053 Reims
Tel: 03 26 77 51 51.
Email: visites-receptions@
ruinart.com.
www.ruinart.com
TP. AN. Open 9AM–6PM.
WS. Reception rooms; cellars
include chalk pits that are
listed as historic monuments.
E, G, D, S, I.

Reims

A historic city

In some ways, the greatest moments of Reims seem to have been in the past. One of the four triumphal gates to the Roman city still remains, the Porta Martis. For more than six centuries, the kings of France were crowned in Reims cathedral.

More recently, Reims has stood in the way of a succession of invading armies from the east. In 1870, for a time it was the headquarters of the Prussian army on its way to capture Paris, and it suffered heavily from bombardment during World War I. The surrender document of the German forces was signed at what is now 12, rue Franklin Roosevelt, on May 7, 1945, to end World War II.

Reims is now an important regional center, though being challenged as the capital of the Champagne trade by Epernay, and having lost out to Châlons-en-Champagne as the administrative center of the *département*. It still plays an important role in the textile trade and is a major shopping center.

From whichever direction you approach the town, it is the cathedral that stands out. It has been described as the most perfect Gothic church building in the world.

The cellars

Of all the wine regions of France, it is in Champagne where branding is the most developed. To support this image, many of the Champagne houses have very sophisticated facilities for welcoming visitors.

While the cellars of Reims may be not as large as some of those of Epernay, some of them have a particular interest, in that they were originally dug in Roman times as chalk pits.

The Montagne de Reims

The Montagne de Reims lies to the south of the city of Reims, though there are some vineyards to the northwest around the village of Merfy. Surprisingly, many of the best vineyards face north—normally, the best exposure to the sun is southeast. Here the dominant grape is the Pinot Noir, which also produces the great red wines of Burgundy.

To join the road that winds through the wine villages of the Montagne de Reims, take the RD380 southwest out of the city in the direction of Château-Thierry. After 8 km (5 miles), turn left onto the D26. This follows the vines around the foot of the hill all the way to the

MERFY

Champagne Chartogne-Taillet
37–39, Grande Rue,
51220 Merfy
Tel: 03 26 03 10 17.

RILLY–LA MONTAGNE

Vilmart et Cie
5, rue des Gravières
51500 Rilly-la-Montagne
Tel: 03 26 03 40 01.
Email: vilmart@
champagnevilmart.com
www.champagnevilmart.com

MAREUIL–LE–PORT

Champagne Comte de Lantage
20, rue de la Chapelle, Cerseuil,
51700 Mareuil-le-Port.
Tel: 03 26 51 11 39.
Email: lantage@lantage.com or
visit@lantage.com
Fax: 03 26 51 11 41.
www.lantage.com
TF. AN for groups of 10+. Open
daily, 9AM–12PM and 2–6PM.

TOURS–SUR–MARNE

Champagne Laurent-Perrier
Domaine Laurent-Perrier,
51150 Tours-sur-Marne.
Tel: 03 26 58 91 22.
Fax: 03 26 58 77 29.
www.laurent-perrier.fr
Tours available; AN.

EPERNAY

Champagne Perrier-Jouët
28, avenue de Champagne,
51200 Epernay.
Tel: 03 26 53 38 00.
Fax: 03 26 54 54 55.
www.perrier-jouet.com

Champagne Mercier
70, avenue de Champagne,
51200 Epernay.
Tel: 03 26 51 22 22.
Email: efauchoux@
mercier.tm.fr
Fax: 03 26 51 22 23.
www.champagne-mercier.fr
TP. AN for 10+ people.
Open daily Mar 16–Nov 14,
9:30–11:30AM and
2–4:30PM. Closed Tues and
Wed, Feb 16–Mar 15 and
Nov 14–Dec 11. Closed Dec
12–Feb 14. 45-minute tours
of cellars available; disabled
access. E, D, G.

Champagne Moët & Chandon
20, avenue de Champagne,
51200 Epernay.
Tel: 03 26 51 20 00.
Email: visites@moet.tm.fr
Fax: 03 26 51 20 21.
www.moet.com
TP. F, E; AN in G, D, I, J,
S, Portuguese, Russian,
Polish, and Chinese. Open
daily (except holidays) from
early March–late Nov,
9:30–11:30AM and 2–
4:30PM; closed weekends in
winter. 1-hour tour available
with tasting included.

beginning of the Vallée de la Marne vineyards near Bouzy.

The first villages belong to what is called la Petite Montagne, and it is not until you have crossed the main N51 road that you come to the 100 percent villages of Mailly and Verzenay, the latter with its well-restored windmill. Below the road on the left lies Sillery, whose wines were, for a long time, the most popular Champagnes in England. Beyond Verzenay, the direction the vineyards face changes, first towards the east and then south, where they slope down towards the river Marne. Among the great villages here is Bouzy, noted for its still, red Coteaux Champenois wine.

One of the finest views in Champagne is that of the Marne Valley from the road that leads directly from Reims to Epernay. To the right is Hautvillers, with its abbey, where Dom Perignon experimented so successfully with the wines of Champagne.

Epernay and the Marne Valley

South of the Montagne de Reims is Epernay, a rather crowded, dull town with, as its great redeeming feature, the magnificent Avenue de Champagne, flanked by some of the greatest names in the wine trade: De

Venoge and Perrier-Jouet, Mercier, and Moët & Chandon.

Some of the cellars are well worth visiting. While these may not be as old as some of those of Reims, they too are cut out of the chalk. The cellars at Mercier are so vast that they have to be visited by electric train.

The Marne Valley

Along the north bank of the river lies a great chain of vineyards stretching to the limits of the Marne *département,* beyond Château Thierry 30 miles to the west of Epernay. The principal grape grown along the Marne Valley is Pinot Meunier. Champagne houses tend to play down the role of Pinot Meunier in their blends while trumpeting that of Chardonnay and Pinot Noir. Pinot Meunier adds softness to the blend and helps to make the Champagne ready to drink younger than if it were just a blend of the other two varieties. It tends to be used more in non-vintage Champagnes than in vintage or prestige *cuvées.* However, Krug always uses a proportion of Pinot Meunier.

Almost facing Epernay are the two highest-rated villages: Aÿ and Mareuil-sur-Aÿ. The drive along this north bank is particularly attractive and provides an opportunity of visiting the Abbey of Hautvillers. In 1822, a member of the Moët family bought the ruined abbey and the company has now created a small wine museum there.

AŸ

Champagne Billecart Salmon
40, rue Carnot,
51160 Mareuil-sur-Aÿ.
Tel: 03 26 52 60 22.
Email: claudia@
champagne-billecart.fr
Fax: 03 26 52 64 88.
www.champagne-billecart.fr
AN. Closed weekends.

Champagne Bollinger
16, rue Jules-Lobet,
51160 Aÿ.
Tel: 03 26 53 33 66.
www.champagne-bollinger.fr

Champagne Gosset
69, rue Jules Blondeau,
51160 Aÿ.
Tel: 03 26 56 99 56.
Email: info@
champagne-gosset.com
Fax: 03 26 51 55 88.
www.champagne-gosset.com

Champagne Philipponnat
13, rue du Pont,
51160 Mareuil-sur-Aÿ.
Tel: 03 26 56 93 00.
Email: info@
champagnephilipponnat.com
Fax: 03 26 56 93 18.
www.champagne
philipponnat.com

The Côte des Blancs

South from Epernay runs the Côte des Blancs, with the vineyards lying on easterly facing slopes below wooded hillsides. As in the Montagne de Reims the soil here is chalk, which drains easily and is ideally suited to the production of sparkling wines. Here the other great grape of Burgundy, the Chardonnay, is grown.

The wine made from this grape adds a certain crisp delicacy to the ultimate blend, and it is not surprising in this age when lighter wines are so much appreciated that Blanc de Blancs Champagne is becoming more popular.

The road for visiting these vineyards is the D10, which branches off the main road to the south of Epernay, 3 km (2 miles) from the center of town. It is an attractive drive through a series of pretty villages dominated by the ridge of sloping vineyards to the east. The villages include Oger, Le Mesnil-sur-Oger, and Vertus.

The two best-known villages are Cramant and Avize. The first of these used to be particularly known for its Crémant de Cramant, a wine with a much less aggressive sparkle than that usually associated with Champagne. However, the term Crémant is no longer permitted for Champagne and is now reserved for sparkling wine from other regions, such as Crémant d'Alsace and Crémant de Loire. This was part of the trade-off in the agreement that allowed the Champagne producers to prevent anyone else using the term *méthode champenoise.* Avize is the home of one of the largest cooperatives in Champagne.

The vineyards of the Côte des Blancs end just beyond the village of Vertus, where there is a most impressive church with a spring beneath it. Just 5 km (3 miles) further south at Bergères-les-Vertus, there is a good view back northward over the vineyards from the top of Mont Saint Aimé, where there are the ruins of an old château.

Chalons-en-Champagne

This is the third important town in Champagne. Although it has many fewer Champagne firms than either

Golden ripe Chardonnay grapes © Olga Vasilkova/Dreamstime.com

CHOUILLY

Champagne Nicolas Feuillatte
Chouilly–BP 210 F-
51206 Epernay.
Tel: 03 26 59 64 61.
Email: service-visites@
feuillatte.com
Fax: 03 26 59 64 62.
www.feuillatte.com
Tasting available; AN.
Reception rooms; disabled access.

VERTUS

Larmandier-Bernier
19 avenue du Général de Gaulle,
51130 Vertus.
Tel: 03 26 52 13 24.
Email: larmandier@terre-net.fr
Fax: 03 26 52 21 00.
www.isasite.net/
champagne-larmandier
AN.

CHALONS-EN CHAMPAGNE

Champagne Joseph Perrier
69, avenue de Paris,
51016 Chalons-en-Champagne.
Tel: 03 26 68 29 51.
Email: contact@
josephperrier.com
Fax: 03 26 70 57 16.
www.joseph-perrier.com
Tastings available.
Open 8AM–12PM and 2–4PM.

BAR-SUR-SEINE

Champagne Veuve A. Devaux
Domaine de Villeneuve,
10110 Bar-sur-Seine.
Tel: 03 25 38 30 65.
Email: champagnedevaux@
wanadoo.fr
Fax: 03 25 29 73 21.

Epernay or Reims, it is the administrative center of the Marne *département*. The leading Champagne company is Joseph Perrier, which was founded in 1825. Despite suffering serious damage in both World Wars, there are a number of old religious and civic buildings that have survived in the center. These include Saint Etienne Cathedral and the Porte Sainte-Croix or Porte Dauphine. The town changed its name from Chalons-sur-Marne at the end of the last century.

Southern Champagne Vineyards

Although the heart of the Champagne vineyards could be said to finish here, there are three substantial enclaves of vines to the south with every right to the name Champagne. Much of the wine disappears into the blends of the big brands of Reims and Epernay, and it is only recently that some of the local growers have begun to make efforts to sell their wines under their own labels.

These vineyards are historical relics of the territories of the Count of Champagne, and indeed at their southern extremity they approach the northern limits of the vineyards of Burgundy.

Of the three vineyard areas, the first, the Côte de Sézanne, is still in the Marne *département* and is effectively a continuation of the Côte des Blancs. The other two areas are in the *département* of the Aube, and for many years had to label their wines in a pejorative way as Champagne Deuxième Zone. They are Bar-sur-Aude and Bar-sur-Seine. Just outside the former are the remains of what used to be a Roman camp on the summit of the Colline Sainte-Germaine. This site had two great advantages: not only was it easily defended, but it was well watered by a spring.

The wine roads in the main part of the Champagne vineyards are well signposted and there are separate routes for the Montagne de Reims, the Marne Valley, and the Côte des Blancs.

LES RICEYS

Champagne Alexandre Bonnet
10340 Les Riceys.
Tel: 03 25 29 30 93.
Fax: 03 25 29 38 65.
www.champagnebonnet.com.
(M. Gérard Rafai). TF.
Open Mon–Fri 8AM–12PM
and 2–6PM. WS. Champagne,
Coteaux Champenois red,
Rosé des Riceys. E.

URVILLE

Champagne Drappier
rue des Vignes,
10200 Urville.
Tel: 03 26 05 13 01.
Email: infos@
champagne-drappier.com
Fax: 03 25 27 41 19.
www.champagne-drappier.com

Food in Champagne

There are relatively few dishes that are native to Champagne, and even fewer traditional dishes that use Champagne in the preparation. Cooking destroys the bubbles that producers have spent a long time putting into the wine. Local recipes include Matelote marnaise, made with local freshwater fish, including pike and eels, and using Coteaux Champenoise, the local still wine. *Potée champenoise* is a substantial dish of chicken, ham, various sausages, and beans. Reims is known for a number of pastries and sweets, including *croquignoles*, a crunchy,

FOR FURTHER
INFORMATION

CIVC

5, rue Henri Martin,
51204 Epernay.
Tel: 03 26 51 19 30.
Email: info@champagne.fr
www.champagne.fr

finger-shaped cookie, and *massepains*, an almond cookie. Local cheeses include Brie, Baguette Laonnaise, Carre de l'Est, and Chaource. Nowadays, Champagne is used in a number of dishes, particularly seafood and chicken.

The Champenois spend a great deal of money and

Bossancourt on the river Aube in Champagne. Photo © Craig Hansen/Dreamstime.com

effort seeking to persuade people that Champagne is a natural partner with a wide range of foods. I remain unconvinced. Champagne is a wonderful aperitif, but still wine is generally a better match with food.

Where to stay and eat

EPERNAY AREA

Best Western-Hotel de Champagne
30, rue Eugène-Mercier.
Tel: 03 26 53 10 60 (H). Fax: 03 26 51 94 63.
www.bestwestern.com

Les Berceaux
13, rue des Berceaux, 51200 Epernay.
Tel: 03 26 55 28 84 (H/R). Fax: 03 26 55 10 36
www.lesberceaux.com

Le Clos Raymi
3, rue Joseph de Venoge, 51200 Epernay.
Tel: 03 26 51 00 58 (H). Email: info@closraymi-hotel.com
Fax: 03 26 51 18 98. www.closraymi-hotel.com

La Table Kobus
3, rue du Dr-Rousseau, 51200 Epernay.
Tel: 03 26 51 53 53 (R). Fax: 03 26 58 42 68.
www.latablekobus.com
Open daily 12–2PM and 5–9:15PM; closed Mon and Sat nights.
Closed first week of Jan and of April, and Aug 1–22.

Royal Champagne
51160 Champillon.
Tel: 03 26 52 87 11 (H/R).
Email: reception@royalchampagne.com
Fax: 03 26 52 89 69. www.royalchampagne.com
Restaurant closed Mon, Tues afternoon, and Dec 24–31.

Hostellerie du Mont Aimé
51130 Bergères les Vertus.
Tel: 03 26 52 21 31 (H/R). www.hostellerie-mont-aime.com
Restaurant closed Sun evening.

Hostellerie La Briquererie
4, route de Sézanne, 51530 Vinay.
Tel: 03 26 59 99 99 (H/R).
Email: briqueterie@relaischateaux.com
Fax: 03 26 59 92 10. www.labriqueterie.com

REIMS AREA

Best Western-Hotel de la Paix
9, rue Buirette. 51100 Reims.
Tel: 03 26 40 04 08 (H).
Email: reservation@hotel-lapaix.fr
Fax: 03 26 47 75 04. www.bestwestern-lapaix-reims.com

Brasserie du Boulingrin
48, rue de Mars, 51100 Reims.
Tel: 03 26 40 96 22 (R). Fax: 03 26 40 03 92.
www.boulingrin.fr
Open Mon—Sat.

Les Crayères
64, boulevard Henry-Vasnier, 51100 Reims.
Tel: 03 26 82 80 80. www.gerardboyer.com
Hotel closed Dec 20—Jan 12; restaurant open daily for
lunch & dinner.

Restaurant le Foch
37, boulevard Foch, 51100 Reims.
Tel: 03 26 47 48 22 (R). Fax: 03 26 88 78 22.
www.lefoch.com
Closed for lunch Sat, Sun night, and Mon.

Château de la Muire/L'Assiette Champenoise
40, rue Paul Vaillant-Couturier, 51430 Tinqueux.
Tel: 03 26 84 64 64 (H/R). Email:
assiette.champenoise@wanadoo.fr
Fax: 03 26 04 15 69. www.assiettechampenoise.com
Restaurant closed Tues lunch and dinner, Wed lunch.

Grand Hotel des Templiers
22, rue des Templiers, 51100 Reims.
Tel: 03 26 88 55 08 (H).
www.jpmoser.com/grandhoteldestempliers.html

CHALONS AREA

Aux Armes de Champagne
31, avenue du Luxembourg, 51460 L'Epine.
Tel: 03 26 69 30 30 (H/R). Fax: 03 26 69 30 26.
www.aux-armes-de-champagne.com

Alsace

Photo on previous page of an Alsacian village in summer © Jean Schweitzer/Dreamstime.com

ALSACE

Through the centuries, Alsace has been the bone over which France and Germany have fought. It is only since the end of World War I that it has been definitively French; indeed, some of the older men fought in the German army. As a result, the area has a happy blend of styles—in the architecture, the food, and the wine. However, the growers that you will meet are proud that they are neither French nor German: they are *Alsacien*.

With the Vosges Mountains as a backdrop, the vineyards of Alsace are among the prettiest in France, and those villages that have not suffered in the succession of Franco-German wars are picture-postcard material. Strasbourg and Colmar are two beautiful towns with imposing buildings and museums. Of all the vineyard regions of France, Alsace is, in many ways, the most satisfying to visit.

TO GET TO ALSACE

Colmar is 444 km (277 miles) east of Paris by N4 to Luneville, then N59 and N415; it is 557 km (348 miles) by the A4 motorway to Strasbourg, then N83; 683 km (426 miles) from Calais via Reims; 290 km (181 miles) by A36 from Beaune.

Varietal wines

The dominant feature on any Alsace wine label is not likely to be the name of a village or a vineyard, but rather a grape variety. Alsace is the only French wine region to consistently use varietal labeling.

Here wines are normally made from one of seven different grapes. Each of these has its own characteristics. Only one, the Pinot Noir,

THE BAS-RHIN

Alsace Willm

SA 32, rue du Dr Sulzer
67140 Barr.
Tel: 03 89 41 24 31.
Email: contact@alsace-willm.com
www.alsace-willm.com
TF for individuals; TP for groups.
AA. Open daily 8AM–12PM and
2–6PM. (Tastings also available at
La Cave, 5 Chemin de la Fecht,
68000 Colmar
Tel: 03 89 30 40 70.
Open Mon–Sat 9AM –7PM,
Sun 9AM–6PM.)

Domaine Klipfel

6, avenue de la Gare,
67140 Barr.
Tel: 03 88 58 59 00.
Email: alsacewine@klipfel.com
Fax: 03 88 08 53 18.
www.klipfel.com
Open Mon–Thurs 8AM–12PM and
1:30–5PM; Fri 8AM–12PM.

Willy Gisselbrecht et Fils

5, route du Vin 67650
Dambach-la-Ville.
Tel: 03 88 92 41 02.
Email: info@vins-gisselbrecht.com
Fax: 03 88 92 45 50.
www.vins-gisselbrecht.com

gives a red, or more often, a deep, refreshing, fruity rosé wine. Two of the white grapes, the Sylvaner and the Pinot Blanc (or Clevner), give wines for everyday drinking. The Sylvaner, found more in the Bas-Rhin, the northerly end of the vineyards, gives a rather full, earthy wine, while the Pinot Blanc makes a lighter, crisp style and is often used in making the local AOC sparkling wine, the Crémant d'Alsace.

The four noble grapes

The four noble grapes are the Pinot Gris—known also as the Tokaji Pinot Gris—the Gewürztraminer, the Muscat, and the Riesling. The Pinot Gris is full, soft, and supple, and often high in alcohol.

The Muscat and the Gewürztraminer both give very full-flavored wine. The Muscat comes from the same grape as many of the great sweet dessert wines of the world; it has a similar taste but is dry. The Gewürztraminer's spicy flavor reminds me of Ogen melons (one of the cantaloupe varieties).

Alsace growers are proudest of their Rieslings. At their best, these are classic, steely, austere wines, whose flavor seems to remain in your mouth forever. Alsace Rieslings age well and good vintages should easily keep 30 to 40 years. Indeed, these Rieslings generally need four or five years of age before they are ready to drink.

All these wines are dry, but, in the greatest years, sweeter wines are sometimes made from late-picked grapes. The label will then say *Vendange Tardive* (late harvest) or, for the very finest and most expensive wines, *Sélection de Grains Nobles*. These last will have been concentrated by noble rot and rate with the finest Sauternes.

Grand cru appellation

In 1975, as part of a continuous quality improvement program, the Alsace growers established a Grand Cru appellation. This is based on the soil and aspect to the sun of individual vineyards. Yields are limited to not more than 65 hl/ha (less than four metric tonnes, or four US tons, an acre), and vines are restricted to "the four noble grapes." Twenty-five sites were selected in 1983; this number has since grown to 50.

The Bas-Rhin

Although the main Alsace wine road starts at Marlenheim to the west of Strasbourg, there is a small enclave of vines near Wissembourg, some 60 km (38 miles) to the north. There is an interesting contrast between the host of vines on the German side of the frontier and the few on the French, where all the grapes are sent to the pretty little Cooperative Cellar at Cleebourg.

On the drive up to Wissembourg, the pottery villages of Soufflenheim and Betschdorf, the Forest of Haguenau, and such charming half-timbered farming villages as Oberseebach and Niederseebach are worth a visit.

Strasbourg

Although Strasbourg is away from the vineyard area, the wine lover can justify a visit there for its numerous *winstuben*, or wine taverns. These play an important part in the daily life of Alsace and are ideal places in which to taste a range of wines by the glass or bottle and to eat the local gastronomic specialties at a reasonable price. Those

interested in architecture must visit the cathedral and the old quarter of the city.

To reach the wine road from Strasbourg, take the main N4 road west. After 20 km (12.5 miles), you come to Marlenheim. It is here that the main vineyards of Alsace begin. The vinous reputation of Marlenheim is based on its red, or more properly rosé, wine. From Marlenheim, the route du vin is clearly marked as it meanders its way south. For the first few miles, the names will probably strike more of a chord with beer drinkers than with wine drinkers as one drives through the village of Mützig and passes the modern Kronenbourg brewery.

Maison Albert Seltz SARL
21, rue Principale,
67140 Mittelbergheim.
Tel: 03 88 08 91 77.
Email: info@albert-seltz.fr
Fax: 03 88 08 52 72.
www.albert-seltz.fr/seltz.html
Open Mon–Fri 8AM–1:00PM and 2–6PM. Wed afternoon and Sat only by appointment. Closed Sun.

Cave de Cléebourg
route du vin,
67160 Cléebourg
Tel: 03 88 94 50 33.
Email: info@cave-cleebourg.com
Fax: 03 88 94 57 08.
www.cave-cleebourg.com
TF for individuals; TP for groups of 15+. Open Mon–Sat 8AM–12PM and 2–6PM; Sun and holidays 10AM–12PM and 2–6PM. Closed Dec 25, Jan 1, and Easter Sunday. Group tours (1.5–2.5 hours) with tastings available. E, G.

Villages of the Bas-Rhin

Rosheim still has fortified gateways dating back to the 14th century. If only to get a good view of the vineyards and the plain of the Bas-Rhin, visit the Mont Sainte Odile above Obernai. Here are the remains of an abbey and a convent to the memory of this 7th-century saint.

Obernai is an attractive town with a beautiful marketplace and 16th-century well. Between Obernai and the next town, Barr, lies a succession of pretty villages tucked into the feet of the Vosges mountains. Of these, I can recommend Ottrott as a local base. Heiligenstein even has its own grape variety, the Clevner de Heiligenstein, a type of Gewürztraminer.

Strasbourg is Alsace's leading city and home to a number of fine restaurants.
Photo by Uwe Blosfeld/Dreamstime.com

Barr is a center of the tanning industry as well as the wine trade. It has an important wine fair each July and is particularly proud of its Gewürztraminer wines. Just to the south comes Mittelbergheim, where the best Sylvaners are made, and Dambach, which has more vineyards than any other village in Alsace.

At the southern extremity of the Bas-Rhin *département*, on a crest of the Vosges, is the remarkable Château du Haut-Koenigsbourg. The ideal location for any Dracula film, this castle was built by Kaiser Wilhelm II at the beginning of the 20th century on the ruins of a Swiss feudal stronghold. The winding road up to it gives some sensational views. Just to the north is the valley of the Giessen, where many of Alsace's well-known white spirits are distilled.

The Haut-Rhin

There is no great difference in the scenery between the Haut-Rhin and the Bas-Rhin, but for the wine lover there is a world of difference in the quality of the wines. With a few notable exceptions, all the great wines of Alsace come from the southern end of the vineyards.

Ribeauvillé

The first wine village in the Haut-Rhin is Saint-Hippolyte, which, like Marlenheim, is known for its red wines. However, the first of the great villages is Ribeauvillé. Perhaps the finest Riesling of Alsace, the Clos Saint Hune, comes from here, and, to balance it out, there is an important bottling plant for mineral water.

The last Sunday in August is known here as the Pfifferday, or Piper's Day. Each year there are colorful festivities, with free wine flowing in the Town Hall Square.

Just south of the village, at Hunawihr, efforts have been made to reintroduce the stork, the bird for which the region is best known. Storks can be seen here during the nesting season.

Riquewihr

Just 4 km (2.5 miles) to the south comes Riquewihr, which must be one of the most beautiful wine villages in the

world. In an area that has
suffered regularly from the
ravages of war, somehow
Riquewihr has managed to
escape, and it remains to
this day a 16th-century
fortified village.

The best time to visit must
be in October during the
vintage, for many of the
cellars of both growers and
merchants are on the main
street, the rue du Général de
Gaulle. To refresh yourself,
some of the growers have
winstuben, where the traditional way of taking the new,
still cloudy, and not fully
fermented wine is with
walnuts and fresh bread.

Mittelwihr and Bennwihr

Riquewihr may have escaped
damage in succeeding wars,
but the same cannot be said
for the neighboring twin
villages of Mittelwihr and
Bennwihr. They were the
scene of some of the fiercest
fighting during World War II
and were almost totally
destroyed. They have now
been rebuilt in traditional
Alsace style.

THE HAUT-RHIN

Domaine Sick-Dreyer
17, route de Kientzheim,
68770 Ammerschwihr.
Tel: 03 89 47 11 31.
Email: edreyer@wanadoo.fr
Fax: 03 89 47 32 60.
www.sick-dreyer.com
Open daily Mon–Fri 9AM–12PM
and 2–6PM; Saturday 9AM–12PM
and 2–4:30PM.
Closed Sun and holidays.

Cave Vinicole Beblenheim
14, rue de Hoen,
68980 Beblenheim.
Tel: 03 89 47 90 02.
Email: info@
cave-beblenheim.com
Fax: 03 89 47 86 85.
www.cave-beblenheim.com

Bestheim
3, rue du Général de Gaulle,
68630 Bennwihr.
Tel: 03 89 49 09 29.
www.bestheim.com

Domaine Marcel Deiss
15, route du vin,
68750 Bergheim.
Tel: 03 89 73 63 37.
Email: marceldeiss@
marceldeiss.com
Fax: 03 89 73 32 67.
www.marceldeiss.com

The Weiss Valley

Shortly after these two villages, the route du vin turns off to
the right up the valley of the Weiss. The first village,
Sigolsheim, was also destroyed in World War II, but
Kientzheim still has a fortified gateway, with a sculpture of a

Paul Blanck et Fils
32, Grande Rue,
68240 Kientzheim.
Tel: 03 89 78 23 56.
Email: blanck-alsace@rmcnet.fr
Fax: 03 89 47 16 45.
www.blanck.com

FE Trimbach
15, route de Bergheim,
68150 Ribeauvillé.
Tel: 03 89 73 60 30.
Fax: 03 89 73 89 04.
www.maison-trimbach.fr
Open 8AM-12PM and
2-5PM. Closed holidays, 1st 3
weeks in Aug, last week in Dec,
1st week in Jan. E, G.

Dopff au Moulin
68340 Riquewihr.
Tel: 03 89 49 09 69.
Email: reservation@
dopff-au-moulin.fr
www.dopff-au-moulin.fr
TP. AN. Open Mon–Fri
8AM–12PM and 2–6PM; Sat–Sun
9AM–12PM and 2–6PM.

Hugel et Fils SA
3, rue de la 1ère Armée
Française, 68340 Riquewihr.
Tel: 03 89 47 92 15.
Email: hugel1639@wanadoo.fr
or info@hugel.com
Fax: 03 89 49 00 10.
www.hugel.com
Groups of up to 10 welcome.
Open daily, Easter to
Christmas, 10AM–12:30PM and
2–6PM.

man's head putting out his
tongue at any assailant, and a
château, which is the base of the
Confrérie Saint-Etienne, the
local drinking brotherhood.
Here they hold regular banquets
and maintain a wine museum.

To the left of the road between
Kientzheim and the next village,
Kaysersberg, lies the Weinbach, a
wine estate that used to belong to
a Capuchin convent.

Kaysersberg

Kaysersberg's name, "Caesar's
Hill," goes back to Roman
times, when it guarded the end
of the most strategic pass
between Gaul and the plains of
Alsace. Many of the buildings
date back to the 15th and 16th
centuries, including a fortified
bridge with a chapel on it. It is
the proud birthplace of Albert
Schweitzer.

In Kaysersberg, the wine road
again turns back on itself, down
the N415, through the important
wine village of Ammerschwihr to
the center of the wine trade of
Alsace, Colmar.

Colmar

This attractive town, with its fine
medieval center, is a good base
for the wine tourist. The
regional wine fair takes place in
August, in the exhibition hall to
the north of the town. There is
no better occasion on which to

taste a full range of wines from throughout the region.

Colmar is an ideal base for visiting the vineyards of Alsace. It is also very beautiful in its own right. Well worth visiting are the old quarter, with its network of canals, and the Musée d'Unterlinden.

A chain of villages

While Colmar makes a convenient break in the Alsace wine road, the hardy traveller will cut across from Ammerschwihr to the walled village of Turckheim, where, every evening in summer, the night-watchman with halberd and lantern in hand walks round telling all the inhabitants to go to bed. The village also has one of the best cooperatives in Alsace.

Eguisheim

Eguisheim is another in the chain of beautiful Alsace villages. Its cobbled streets are alight with flowers, and even its cooperative cellar, the largest in Alsace, blends into the general picture. The village's most famous son is Pope Leo IX, who was Supreme Pontiff during the middle of the 11th century. Above Eguisheim, halfway up the hillside, lies Husseren-les-Châteaux, itself dominated by the ruins of three castles on the Vosges skyline.

Rouffach

The wine villages continue in a chain on the slopes above the fast-moving traffic of the N83. This skirts the pretty village of Rouffach, whose wines were described a quarter of a century ago as having a "spiritual" bouquet.

One of its vineyards, the Clos St-Landelin, has a microclimate that is claimed to be the driest in all of

Preiss-Jean-Zimmer
42, rue General de Gaulle,
68340 Riquewihr.
Tel: 03 89 47 92 58.
Fax: 03 89 47 99 39

Rolly Gassman
2, rue de l'Eglise,
68590 Rorschwihr.
Tel: 03 89 73 63 28.
Email: rollygassmann@
wanadoo.fr

Daniel Wiederhirn
7, rue du Cheval,
68340 Riquewihr.
Tel: 03 89 47 92 10.
Fax: 03 89 49 06 45.

France. (Saint Landelin was an itinerant Irish monk who came to convert the Germans during the 4th century and founded a monastery just across the Rhine in the Black Forest in Germany.)

Guebwiller

Of all the Alsace wine towns, Guebwiller must be the least attractive. It owes its size, and its wealth, to the textile machinery factories of the Schlumbergers. Since the time of the French Revolution, this family has built up what is now the largest single wine domain in Alsace—and the largest single hillside wine property in France. This now extends to 140 hectares (340 acres), spread along south-facing slopes overlooking the town. It is so steep in places that tractors are unable to work the vines and a team of twelve horses is still kept for the purpose (and for a natural supply of manure).

The end of the wine road

Towards its southern end, the route du vin seems to lose its purpose for a while, as the vineyards become fewer and the landscape becomes dominated by the potash mines in the plain. However, it comes to a glorious finale with the Rangen vineyard, of volcanic soil, overlooking the town of Thann.

Most of the wine villages of Alsace that the traveller may wish to visit lie in a narrow strip along the flanks of the Vosges, and there is no easy circuit that can be made. Nevertheless, because of their wines, their beauty, and their hospitality, even the shortest visit to any part of them is always rewarding.

A Land of Plenty

Well endowed with agri-cultural and natural resources, Alsace has its own distinctive regional cuisine—one of the most distinctive in France. It can call upon fish from the tributaries of the Rhine, as well as game from the Vosges forests. The food is a hearty blend of much that is best from the cooking of both France and Germany. As a local saying has it, "The Frenchman likes to eat well, the German likes to eat a lot, the *Alsacien* likes to eat well—and a lot."

Vignobles René Muré Clos St Landelin
RN83, 68250 Rouffach.
Tel: 03 89 78 58 00.
Email: rene@mure.com
Fax: 03 89 78 58 01.
www.mure.com
Cellar open Mon–Fri
8AM–7PM; Sat 9AM–12PM
and 2–6:30PM.

Cave Cooperative of Turckheim
16, rue de Tuileries,
68230 Turckheim.
Tel: 03 89 30 23 60.
Email: brandt@
cave-turckheim.com
www.cave-turckheim.com
AN for groups. Open Mon-–Sat 8AM–12PM and 2–6PM;
Sun 10AM–12PM and 3–6PM.

Zind Humbrecht
4, route de Colmar,
68230 Turckheim.
Tel: 03 89 27 02 05.
Email: o.humbrecht@
wanadoo.fr
Fax: 03 89 27 22 58.
perso.wanadoo.fr/jean-michel.parault/alsace5.html

Vins Josmeyer
76, rue Clemenceau,
68920 Wintzenheim.
Tel: 03 89 27 91 90.
Email: contact@josmeyer.com
Fax: 03 89 27 91 99.
www.josmeyer.com
Shop open Mon–Fri 9AM–1PM
and 2–6PM; Sat 9AM–1PM;
closed Sun and holidays.

Leon Beyer
8, place Château St Léon,
68420 Eguisheim.
Tel: 03 89 23 16 16.
Email: contact@leonbeyer.fr
www.leonbeyer.fr
WS. Open daily 10AM–12PM
and 2–6PM except Wednesdays.
Closed Jan–Feb. 10 people max.
Office: Tel: 03 89 21 62 30.
Fax: 03 89 23 93 63.
Closed Aug 6–30.

**Vins Wolfberger Cave
Vinicole Eguisheim**
6, Grand' Rue,
68420 Eguisheim.
Tel: 03 89 22 20 20.
Email: wolfberger@wanadoo.fr
Fax: 03 89 23 47 09.
www.wolfberger.com

Domaines Schlumberger
100, rue Theodore Deck,
68501 Guebwiller.
Tel: 03 89 74 27 00.
Email: duschlum@aol.com
Fax: 03 89 74 85 75.
www.domaines-
schlumberger.com
Tasting room open Mon–Sat
(May–Oct) 8AM–12:30PM and
1:30–5PM. Closed weekends
Nov–Apr.

Vins Kuentz-Bas
14, route du vin,
68420 Husseren-les-Châteaux.
Tel: 03 89 49 30 24.
Email: kuentz-bas@calixo.net
Fax: 03 89 49 23 39.
www.kuentz-bas.fr
AN for groups. Open daily,
Mon–Sat 9AM–12PM and 1–6PM,
in summer; in winter, Sat only
by appointment.

Typical dishes include *choucroute* (pickled cabbage with various meats and sausages), *backoefe* or *baeckeoffe* (lamb, pork, and vegetables baked in the oven), *spätzle* (a cross between noodles and pasta that is served as an accompaniment with many dishes), and onion tart. *Foie gras*, particularly fresh, is also featured widely. Alsace is also renowned for baking.

Tarte Flambée, an Alsacian specialty. Photo © Dreamstime.com

Kugelhopf is similar to a brioche but can be both sweet or savory, while apple strudel is another popular dish.

Alsace has a number of very fine restaurants. As is usually the case, the further up the price and quality scale you go the more refined and delicate the dishes. For those wishing to try the local wines and not wanting to eat too heavily, *winstuben* serve simple dishes and wines by the glass as well as the bottle. With fine food and wine at fair prices, Alsace is a happy hunting ground for the thrifty gastronome.

Where to stay and eat

Aux Armes de France

1, Grande Rue, 68770 Ammerschwihr.
Tel: 03 89 47 10 12 (H/R). Fax: 03 89 47 38 12.
www.aux-armes-de-france.com

Au Fer Rouge

5, Grande Rue, 68000 Colmar.
Tel: 03 89 41 37 24 (R).
Email: au.fer.rouge@calixo.net
Fax: 03 89 23 82 24. www.au-fer-rouge.com
Lunch: 12–1:45PM. Dinner: 7:15–9:45PM. Closed Sun lunch,
Mon; closed Feb 19–Mar 2.

Restaurant Jean-Yves Schillinger

17, rue de la Poissonnerie, 68000 Colmar.
Tel: 03 89 21 53 60 (R). www.jean-yves-schillinger.com
Lunch: 12–2:30PM. Dinner 7–10:30PM.
Closed Mon lunch, Sun.

Wistub Brenner

1, rue de Turenne, 68000 Colmar.
Tel: 03 89 41 42 33 (R).
www.linternaute.com/restaurant/restaurant/82/
wistub-brenner.html
Open daily 12–2PM and 7–10PM, except Tues and Wed.
Closed June 20–29; Nov 15–24; Dec 24–Jan 2; and Feb 6–23.

Le Chambard

9–13, rue du Général de Gaulle, 68240 Kayserberg.
Tel: 03 89 47 10 17 (H/R). Email: info@lechambard.fr
Fax: 03 89 47 35 03. www.lechambard.fr

Auberge de l'Ill

rue de Collonges-au-Mont-d'Or, 68970 Illhaeusern.
Tel: 03 89 71 89 00 (H/R).
Email: aubergedelill@aubergedelill.com
Fax: 03 89 71 82 83. www.auberge-de-l-ill.com

Le Cerf

30, rue du Général de Gaulle, 67520 Marlenheim.
Tel: 03 88 87 73 73 (H/R). Email: info@lecerf.com
Fax: 03 88 87 68 08. www.lecerf.com
Restaurant open for lunch and dinner Thurs–Mon,
closed Tues and Wed.

Le Haut-Ribeaupierre

1, route de Bergheim, 68150 Ribeauvillé.
Tel: 03 89 73 87 63 (H/R). Fax: 03 89 73 88 15
Closed Tues and Wed, and Jan 1–31 and June 1–7.
Open Sat night and Sun; open in August.

La Table du Gourmet

5, rue de la Iere Armée, 68340 Riquewihr.
Tel: 03 89 49 09 09. Email: table@jbrendel.com
Fax: 03 89 49 04 56. www.jlbrendel.com
Lunch: 12:15–1:45PM. Dinner 7:15–9:15PM.
From April–Nov 15, open for dinner daily, except Tues;
open for lunch Fri–Mon. From Nov 15–April, open Thurs
evening–Mon. Closed Jan 6–Feb 13.

WINE FESTIVALS

The festival season starts on May 1 and ends in late October, with a peak period in July and August. There are approximately 45 festivals each year. The main one is the regional wine fair at Colmar at the beginning of August.

FOR FURTHER INFORMATION

CIVA Maison des Vins d'Alsace
12, ave de la Foire-aux-Vins, 68012 Colmar.
Tel: 03 89 20 16 20 or c.i.v.a.@rmcnet.fr
www.vinsalsace.com

Burgundy

BURGUNDY

I f one vineyard region in France has the image of living
life to the fullest, it is Burgundy. There is no doubt
that it is a land devoted to wine—and hearty food.

Burgundians are proud of their history; once their
Dukes ruled territory that stretched as far as what is now
Belgium. They are proud, too, of their wines, and happy
to show them off and talk about them to visitors who show
a genuine interest. Burgundy has a reputation for its
hospitality as well as its food and wine.

The vineyards of Burgundy are shared between three
different departments—the Yonne, Côte d'Or, and Saône

Above: View of Burgundy, France by Laura Frenkle/Dreamstime.com

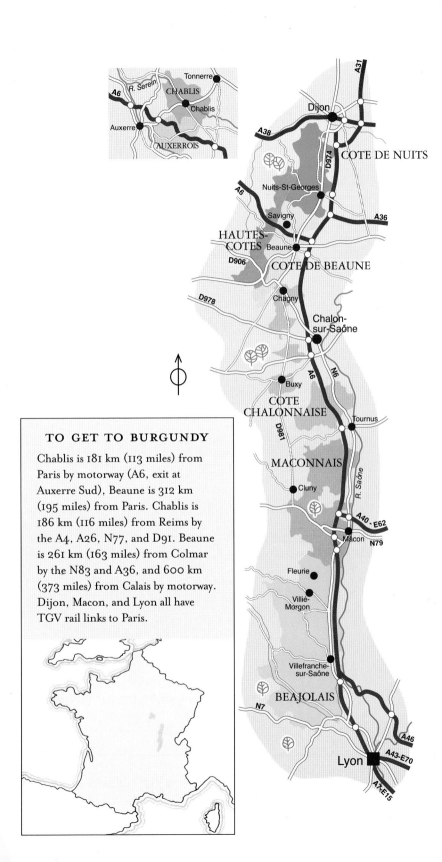

Tonnerre

CHABLIS

A6   R. Serein

Auxerre   Chablis

AUXERROIS

A31

Dijon

A38   **D974**   **COTE DE NUITS**

A6   Nuits-St-Georges

A36

Savigny

HAUTES-COTES   Beaune

D906   **COTE DE BEAUNE**

D978   Chagny

Chalon-sur-Saône

Buxy   **A6**   **N6**

COTE CHALONNAISE

D981   Tournus

R. Saône

MACONNAIS

Cluny

A40 - E62

Mâcon   **N79**

Fleurie

Villié-Morgon

Villefranche-sur-Saône

BEAJOLAIS

N7

A46

Lyon   **A43-E70**

A7 - E15

TO GET TO BURGUNDY

Chablis is 181 km (113 miles) from Paris by motorway (A6, exit at Auxerre Sud), Beaune is 312 km (195 miles) from Paris. Chablis is 186 km (116 miles) from Reims by the A4, A26, N77, and D91. Beaune is 261 km (163 miles) from Colmar by the N83 and A36, and 600 km (373 miles) from Calais by motorway. Dijon, Macon, and Lyon all have TGV rail links to Paris.

et Loire—and between four separate and largely distinct regions: Chablis and the Auxerrois, the Côte d'Or, the Côte Chalonnaise, and the Mâconnais.

While the reputations of the wines of Burgundy and Bordeaux may be on a par, in an average vintage Bordeaux produces two and a half times as much wine. As an analogy, consider the total production of Burgundy to be one bottle of wine. Out of that bottle, just one glassful comes from the Yonne and the Côte d'Or—those vineyards that have made Burgundy's reputation with such wines as Chablis, Meursault, Nuits-Saint-Georges, Beaune, Pommard, and Gevrey-Chambertin.

By far the bulk of the production comes from the vineyards of the Beaujolais and the Mâconnais. Because of their very small production, the great wines of Burgundy are never cheap.

A voyage of discovery

With their system of *grand* and *premier crus*, Chablis and the Côte d'Or are the most classified vineyards in the world. Small differences of soil, slope, and exposure to the sun determine whether a vineyard has *grand*, *premier*, or merely *village* status. These small differences of site should make a difference in quality—they certainly make a difference in price.

Even in the Côte d'Or with its world-famous vineyards such as Montrachet and Romanée Conti, there are lesser-known vineyards to explore whose wines often offer better value than the stellar names. Here, then, is one of the attractions of the region: seeking out the lesser-known wines and the good restaurants off the beaten track. There are fine discoveries to be made in the small villages away from the main roads.

The increase in the number of hotel rooms in such towns as Beaune and Nuits-Saint-Georges bears witness to their popularity as tourist centers. See there what has to be seen—but there is much else in Burgundy.

Abstract of burgundy wine. Photo by Frank Farrell/Dreamstime.com

FOR FURTHER
INFORMATION

BIVB
12, blvd Bretonnière,
BP 150, 21204 Beaune.
Tel: 03 80 25 04 80.
E-mail: bivb@wanadoo.fr
www.bivb.com

CHABLIS

Jean-Marc Brocard
3, route de Chablis,
89300 Préhy.
Tel: 03 86 41 49 00.
Email: info@brocard.fr
Fax: 03 86 41 49 09.
www.brocard.fr
Chais/cellar open Mon–Sat
9:30AM–12:30PM and 3–7PM.
Shop (place Charles de Gaulle,
89800 Chablis; tel 03 86 42
45 76) open Mon–Sat
9:30AM–12:30PM and 3–7PM;
Sun 10AM–2 PM.

La Chablisienne
8, blvd Pasteur,
89800 Chablis.
Tel: 03 86 42 89 89.
Email: chab@chablisienne.fr
Fax: 03 86 42 89 90.
www.chablisienne.com
Open daily Jan 1–Mar 31
9:30AM–12:30PM and 2–6PM.
Open daily April 1–Dec 31
9:30AM–12:30PM and 2–7PM.
Open holidays.

Domaine Daniel Etienne Defaix
14, rue Auxerroise,
89800 Chablis.
Tel: 03 86 42 14 44.
Email: chateau@
chablisdefaix.com
Fax: 03 86 42 48 56.
www.chablisdefaix.com

Jean Durup Père et fils
4 Grande Rue,
89800 Maligny.
Tel: 03 86 47 44 49.
Email: info@durup-chablis.com
Fax: 03 86 47 55 49.
www.durup-chablis.com

Chablis

When you first see the small town of Chablis, there is a certain feeling of anti-climax. It seems surprising that such a little place should have become synonymous throughout the world with dry white wine. While there may still be vast quantities of so-called Chablis produced in California, the real thing comes from around 4,500 hectares planted just here and in a few surrounding villages.

Renaissance of Chablis

Historically, the reputation of Chablis was based on its location on the river Serein, for the wines could simply be shipped downstream to the ever-thirsty market of Paris. However, the soil is poor and the climate severe, so when the added burden of the phylloxera plague arrived at the end of the last century, many of the vineyards were simply abandoned and allowed to return to scrub. It is only during the past thirty years or so, when increased demand and improved techniques have made replanting profitable, that the true renaissance in Chablis has occurred.

Classification

There is a rigid hierarchy in the classification of the wines of Chablis. At the top come the seven *grand cru* vineyards, and

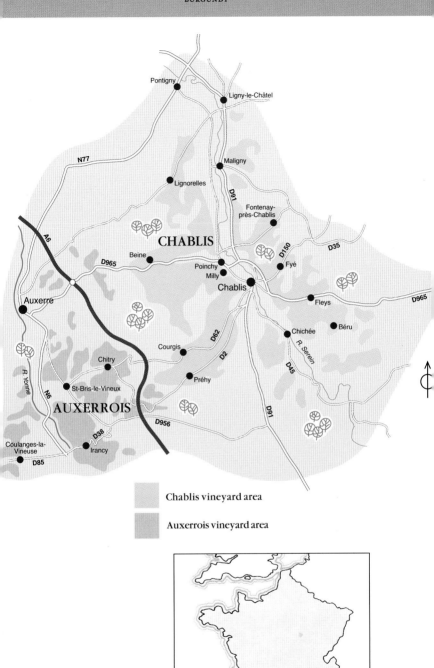

Chablis vineyard area

Auxerrois vineyard area

Domaine des Malandes
63, rue Auxerroise,
89800 Chablis.
Tel: 03 86 42 41 37.
Email: contact@
domainedesmalandes.com
Fax: 03 86 42 41 97.
www.domainedesmalandes.com

Christian Moreau
26, ave d'Oberwesel,
89800 Chablis.
Tel: 03 86 42 86 34.
Email: contact@
domainechristianmoreau.com
Fax: 03 86 42 84 62.
www.domainechristian
moreau.com
AN.

Domaine Vocoret et Fils
40, route d'Auxerre,
89800 Chablis.
Tel: 03 86 42 12 53.
Email: domaine.vocoret@
wanadoo.fr
Fax: 03 86 42 10 39.
www.vocoret.com

**FOR FURTHER
INFORMATION**

CIVC
5, rue Henri Martin,
51204 Epernay.
Tel: 03 26 51 19 30.
Email: info@champagne.fr
www.champagne.fr

these lie together on one south-facing slope just a few hundred meters to the north of the town, across the river Serein.

From left to right, as you face the hillside, they are Bougros, Les Preuses, Vaudésir, Grenouilles, Valmur, Les Clos (the largest and my favorite), and Blanchots.

Next there come a host of *premiers crus*. These lie on southerly facing slopes on both sides of the river and in the small valleys that run off it. Perhaps the best-known *premier cru* wines are Montée de Tonnerre Fourchaume, Vaillons, and Montmains.

Ordinary Chablis comes from a number of small surrounding villages, where the stony soil is a limestone based on shells that predate human habitation. Finally comes Petit Chablis, made in villages on the fringe of the area.

Recent changes

As replanting has taken place, the area under vines and the total crop have increased considerably in recent times, more than 10 times in the past 40 years and 4 times in the last 20.

The Chardonnay is the only grape allowed for making the wines of Chablis, and traditionally it gives a steely, dry wine that is the ideal match for shellfish, especially oysters. Over the past few

WINE FESTIVALS

Les Pastorales Chablisiennes,
1st weekend in May.
Chablis Wine Festival,
4th weekend in Nov.

FOR FURTHER
INFORMATION

BIVB Le Petit Pontigny
1, rue de Chichée,
89800 Chablis.
Tel: 03 86 42 42 22.
www.bivb.com

William Fèvre
21, avenue d'Oberwesel,
89800 Chablis.
Tel: 03 86 98 98 98.
Email: france@
williamfevre.com.
Fax: 03 86 98 98 99

Domaine Alain Geoffroy
4, rue de l'équerre, Beines,
89800 Chablis.
Tel: 03 86 42 43 76.
Email: info@
chablis-geoffroy.com
Fax: 03 86 42 13 30.
www.chablis-geoffroy.com
TF. AN on Sat & for groups.
Open Mon–Fri 8AM–12PM
and 2–5PM. WS. Wine and
corkscrew museum, reception
rooms.

**Michel Laroche
L'Obédiencerie**
22, rue Louis-Bro,
89800 Chablis.
Tel: 03 86 42 89 00.
Email: winebar@
larochewines.com
Fax: 03 86 42 89 29.
www.larochewines.com
Open Mar–Dec, Mon–Wed
11:30AM–5PM; Thurs–Sat
11:30AM–5PM and 7–10PM;
closed Sun. Closed Dec
23–Feb 27. Also wine bar,
restaurant & shop at 18 rue
des Moulins, Chablis.

Château Long-Depaquit
45, rue Auxerroise,
89800 Chablis.
Tel: 03 86 42 11 13.
Fax: 03 86 42 81 89
www.grandscruschablis.com/
an_domaine_depaquit.htm

years, the style of the wines of
Chablis has gently altered,
perhaps as a result of the
demands of the market. True
austerity seems to be something of the past; nowadays a
degree of softness is often
present.

The town of Chablis

Despite the fact that during the
last war it suffered as a result of
an extempore air raid by the
Italian air force, much of old
Chablis survives. There are a
number of houses dating back
to the 14th and 15th centuries,
as well as the Porte Noël, which
was rebuilt in 1770.

At the end of a series of
narrow streets, the door of the
parish church, begun in the
13th century, is covered with
horseshoes. These are
offerings to Saint Martin, the
patron saint of horsemen and
all things equestrian.

The Yonne

Historically, the Yonne Valley was the part of Burgundy with the greatest number of vineyards. A combination of the extreme climate, phylloxera, the coming of the railway (enabling wines to be brought to Paris cheaply from the vineyards of the south of France) as well as the increasing availability of other forms of employment led to the valley's being almost totally abandoned, apart from a hard core at Chablis.

Now, there is a renaissance in the wines of the Yonne, as well as in the wines of Chablis. While there are about 4,000 hectares (9,680 acres) of Chablis vineyards, there are a further 1,000 hectares of vineyards producing a variety of other wines. The viability of these new vineyards is largely underwritten by "farm-gate sales" to the hordes of Parisians who descend on the region every weekend seeking to replenish their wine cellars.

THE YONNE

EARL Colinot
1, rue des Charitas,
89290 Irancy.
Tel: 03 86 42 33 25.

Ghislaine et Jean-Hugues Goisot
30, rue Bienvenu-Martin,
89530 St-Bris-le-Vineux.
Tel: 03 86 53 35 15.

Caves de Bailly
Hameau de Bailly,
89530 St-Bris-le-Vineux.
Tel: 03 86 53 77 77.
Email: home@caves-bailly.com
Fax: 03 86 53 90 84.
www.caves-bailly.com
TF. AN for groups. Cellar open year round Mon–Fri 8AM–12PM and 2–6PM year. Weekends and holidays in Jan and Feb, open 2:30–6PM; from Mar–Dec 10AM–12PM and 2:30–6PM. Guided tours (for fee, includes tasting) Apr–Oct daily from 2:30–5PM; from Nov–Mar on weekends/holidays from 4–5PM. WS. Sculpture exhibit in Aug. G, D, E.

WINE MUSEUM

Le Musée du Vieux Pressoir et de la Vigne de Coulanges La Vineuse
46, rue André Vildieu, 89580 Coulanges la Vineuse.
Tel: 03 86 42 54 48. Fax: 03 86 42 51 77.
www.yonne-89.net/MusCoulangV.htm
Open Jun 1–Sept 30 Wed–Fri 8AM–12PM and 2–6PM; AN
Sun–Tues. Open Oct 1–May 31 Mon–Thurs 8AM–12PM and
2–5:30PM; AN Fri–Sun. AN for groups.

Crémant de Bourgogne

Perhaps the most exciting development has taken place in a former quarry and in the mushroom cellars in the village of Bailly on the banks of the river Yonne, just off the N6, south of Auxerre. Here, in 1972, 80 growers banded together to form a company to produce sparkling Crémant de Bourgogne. With a stock of some 5 million bottles and an average of 2,000 visitors a week, this has now become a very large-scale operation.

A local specialty

Up a steep, narrow road behind Bailly lies the mother village of Saint-Bris-le-Vineux, which is by far the most important vineyard village in the Yonne *département*, outside the Chablis vineyards. The streets are full of growers' houses, with narrow, deep cellars beneath them. Many of the growers make wines from Chardonnay and Aligoté grapes, but there is also a local specialty, the Sauvignon de Saint-Bris. This is the only place in Burgundy where this grape is grown; it gives a wine that is similar in style to Sancerre.

Just 4 km (2.5 miles) away is the village of Chitry-le-Fort, renowned for its Bourgogne Aligoté. Here there is a fortified church dating back to the 13th century.

The vineyards of Irancy are intermingled with cherry orchards, and they produce a full-bodied red wine from the Pinot Noir and the César, a traditional local grape. The soil is very similar to that of Chablis, and oyster fossils can be picked up everywhere. The vines are in a natural amphitheater, which is a sun trap. On the west bank of the river Yonne lie two vineyard villages, Coulanges-la-Vineuse and Vaux.

Auxerre

The most important town in the region is Auxerre, which has a very pretty old quarter and the Gothic cathedral of Saint Stephen. There is also a 15th-century clock tower, with not only a sundial, but also a moondial.

The Côte d'Or

When one thinks of the wines of Burgundy, the first to come to mind are probably those of the Côte d'Or. This is a ridge that runs southwards from Dijon to just beyond Santenay. The protected, southeast-facing slopes are ideal for vines. The vineyards are classified in ascending order of quality: regional (e.g. Bourgogne), village (Gevrey-Chambertin), *premier cru* (Gevrey-Chambertin 1er Cru Clos Saint Jacques), and *grand cru* (Chambertin). A *grand cru* stands on its own without the village name. Although Côte d'Or only represents a small proportion of the total production, most of the great names are here.

No one knows for certain when the vines were first planted here. There is evidence that the local inhabitants enjoyed wine as long ago as 500 BC; the difficult part of the tin road—from Cornwall to the eastern Mediterranean—lay between the headwaters of the river Seine and its tributaries and the valley of the river Saône. Here the Aedui, predecessors of the Burgundians, acted as porters—and they took wine as a significant part of their pay.

In about 400 BC a vast number of the Aedui crossed the Alps and settled in northern Italy. When they returned to Burgundy a century and a half later, they probably brought vines and knowledge of wine-making with them. It is certain that during the Roman occupation many wine estates were established in what are the better-known vineyard villages.

TO GET TO THE CÔTE D'OR

From Chablis by the D91, A6, and A38, Dijon is 135 km (85 miles) and by the D91 and A6, Beaune is 130 km (81 miles).

The wine of prince and prelate

With Burgundy's importance as an independent kingdom, and then as a semi-autonomous duchy, the reputation of its wines spread far and wide. Their fame was also helped by the fact that for more than 600 years all the most famous vineyards belonged to either the nobility or the church, so the wines were drunk in all the most important royal and ecclesiastical circles in Europe.

Dijon

Dijon, the administrative and commercial capital of Burgundy, now has comparatively little to do with the wine trade. Industrial expansion has left little of the vineyards that it used to boast. However, it still has a high gastronomic reputation for its liqueurs—particularly the

House at countryside in Côte d'Or, Burgundy.
Image © Bernard Breton/Dreamstime.com

crême de cassis de Dijon—a controlled appellation, its gingerbread, and its mustards. These and many other products are on show at the Dijon Gastronomic Fair, which takes place each year in early November.

The town center is still full of old streets, most of them just a short walk from the tourist office in the Place Darcy.

The cathedral of St-Bénigne is the fourth church on the site and dates from the end of the 13th century. Originally a Benedictine abbey, what used to be the monks' dormitory is now an archaeological museum.

Other churches that should be visited include Notre-Dame, St-Jean, and St-Michel. The former Palace of the Dukes of Burgundy now houses the town hall and what some people consider to be the best art gallery in France outside Paris.

DIJON CASSIS

Gabriel Boudier
14, rue de Cluj,
21007 Dijon.
Tel: 03 80 74 33 33.
Email: information@
boudier.com
Fax: 03 86 74 88 88.
www.boudier.com

The Côte de Nuits

The Côte d'Or divides into two sections: the narrower Côte de Nuits in the north, largely making red wine, and the broader Côte de Beaune in the south, making both red and white.

A choice of routes

Driving south from Dijon along the Côte d'Or, there is a choice of three roads. If you are in a hurry, take the A31 motorway and then, to visit the vineyards, take the exit either at Nuits-Saint-Georges or at Beaune. Alternatively, take the D974 main road, which has lesser vineyards on either side, or D122, the *Route des Grands Crus*, which slowly wanders through the famous wine villages of Burgundy.

Chenôve

To join the *Route des Grands Crus*, take the D974, and after some 5 km (3 miles), at Chenôve, turn right at the L'Escargo-tière restaurant.

The vineyards of Chenôve have suffered greatly from the expansion of the city of Dijon and there are now only a quarter of the growers that there were 25 years ago. The most important feature in the village is the former press house of the Dukes of Burgundy, with two enormous wine presses dating back to 1238.

The first vineyard village of importance is Marsannay-la-Côte, which has traditionally been known for the best rosé wines in Burgundy. It has recently been granted its own village appellation for white and red wines, so there is a real danger that the rosé wines may slowly disappear, although Marsannay red and white can only come from the slopes, whereas the rosé can also come from the flatter, gravel vineyards. The next village, Couchey, also has the right to sell its wines under the name of Marsannay.

Fixin: a souvenir of Napoleon

Fixin may be said to be the first village on the Côte to produce great red wines, with the Clos de la Perrière probably being the outstanding vineyard. For Imperialists, the village is a living memory to the Emperor Napoleon, thanks to an adopted son of the village, Claude Noisot. He shared Napoleon's exile at Elba and fought at the battle of Waterloo. In later life, Napoleon became his fixation. He renamed a local vineyard Clos Napoleon and created a park in his memory, with, eventually, a museum, a florid statue of the emperor rising to lead the world again, and his own tomb, where he was buried, standing on guard.

Gevrey-Chambertin

After Brochon comes Gevrey-Chambertin, perhaps the capital of the red wines of Burgundy. Gevrey-Chambertin is the largest village appellation in the Côte de Nuits. Driving along on

CORGOLOIN

Domaine d'Ardhuy
Clos des Langres,
21700 Corgoloin.
Tel: 03 80 62 98 73.

COUCHEY

Derey Frères
1, rue Jules-Ferry, Couchey,
21160 Marsannay-la-Côte.
Tel: 03 80 52 15 04.

CIXIN

Domaine P. Gelin
2, rue du Chapitre,
21220 Fixin.
Tel: 03 80 52 45 24.

GEVREY-CHAMBERTIN

Domaine du Clos de Tart
Morey-Saint-Denis 21220
Gevrey-Chambertin.
Tel: 03 80 34 30 91.

the southern side of the village, the vineyards read like a roll call of honor: Mazis-Chambertin, Ruchottes-Chambertin, Clos de Bèze, le Chambertin, and Latricières-Chambertin. All of these are classified *grand cru*. On looking at the soil there is little to show that where the sign reads "Ici commence le Chambertin," real greatness begins. All along the Côte d'Or the *grand cru* vineyards are on the same part of the slope—the best drained and the best exposed to all the rays of sunshine available in this northern wine region.

Morey

Like many of the villages of Burgundy, Morey tacked onto its name that of its most famous vineyard, the Clos Saint Denis, becoming Morey-Saint-Denis. Its other greatest vineyards

MARSANNAY-LA-CÔTE

Domaine Bruno Clair

5, rue du Vieux-Collège,
21160 Marsannay-la-Côte.
Tel: 03 80 52 28 95.
Email: brunoclair@wanadoo.fr
www3.sympatico.ca/demersh

Domaine Fougeray de Beauclair

44, rue de Mazy,
21160 Marsannay-la-Côte.
Tel: 03 80 52 21 12.
Email: fougeraydebeauclair@
wanadoo.fr
Fax: 03 80 58 73 83.
www.fougeraydebeauclair.fr

Château de Marsannay

Route des Grands-Crus,
21160 Marsannay-la-Côte.
Tel: 03 80 51 71 11.
Email: chateau.marsannay@
kriter.com
Fax: 03 80 51 71 12.
Open Sunday except during
winter.

are Clos de la Roche, Clos de Tart, and Clos des Lambrays.

Chambolle-Musigny

Morey shares the vineyard of Bonnes-Mares with its neighbor, Chambolle-Musigny. Here the finest wines come from le Musigny, which makes a minute quantity of white wine each year, in addition to an outstanding red. In the center of the village is a magnificent lime tree planted on the instructions of Sully, Henri IV's minister.

Clos de Vougeot

Down the slope from the vineyard of le Musigny is the Clos de Vougeot, a walled vineyard founded in the 12th century by the monks of Cîteaux. Within the *clos* of 50 hectares (120 acres), there are almost 80 owners, each making his own wine. Unfortunately, this means that the wines vary greatly in quality.

The château, which now belongs to the Confrérie des Chevaliers du Tastevin, was originally built as the press house and cellars for the monks. It is now used for various grand dinners and celebrations. Vougeot's second castle, the Château de la Tour, was built at the end of the 19th century. The "new" château has beneath it some magnificent cellars dating back to the 15th century. Unfortunately, it is not open to the public.

In the narrow streets there is a particularly fine collection of vineyard owners' houses. One in the rue Sainte Barbe has a wooden balustrade more than 400 years old.

After Vougeot, the next vineyards belong to the village of Flagey-Echezeaux. Because the village lies to the east of the main road and is undistinguished, its claim to fame must be its two *grands crus*: les Echezeaux and les Grands Echezeaux. Its lesser wines can be sold under the name of the next, and infinitely more famous, village of Vosne-Romanée.

Vosne-Romanée

In the crown of the red wines of Burgundy, this must be the diamond in the center. Its wines have gained a justified reputation for their unrivalled finesse and bouquet. While some would claim that the Romanée-Conti is the finest, others would vote for La Tâche. Close behind come other great wines, such as La Romanée, Romanée-Saint-Vivant, Richebourg, and La Grande Rue.

Romanée-Conti and La Tâche belong exclusively to the Domaine de la Romanée-Conti, La Romanée to the Liger-Belair family, and La Grande Rue to the Lamarche domain. Given these circumstances, each bottle is allocated carefully—and at a price.

Once again, there is little to distinguish these noble plots of earth. To visit them, you go up the narrow lane by the side of the church. On the slope in front of you, a simple cross marks Romanée-Conti.

Nuits-Saint-Georges

Because the main road skirts the fringes of Nuits-Saint-Georges, few visit the town itself. Besides its host of merchants' cellars (Nuits comes second only to Beaune in importance in the Burgundy wine trade), there is the beautiful 13th-century church of Saint Symphorien.

Though much of it has been destroyed in a succession of wars, the town still maintains a bustling air of history. The fame of its wines owes a great deal to the prescriptions of the royal physician Fagon, who cured Louis XIV of a fistula by liberally dosing him with Nuits. In honor of this, the main street is now named after him.

The importance of the town and its wines have led to this northern part of the Côte d'Or vineyards being called the Côte de Nuits.

NUITS–SAINT–GEORGES

Bourgognes Faiveley
8, rue du Tribourg,
21701 Nuits-St-Georges.
Tel: 03 80 61 04 55.
Email: info@
bourgognes-faiveley.com
Fax: 03 80 62 33 37.
www.bourgognes-faiveley.com

Domaine Moillard
route Nationale 74,
21700 Nuits-St-Georges.
Tel: 03 80 62 42 20.
Email: contact@moillard.fr
www.moillard.fr
Shop: 8 Place de la Halle,
21200 Beaune,
03 80 22 53 45.

Morin Père et Fils
9, quai Fleury,
21700 Nuits-St-Georges.
Tel: 03 80 61 19 51.
Email: caves@
morinpere-fils.com
Fax: 03 80 61 05 10.
TP. Open 9AM–12PM and
2–6PM year round; 9AM –7PM
Apr 1–Oct 31.
Closed Dec 25–Jan 1

Domaine Daniel Rion,
RN 74, 21700 Prémeaux.
Tel: 03 80 62 31 28.
Email: contact@
domaine-daniel-rion.com
Fax: 03 80 61 13 41.
www.domaine-daniel-rion.com
Two tasting cellars and shop
open daily.
Tel: 03 80 61 26 16.

Prémeaux

South of Nuits, the next village
is Prémeaux. In its boundaries
many of the finest *premier cru*
wines of Nuits-Saint-Georges,
including the Clos de l'Arlot
and the Clos des Argillières, are
produced. Prémeaux also has a
number of natural springs, and
until 1970 the water from one of
them was marketed commer-
cially. Its medical properties were
recognized in Roman times.

Comblanchien and Corgoloin

The Côte de Nuits ends with the
two villages of Comblanchien
and Corgoloin. Sadly, neither
has been able to establish an
individual reputation for its
wines, and they are sold simply
as Côte de Nuits Villages.

Comblanchien is perhaps
better known now for its
"marble" (actually a variety of
limestone that looks like
marble), which was widely used
in the construction of the
Paris Opéra and Orly airport.

The name of the last vineyard
on the Côte de Nuits, the Clos
de Langres, is an indication of
the former importance of the
church in the history of
viticulture. It used to be the
property of the bishop and
chapter of Langres (a town to the
north of Dijon) who, until the
French Revolution, were the
largest vineyard owners in

Burgundy, after the Cistercian order of monks.

Côte de Beaune: Ladoix to Beaune

The Route des Grands Crus on the Côte de Nuits is relatively easy to follow because the villages form a straight line. On the Côte de Beaune, by way of contrast, there are numerous twists and turns and often a choice of roads. This first section to the north of Beaune is dominated by an instantly recognizable landmark: the imposing, conical hill of Corton.

Corton and Corton-Charlemagne

The first village one comes to is Ladoix-Serrigny; the reputation of wines under its own name comes below those that it makes on its higher slopes, which can be sold under the *grand cru* names of Corton-Charlemagne for white wines and, with rare exceptions, Corton for red. (One exception is the Cuvée Paul Chanson belonging to the Hospices de Beaune, which is a white wine coming from Corton-Vergennes.)

To the left of the main road, as you come out of the village, there is an 11th-century chapel, probably built for pilgrims on their way to Santiago de Compostella.

VOSNE-ROMANÉE

Domaine François Lamarche
9, rue des Communes,
21700 Vosne-Romanée.
Tel: 03 80 61 07 94.
Email: domainelamarche@
wanadoo.fr
www.domaine-lamarche.com

Domaine Mongeard-Mugneret
14, rue de la Fontaine,
21700 Vosne-Romanée.
Tel: 03 80 61 11 95.
Email: domaine@mongeard.com
Fax: 03 80 62 35 75.
www.mongeard.com
WS; tasting with purchase. AN.
Open Mon–Fri 8–11:30AM and
2–5PM. Closed in Aug. Associated with the Hôtel le Richebourg in Vosne Romanée,
www.hotel-lerichebourg.com.

**Domaine Armelle et
Bernard Rion**
8, route Nationale,
21700 Vosne-Romanée.
Tel: 03 80 61 05 31.
Email: rionab@wanadoo.fr
Fax: 03 80 61 34 60.
www.domainerion.com
TP. AN for groups (up to 50).
Open Mon–Sat 8AM–12PM and
2–6PM. No disabled access. E.

VOUGEOT

Château de la Tour
Clos de Vougeot,
21640 Vougeot.
Tel: 03 80 62 86 13.
Email: contact@
chateaudelatour.com
Fax: 03 80 62 82 72.
www.chateaudelatour.com
TP; TF with purchase. AN
for groups of 8+. Open
Easter–mid-Nov daily, except
Tues, 10AM–6PM. WS. E.

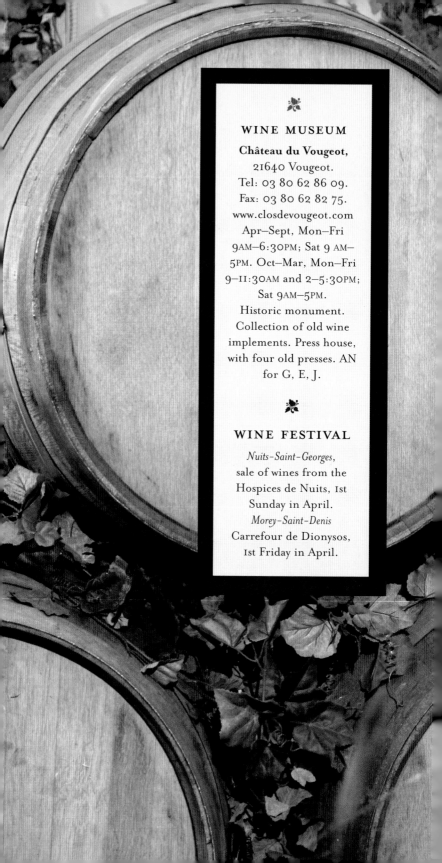

❧

WINE MUSEUM

Château du Vougeot,
21640 Vougeot.
Tel: 03 80 62 86 09.
Fax: 03 80 62 82 75.
www.closdevougeot.com
Apr–Sept, Mon–Fri
9AM–6:30PM; Sat 9 AM–
5PM. Oct–Mar, Mon–Fri
9–11:30AM and 2–5:30PM;
Sat 9AM–5PM.
Historic monument.
Collection of old wine
implements. Press house,
with four old presses. AN
for G, E, J.

❧

WINE FESTIVAL

Nuits-Saint-Georges,
sale of wines from the
Hospices de Nuits, 1st
Sunday in April.
Morey-Saint-Denis
Carrefour de Dionysos,
1st Friday in April.

Aloxe-Corton

Aloxe-Corton, in addition to its *grand cru* vineyards, boasts the colorfully roofed Château Corton-André, built at the end of the last century, and the more sober Château Corton-Grancey, belonging to wine company Louis Latour. Behind it, carved out of a quarry, are perhaps the finest cellars in Burgundy, with the estate press house above.

Pernand-Vergelesses

The third of the villages producing Corton and Corton-Charlemagne is Pernand-Vergelesses. Tucked into a narrow valley in the hillside, it is perhaps the least spoiled of all the wine villages of the Côte d'Or, with some beautiful growers' houses. Above the village there is a classic panoramic view over the vineyards and Beaune. A steep, narrow road up from the village takes you to the viewpoint. There are picnicking facilities as well as a statue to the Virgin Mary.

Savigny and Chorey-lès-Beaune

Savigny is particularly known for its red wines. In the valley lies an imposing château, which was rebuilt at the beginning of the 18th century and which now houses a car museum. Leading up from the village is the valley of the Fontaine Froide, a beautiful drive for those tired of looking at vineyards. At the top of the valley lies the pretty village of Bouilland, with its excellent restaurant, the Vieux Moulin.

On the plain, beyond the D974, is the village of Chorey-lès-Beaune, where a number of important estates are based. The church has a belfry in the "foreign" style of Franche-Comté, and there is a picturesque château surrounded by a moat.

The Town of Beaune

Beaune is one of the most satisfying wine towns to visit because of its compactness. It is still circled by its town walls, built in the 13th and 14th centuries, and, while the town has now expanded far beyond this military corset, most that is of interest lies within. The origins of the town go back to Roman days, and on a town plan one can still see the circular trace of the *oppidum*.

CHOREY-LÈS-BEAUNE

Domaine Dubois-Cachat
2, Grande Rue,
21200 Chorey-lès-Beaune.
Tel: 03 80 22 27 83.
Fax: 03 80 22 27 83.

Domaine Château de Chorey-lès-Beaune
21200 Beaune.
Tel: 03 80 22 06 05.
Email: contact@
chateau-de-chorey-les-beaune.fr
Fax: 03 80 24 03 93.
www.chateau-de-chorey-les-beaune.fr
Château and B&B.

LADOIX

Caves des Paulands
route Nationale 74,
21420 Aloxe-Corton.
Tel: 03 80 26 41 05.
Email: paulands@wanadoo.fr
Fax: 03 80 26 47 56.
www.lespaulands.com
Open Sunday. Caves, hotel, restaurant.

PERNAND-VERGELESSES

Domaine P Dubreuil-Fontaine Père et Fils
rue Rameau-Lamarosse,
21420 Pernand-Vergelesses.
Tel: 03 80 21 55 43.
Tel: 03 80 21 55 43.
Email: domaine@
dubreuil-fontaine.com
Fax: 03 80 21 51 69.
www.dubreuil-fontaine.com
AN. Open Mon–Fri 9AM–12PM and 2–6PM; Sat 9AM–12PM.

Roger Jaffelin et Fils
21400 Pernand-Vergelesses.
Tel: 03 80 21 52 43.

In these days of peace, the walls and towers of the fortifications are used to store wine, and while expanding business and modern machinery have led many companies to construct new premises outside the town, most of the important ones still have their offices and much of their stock in the town center. While Bouchard Père et Fils and Chanson Père et Fils store their wine in the bastions with walls up to seven meters (22 ft) thick, other companies, such as Patriarche and Ponnelle, use dispossessed religious properties. Drouhin has the former cellars of the Dukes of Burgundy.

The Hôtel-Dieu

Among the architectural gems of the town, the most famous is the Hôtel-Dieu, built in 1443 by Nicolas Rolin, chancellor of the Duchy of Burgundy, as a "hospital for the accommodation and assistance of the poor and the sick." Built in the Flemish style, with high, colorful roofs, around a beautiful courtyard, its treasures include a polyptych of the Last Judgment by Roger van der Weyden.

The Hôtel-Dieu forms part of the Hospices de Beaune (the other part is the Hospice de la Charité in the rue de Lorraine), financed by considerable

The historic Hôtel-Dieu in the center of Beaune was built in 1443. The famous annual Hospices de Beaune wine auction is held here. Photo © David Hughes/Dreamstime.com

BEAUNE

Louis Jadot
21, rue Eugène-Spuller,
21200 Beaune.
Tel: 03 80 22 10 57.
Email: contact@louisjadot.com
Fax: 03 80 22 56 03.
www.louisjadot.com
Tastings available only for
individuals, not groups; AN. E.

Domaine Albert Morot
Château de la Creusotte
21200 Beaune.
Tel: 03 80 22 35 39.

Patriarche Père et Fils
5, rue du Collège,
21200 Beaune.
Tel: 03 80 24 53 01.
Tel: 03 80 24 53 79 or 87.
Fax: 03 80 24 53 11.
www.patriarche.com
TP. AN for groups of 20+.
Open daily 9:30–11:30AM and
2–5:30PM. From Nov–Mar,
closes at 5PM. Variety of tours,
both audio-guided and guided,
available for groups. WS. Closed
Dec 24, 25, 31, and Jan 1.

Caves Exposition Reine
Pédauque Porte Saint Nicolas
21200 Beaune.
Tel: 03 80 22 23 11.
www.reine-pedauque.com

Albert Ponnelle Clos
Saint-Nicolas
38 Faubourg St-Nicolas,
21200 Beaune.
Tel: 03 80 22 00 05.
Email: info@ponnelle.com
Fax: 03 80 24 19 73.
www.albertponnelle.com

endowments, including an important estate of vineyards, whose wine is auctioned off each year on the third Sunday in November.

In the picturesquely named rue d'Enfer (Hell Street) is the former Palace of the Dukes of Burgundy, which now houses an attractively laid out wine museum. Close to this is Notre-Dame, the parish church of Beaune. Other buildings of interest include the town hall in what used to be the cloister of an Ursuline convent and, beyond the town wall on the road to the north, the simple 13th-century church of Saint Nicolas.

To the west of the town, on the flanks of the hillsides split by two valleys, lie the vineyards that have made Beaune so rich and spread its name through-out the world. While nearly all the wine made here is red, the variety of soils and micro-climates give a variety of styles that is unmatched by any other commune in Burgundy. There are devotees of the Grèves vineyard, of the Clos des Mouches, of Bressandes, and of Fèves; each gives a great wine in its individual style.

Beaune now has plenty of hotel options, with a number of individual hotels and national chains. Many of the new hotels are on the outskirts of Beaune, often close to the motorway.

MUSEUMS

Hôtel-Dieu: Le Musée des Hospices Civils de Beaune.
Tel: 03 80 24 45 00.
Email: hospices.beaune@wanadoo.fr
Fax: 03 80 24 45 99.
www.hospices-de-beaune.tm.fr
Museum open daily 9AM–6:30PM.

Musée du Vin de Bourgogne
Hôtel des Duos, rue d'Enfer,
21200 Beaune.
Tel: 03 80 22 08 19.
Email: musees@mairie-beaune.fr
Fax: 03 80 24 56 20.
www.musees-bourgogne.org.
Open daily Apr 1–Nov 30 9:30AM–6PM;
Dec 1–Mar 31 9:30AM–5PM. Closed Dec
25 and Jan 1; closed Tues from
Dec 1–Mar 31.

WINE FESTIVALS

Beaune Foire de Beaune
end May–1st week of June
Les Trois Glorieuses, weekend of 3rd Sunday in
November; auction of Hospices wines on
the Sunday.

FOR FURTHER INFORMATION

BIVB
12, boulevard Bretonnière,
21200 Beaune.
Tel: 03 80 25 04 80.
www.bivb.com

AUXEY-DURESSES

Domaine Roy Auxey-Duresses
route de Beaune
21190 Auxey-Duresses.
Tel: 03 80 21 22 37.
Email: domaine.roy@free.fr
Fax: 03 80 21 23 71.
domaine.roy.free.fr
AN for groups. Open
Mon–Fri 9am–12pm and
2–7pm; Sat 9am–12pm.
AN Sat afternoon, Sun, and
holidays.

CHASSAGNE-MONTRACHET

Bernard Colin et Fils
22, rue Charles-Pacquelin,
21190 Chassagne-Montrachet.
Tel: 03 80 21 92 40.

Fernand and Laurent Pillot
2, place des Noyers,
21190 Chassagne-Montrachet.
Tel: 03 80 21 99 83.
Email:contact:@vinpillot.com
WS; TF with wine purchase.
AN. Open Mon–Sat
8AM–6PM. E. Visit tasting
room only, not winery.

Domaine Jean Pillot et Fils
RN6,
21190 Chassagne-Montrachet.
Tel: 03 80 21 92 96.

Côte de Beaune: Beaune to Santenay

Pommard

The first vineyard village after Beaune is Pommard, famous throughout the world for its full-bodied red wines. The main street winds off to the right from the D973, with growers' houses on both sides. The village has three châteaux, two of which have now been united as the Château de Pommard and belong to the Laplanche family. The oldest is the Château de la Commaraine belonging to the Jaboulet-Vercherre family and backing on to the attractive Clos de la Commaraine vineyard.

Volnay

As another village standing back from and above the main road, Volnay maintains an agreeable calm, with its finest vineyards lying out on the slope in front of it.

In historical times, the dukes of Burgundy spent the summers in the château that they built here, though unfortunately its destruction was ordered by Cardinal Richelieu. Traditionally, each May Day a shooting competition was held within the village, with the winner being able to style himself as "king" and gain exemption from certain taxes.

Monthélie

To find the village of Month-élie, you must turn right off the main road on to the D23. Monthélie is a village of narrow streets and wine-growers' houses spread down the hillside, with a reputation of poverty, because there are no sources of water on its territory. Because it's slightly off the main road, its wines don't have the quality image that they rightly deserve, so they are often a very good value.

White Wines of the Côte de Beaune

While there are some who might claim that Burgundy does not produce the finest red wines of France, there are few who would say that it does not make the best dry white wines. Here come together the perfect blend of soil, climate, and the Chardonnay grape to give great wines with fruit and flavor.

The village of Aloxe-Corton produces great white wines in the Charlemagne vineyard, but it is the three villages of Meursault, Puligny-Montrachet, and Chassagne-Montrachet that have the reputation for making the best of the white wines.

Meursault

Although there are no *grands crus* in Meursault, there are a number of well-known *premiers*

MEURSAULT

Vincent Girardin Les Champs Lins
21190 Meursault.
Tel: 03 80 20 81 00.
Email: vincent.girardin@vincentgirardin.com
Fax: 03 80 20 81 10.

Château de Meursault
21190 Meursault.
Tel: 03 80 26 22 75.
Email: chateau.meursault@kriter.com
Fax: 03 80 26 22 76.
www.chateau-meursault.com
TP. Open 9:30AM–12PM and 2:30–6PM in winter; in summer, open 9:30AM–12:30PM and 2–6PM. Tours for groups of 25–50, including 5-wine tasting. Painting gallery, video. E.

François Rapet et Fils
rue Sous-le-Château,
21190 Saint-Romain.
Tel: 03 80 21 22 08.

Domaine Jacques Prieur
6, rue des Santenots, Les Herbeux, 21190 Meursault.
Tel: 03 80 21 23 85.
Email: gaillard.f@rodet.com
Fax: 03 80 21 29 19.
www.prieur.com

Caves Ropiteau Frères
Cour des Hospices,
21190 Meursault.
Tel 03 80 21 24 73.
Email: info@caves-ropiteau.com
Fax: 03 80 21 24 73.
www.caves-ropiteau.com
T. Groups AN. Open daily 9:30AM–6:30PM from Easter to the 3rd weekend of November. WS. E; for G & D AN.

MONTHELIE

Domaine Michel Dupont-Fahn
Clos des Toisières,
21190 Monthélie.
Tel: 03 80 21 26 78.

POMMARD

Domaine de Montille
12, rue du Pied-de-la-Vallée,
21190 Volnay.
Tel: 03 80 21 62 67.
Email: e.demontille@
wanadoo.fr

Château de Pommard
21630 Pommard.
Tel: 03 80 22 07 99.
Email: accueil-caveau@
chateaudepommard.fr
Fax: 03 80 24 65 88.
www.chateau-de-
pommard.tm.fr
T. AN only for groups during
season; off season AN. Open
daily end of Mar–3rd Sun in
Nov, daily 9AM–6:30PM. WS.

PULIGNY–
MONTRACHET

Chartron et Trebuchet
13 Grande Rue,
21190 Puligny-Montrachet.
Tel: 03 80 21 32 85.
Email: j.delannoy@
chartron-trebuchet.com
www.chartron-trebuchet.com

crus such as Les Charmes, Les
Genevrières, Les Gouttes d'Or,
and Les Perrières. Meursault is
a useful center for visiting the
vineyards of the Côte d'Or.
There are a number of small
hotels and restaurants and a
camping site.

The village has two châteaux.
The older, dating from the
14th century, was largely
destroyed in 1478; what
remains now forms part of the
town hall. The Château de
Meursault is built above the
14th-century cellars of the
Cistercian monks. Here there is
now an art gallery and the
chance to taste a range of fine
burgundies from Patriarche.

Puligny-Montrachet

Puligny-Montrachet is a much
quieter village, with its two
squares ringed by imposing
private houses. It also has two
châteaux. The "old" one was
partly dismantled and sold off to
antique dealers during World
War I. The "Château de Puligny-
Montrachet" dates back to the
middle of the 18th century.

The great vineyards lie behind
the village. Two *grands crus*,
Chevalier-Montrachet and Bien-
venues-Bâtard-Montrachet, lie
solely within the boundaries; two
others, le Montrachet and
Bâtard-Montrachet, it shares with
its neighbor, Chassagne.

Le Montrachet

Le Montrachet is consi-
dered by many to be the
world's greatest dry white
wine. The vineyard is just
under 8 hectares (20 acres)
in size and has 15 different
owners, with their own
parcels of vines. In an
average year, one of these
may produce no more than
a single barrel—yet each
bottle may sell at £100
($150) or even more.

Chassagne-Montrachet is
best known for its white
wines, but it actually produces more red wine, much
of it of a very high quality.

Santenay

From Chassagne, the
vineyard road, the D113A,
curves round the hillside to
the last of the major
vineyard villages, San-
tenay. Here mainly red
wines are made.

So far, we have kept
along the straight road
through the vineyards.
However, there are villages
lying off that road in the
valleys to the west. From
Meursault, the D17E leads
first to Auxey-Duresses,
known for its red and white

SAINT-AUBIN

Hubert Lamy
rue des Lavières,
21190 Saint-Aubin.
Tel: 03 80 21 32 55.
Email: domainehubertlamy@
wanadoo.fr
Fax: 03 80 21 38 32.
www.perso.wanadoo.fr/
domaine.hubert.lamy

VOLNAY

Rossignol-Février
rue du Mont,
21190 Volnay.
Tel: 03 80 21 64 23.
Email: rossignol-fevrier@
wanadoo.fr
Fax: 03 80 21 67 74.
Closed Sunday.

Rossignol-Jeanniard
rue du Mont,
21190 Volnay.
Tel: 03 80 21 62 43.
Email: domaine-rossignol-
jeanniard@wanadoo.fr

WINE FESTIVALS

Meursault

La Trinquée de Meursault,
2nd Saturday in September
La Paulée de Meursault,
Monday of the 3rd weekend in
November

wines. Next comes the attractive village of St-Romain, which is
split into two parts, one on a rocky escarpment, the other in
the valley below.

The D906, which was the main road from Paris to the south until the motorway was built, leads up to the village of Gamay, which gave its name to the grape, and St-Aubin, which produces excellent red and white wines. It is in villages like these that real bargains are to be found.

The Hautes-Côtes

Behind the main vineyards of the Côte d'Or lie the vineyards of what is known as the Hautes-Côtes. Here there are not just vines, but also meadows and plantings of soft fruit, particularly blackcurrants for the *crème de cassis* liqueur. Most of the wine is red, though there is also a little white, and much of it is made at the cooperative of the Hautes-Côtes, which is on the D974, on the southern outskirts of Beaune.

The scenery is spectacular. From the top of the cliff at Orches you look down on St-Romain, the valley leading down to Meursault, the plain of the Saône, the Jura Mountains, and on a very clear day, Mont Blanc. There is the Château de la Rochepot, nestling in against the hillside; the Pas Saint Martin, near Mandelot, where the saint is reputed to have escaped from the Devil by jumping across the valley; the pretty town of Nolay, with its 14th-century market hall; and Bévy, with the biggest vineyard area of all, where a local wine merchant reclaimed land that had been scrub for generations.

This is the quieter, less commercial face of Burgundy, where time seems less important. Many of the growers also own vines in the more fancied villages of the Côte—but their prices always seem more reasonable because they do not have a fashionable address.

To taste a range of the wines and simple local food, there is no better place to go than the Maison des Hautes-Côtes, a joint venture of a number of growers at Marey-lès-Fussey on the D8, in the hills above Corgoloin.

The Côte Chalonnaise

For too long the wines of the Côte Chalonnaise have been underappreciated, but over the past 20 years there have been two moves to give them more of an individual personality. First, the Aligoté wines from the small village of Bouzeron have been able to call themselves *appellation Bouzeron*—and no other village in Burgundy has been permitted to use its name in this way.

Secondly, up just one level, the red and white wines have been able to add Côte Chalonnaise to their generic name of Bourgogne. This is important; the wines from the local vineyards, apart from those from the four village appell-ations of Rully, Mercurey, Givry, and Montagny, had too often disappeared into the blending vats of the large merchants. Unusually for France, the Côte Chalonnaise wines must pass a strict quality test before they can be labeled Côte Chalonnaise.

Chagny

The starting point for a visit to the vineyards of the Côte Chalonnaise must be the town of Chagny. From there, take the D981 road to the south, though you should take regular diversions to the right to visit the wine villages.

HAUTES-CÔTES DE BEAUNE

Domaine Mazilly Père et Fils
route de Pommard, Meloisey,
21190 Meursault.
Tel: 03 80 26 02 00.

Les Caves des Hautes-Côtes
route de Pommard,
21200 Beaune.
Tel: 03 80 25 01 00.

HAUTES-CÔTES DE NUITS

Domaine Patrick Hudelot
21700 Villars-Fontaine.
Tel: 03 80 61 50 37.
Email: contact@
domaine-patrick-hudelot.com
www.domaine-patrick-
hudelot.com

**Domaine de Montmain
Villars-Fontaine**
21700 Nuits-St-Georges.
Tel: 03 80 62 31 94.
Email: bernard.hudelot@
wanadoo.fr
Fax: 03 80 61 02 31.

**Domaine Thévenot-le-
Brun et Fils
Marey-lès-Fussey**
21700 Nuits-St-Georges.
Tel: 03 80 62 91 64.
Email: thevenot-le-brun@
wanadoo.fr
www.thevenot-le-brun.com

BOUZERON

Chanzy Frères
1, rue de la Fontaine, 71150
Tel: 03 85 87 23 69.
Email: daniel@chanzy.com
Fax: 03 80 87 62 12.
www.chanzy.com
Open Mon–Fri 8AM–12PM and
2–6PM; Sat AN. Closed Sun,
holidays, and Aug 8–Aug 20.

A et P Villaine
2, rue de la Fontaine, 71150
Tel: 03 85 91 20 50.
Email: dom.devillaine@
wanadoo.fr; www.de-
villaine.com
AN. Closed holidays, Jul
25–Aug 17, and Dec 24–Jan 4.

GIVRY

Michel Sarrazin et Fils
Charnailles, 71640 Jambles.
Tel: 03 85 44 30 57.
Email: sarrazin@wanaddo.fr

Bouzeron

Of these villages, the first is Bouzeron, already mentioned for its Aligotés. The monks of Cluny were the first to establish the reputation of Bouzeron's wines, but now Bouchard Père et Fils and Aubert de Villaine, one of the co-owners of the Domaine de la Romanée-Conti, have important holdings here. The quality of the best Aligoté from Bouzeron shows that these wines are fit for more than being the traditional base for *kir*—a measure of *crème de cassis* topped up with white wine.

Classified vineyards

As in the Côte d'Or, some particularly well-sited vineyards in the four leading villages—Givry, Mercurey, Montagny, and Rully—are classified as *premier cru*. However, there are no *grands crus* in the Côte Chalonnaise.

Rully

There is a rather steep and narrow road to the next village, Rully, but the faint-hearted may prefer to return to Chagny first. Rully has suffered badly in history, and its reputation for wines has improved largely as a result of the efforts of its dynamic mayor, Jean-François Delorme. As well as making fine red and white wines, it is also a center of the sparkling-wine trade.

Mercurey

The best-known wines of the Côte are Mercurey, and they

come from a cluster of small villages, of which Mercurey is one. It is also the most important wine-producing commune in the Côte. It is known especially for its red wines, which have an equal standing to many from the Côte d'Or. There are certain "château" wines with a good reputation. The one most often found is the Château de Chamirey, from local merchant Antonin Rodet.

Givry and Montagny

Givry, too, is well known for its red wines, though it produces much less than Mercurey. It was a favorite of Henri IV (who always seemed to be prepared to endorse the local wine), and he may well have used it as an aid in his courtship of his local girlfriend, Gabrielle d'Estrées.

The last of the wines of the Côte Chalonnaise is Montagny. This is just white wine from the vineyards around the small town of Buxy, where there is a tasting cellar in the Tour Rouge.

The Mâconnais

If you continue along the D981 road that has taken you through the vineyards of the Côte Chalonnaise, you cross the boundary into the vineyards of the Mâconnais at the village of

MERCUREY

Antonin Rodet
Domaine du Château de Chamirey, 71640
Tel: 03 85 98 12 12.
Email: rodet@rodet.com
www.rodet.com

Hugues et Yves Suremain
Domaine de Bourgneuf, 71640
Tel: 03 85 45 20 87.
Email: contact@
domaine-de-suremain.com
www.domaine-de-suremain.com
AN.

Maison du Vin de Mercurey
Château du Garnerot, 71640
Tel: 03 85 45 22 99.
Fax: 03 85 45 24 88.
T. WS.

WINE FESTIVALS
Concours des Vins de la Côte Chalonnaise et du Couchois, second Saturday in January (location varies).
Chagny Wine Fair, around 15 August, 4–5 days.

FOR FURTHER INFORMATION

Maison du Vin Picard Bourgognes
route de Saint-Loup de la Salle, 71150 Chagny.
Tel: 03 65 87 51 00.

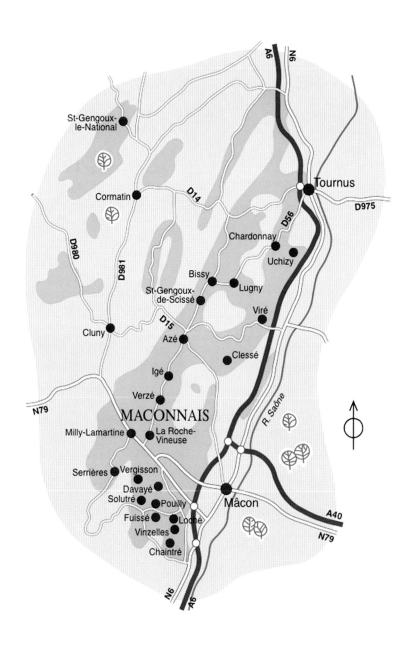

Saint-Gengoux-le-National. The road eventually leads on to the small town of Cluny.

Cluny

While Cluny may not appear to play an important role in the current world of wine, this has not always been the case. Little remains of the great abbey, once the headquarters of the Benedictine order responsible for much of the early vineyard planting in Burgundy.

Cluny is on the western fringes of the vineyard area, which broadly lies in the triangle between Cluny and two towns lying on the river Saône: Tournus and Mâcon.

Saints and churches

For those interested in ecclesiastical architecture, the area is particularly known for its Romanesque churches, dating back to the 12th century. Those of Donzy and Blanot are particularly beautiful. Tournus is best known for the magnificent church of Saint Philibert.

The Mâconnais is not solely dedicated to the production of wine. To the west of Mâcon is the town of Charolles, which has given its name to the well-known breed of cattle, the Charolais. There are also many herds of goats.

Historically the region was known for red wines made from Gamay and Pinot Noir. Now most of the production is in white wine from the Chardonnay. Because this is a region of polyculture, most of the growers take their grapes to the local cooperative cellar. Many of these have tasting cellars for

MONTAGNY

Cave des Vignerons de Buxy
La Buxynoise, Les Vignes de la Croix,
71390 Buxy.
Tel: 03 85 92 03 03.
Email: labuxynoise@cave-buxy.fr
Fax: 03 85 92 08 06.
TF. Open Tues–Sat year round (Mon–Sat in summer) 9AM–12PM and 2–6PM.

RULLY

André Delorme
rue de la République,
71150 Rully.
Tel: 03 85 87 10 12.
Fax: 03 85 87 04 60.
www.andre-delorme.fr

Jérôme Noël-Bouton
Domaine de la Folie
71150 Chagny.
Tel: 03 85 87 18 59.
www.domainedelafolie.com

Maison des Vins de la Côte Chalonnaise
Promenade Ste-Marc,
71100 Châlon-sur-Saone.
Tel: 03 85 41 64 00.
Fax: 03 85 41 99 83.
T. Open 9AM–7PM daily except Sun and holidays. WS.

TO GET TO THE MÂCONNAIS

Tournus is 53 km (33 miles) from Beaune and 364 km (266 miles) from Paris by the A6. Mâcon is 83 km (52 miles) from Beaune and 395 km (247 miles) from Paris. Mâcon may be reached by TGV train from Paris.

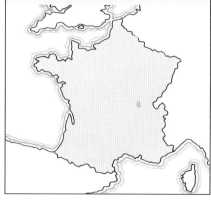

the promotion of their wines to passing tourists.

Mâcon-Villages

Much of the wine from the peripheral vineyards in the area has a right only to the simple appellation "Mâcon." In the heart of the area, though, there are 36 villages that have the right to sell their wine either as Mâcon-Villages, or by attaching the village name to Mâcon, such as Mâcon-Lugny or Mâcon-Viré. Two of the villages have given their names to grape varieties, Chasselas and Chardonnay, while one of them, Milly, has added the name of its most famous son, the poet Lamartine.

To visit the vineyards of the Mâcon-Villages, a simple route would be to leave Tournus by the D56 and drive through Chardonnay and Lugny. From there, take the D82 and the D85 to Igé and La-Roche-Vineuse. After a brief detour to Milly-Lamartine, where the poet lost a fortune in making wine, you can take the main N79 road into Mâcon.

An alternative, and slightly shorter, route would be from Chardonnay to Uchizy, Viré, and Clessé, arriving in Mâcon from the north. Either way is a pleasant pastoral drive through a gentle, rolling landscape.

More affordable wines

Now that many of the white wines of Burgundy have become very expensive, it is worthwhile looking at those from the Mâconnais. These are made from the same grape, the Chardonnay, and they bear a family resemblance to their rather more aristocratic cousins from Chablis and the Côte d'Or. It is in areas such as this that real discoveries are to be made, for, apart from the larger cooperatives, there are a number of smaller growers who are justifiably proud of what they make.

Greatest wines of the Mâconnais

To the west and south of Mâcon are the vineyards of Pouilly-Fuissé and its satellites, Pouilly-Vinzelles, Pouilly-Loché, and St-Véran.

Here, a combination of soil, exposure of the vineyards, and climate create white burgundies with their own character. While still dry, they have a soft richness that makes them very appealing, and they have a particularly strong following in the US. Pouilly-Fuissé is the most famous of these wines and has been very successful despite its hard-to-pronounce name. Although sweet wines are not typical of the area, they are occasionally made in very hot years.

Mâcon

These vineyards lie on the doorstep of Mâcon, a beautiful town despite the fact that its buildings have suffered badly over the centuries. It is the administrative capital for the region and its wines. It has had a wine fair since the first half of the 14th century and, since 1933, has held the annual French National Wine Fair, where wines from all over France, and often further afield, can be tasted for a nominal sum.

For the motorist hurrying down the motorway to the beaches of the Mediterranean or the Alpine ski slopes, Mâcon can make a convenient halt, with its many fine restaurants and hotels. If there is no time to visit the neighboring vineyards, a full range of the local wines can be tasted, with or without a light meal, at the Maison des Vins, on the way into town from the north.

A famous crag

The vineyard skyline of Pouilly-Fuissé is dominated by two dramatic crags, the rocks of Vergisson and Solutré, the second of which has a colorful legend attached to it: the

CLESSÉ

Gautier and Jean Thévenet
Quintaine-Clessé
Domaine de la Bongran,
71260 Clessé.
Tel: 03 85 36 94 03.
Email: contact@bongran.com
Fax: 03 85 36 99 25.
www.bongran.com
AN.

FUISSÉ

Château de Fuissé
71960 Fuissé.
Tel: 03 85 35 61 44.
Email: domaine@
chateau-fuisse.fr. For tours,
email: benedicte@chateau-
fuisse.fr.
Fax: 03 85 35 67 34.
www.chateau-fuisse.fr
Open 8AM–12PM and
1:30–5:30PM. WS.

IGÉ

Cave des Vignerons d'Ige
rue du Tacot,
71960 Igé.
Tel: 03 85 33 33 56.
Email: info@
lesvigneronsdige.com
Fax: 03 85 33 41 85.
www.lesvigneronsdige.com
AN for groups. Open
Mon–Sat 8AM–12PM and
2–6PM; Sun and holidays
10AM–12PM and 2–7PM. WS.
Can also visit the Museum of
Vine & Wine in the Chapelle
de Domange.

prehistoric people used to drive herds of horses to their death over the edge. The truth is more prosaic. The human settlement was located at the foot of the precipice, and it is this that accounts for the mounds of animal bones found there.

Pouilly-Fuissé

The vineyards of Pouilly-Fuissé are in a natural amphi-theater of vines spread between the four villages of Vergisson, Solutré, Fuissé, and Chaintré. The wines are all dry and white, though they have a deep richness of body that is not found elsewhere in Burgundy.

The wines of Pouilly-Fuissé are the most expensive. Fortunately, there are a small number of alternative, if lesser, wines from the same region: Pouilly-Loché, Pouilly-Vinzelles, and St-Véran.

Vineyard circuit

The circuit of these vineyards of the southern Mâconnais is short and simple, though rather winding. Leave Mâcon by the D54, and shortly after passing under the motorway, fork right to Davayé and Vergisson. On the far side of the village, turn left and drive around the back of the rock of Solutré to the village of the same name.

From Solutré, the road leads to Pouilly and the picturesque village of Fuissé, where there is a sign saying, "A hundred growers bid you welcome." Château de Fuissé makes some of the best wine. Here there is a narrow lane down to Loché and Vinzelles, but it is probably easier to drive around via Chaintré. From here, the choice is either a return to Mâcon or to move on to the Beaujolais.

The Beaujolais

For many wine lovers, the Beaujolais is the most enjoyable of all wine regions. It has a relaxed atmosphere that is all its own. It is a place where the importance of time seems to be eternally diminished, and thus, it is the wrong place for those who want to break away from the motorway just to gain a small sample of its flavor.

The flavor of the Beaujolais is not just its wine or its countryside—a succession of rounded hills leading ultimately to the beginnings of the Massif Central. These hills make this one of the most attractive of the French wine regions. Beaujolais is also the red-roofed villages round the squares, where the click of boules is rivaled by the clink of bottle on glass at the tables outside the welcoming bars.

A wine to be enjoyed
Beaujolais, as a wine, does not seek to be taken too seriously. It is there to be enjoyed, and if it is difficult to prove the local claim that Beaujolais is the only wine that can quench a thirst, there is every incentive to put it to the test by taking another glass... and another.

Even with detailed instructions, it is easy to get lost, for the contours do not permit straight roads, and in any case they might speed up the pace of life. The Clochemerle novels of Gabriel Chevalier are not an exaggeration of that life in the Beaujolais, but rather a loving look at it.

Geography of the Beaujolais
Broadly speaking, the Beaujolais can be divided into two parts. In the south, beyond Villefranche-sur-Saône, is the Bas-Beaujolais. Here the soil is largely sandy, and lighter, earlier-maturing wines are made. Many of these are

LUGNY
Cave de Lugny
rue des Charmes, 71260 Lugny.
Tel: 03 85 33 22 85.
Email: commercial@
cave-lugny.com
Fax : 03 85 33 26 46.
www.cave-lugny.com
Open daily Apr–Sept
8:30AM–12:30PM and 1:30–
7PM. Closed Sun and holidays.

OZENAY
Château de Messey
Messey, 71700 Ozenay.
Tel: 03 85 51 33 83.
Email: chateau@demessey.com
Fax: 03 85 51 33 82.
www.demessey.com
Closed January. Guest cottages
and B&B available in vineyard.

VINZELLES
Cave des Grands
Crus Blancs 71680 Vinzelles.
Tel: 03 85 35 61 88.
Email: contact@
cavevinzellesloche.com
Fax: 03 85 27 05 71.
www.cavevinzellesloche.com.
Open daily.

VIRÉ
André Bonhomme
rue Jean-Large, 71260 Viré.
Tel: 03 85 27 93 93.
Fax: 03 85 27 93 94.

Cave de Viré La Passion Partagée
Cave de Viré, En Vercheron,
71260 Viré.
Tel: 03 85 32 25 50.
Email: contact@
cavedevire-bourgogne.com
Fax: 03 85 32 25 55.
www.cavedevirebourgogne.com
Open Mon–Fri 8AM–12PM and
2–6PM.

released in mid-November as
Beaujolais Nouveau.

In the north, between Mâcon
and Villefranche, the soil is
more granitic. From here come
the fuller, fruitier wines of the
Beaujolais-Villages, and here
are the ten crus, those villages
that can sell their wine just
under their own names. These
are, from north to south: St-
Amour, Juliénas, Chénas,
Moulin-à-Vent, Fleurie, Chiroubles, Morgon, Regnié,
Brouilly, and Côte-de-Brouilly.

Throughout the region, the
red wines are made with just
one grape, the Gamay. The
Gamay is despised in the rest of
Burgundy, but in the Beaujolais
it is king. A small amount of
Beaujolais white is made from
Chardonnay.

Alternative routes
The main road, the N6, skirts
the eastern fringes of the
Beaujolais vineyards. While the
villages along it may house
many of the most important
wine merchants of the region,
and while there may be the
occasional tasting cellar to
cause the hurried motorist to
halt for a while, to taste and
perhaps to buy, this is not the
Beaujolais.

There is a choice of three
different Beaujolais "routes,"
which are clearly marked. Two
of these lie between Mâcon and

❧

WINE FESTIVALS

Mâcon Concours des Vins de la Saint Vincent, nearest Saturday to January 22. *Exhibition Center French National Wine Fair*, around May 20 (10 days). *Lugny Haut Mâconnais Wine Fair*, Saturday before Palm Sunday.

❧

FOR FURTHER INFORMATION

La Maison des Vins de Mâcon 484, avenue Maréchal de Lattre de Tassigny, 71000 Mâcon. Tel: 03 85 22 91 11.

BIVB 520, avenue Maréchal de Lattre de Tassigny, 71000 Mâcon. Tel: 03 85 38 20 15. Email: bivb@wanadoo.fr www.bivb.com

THE BEAUJOLAIS

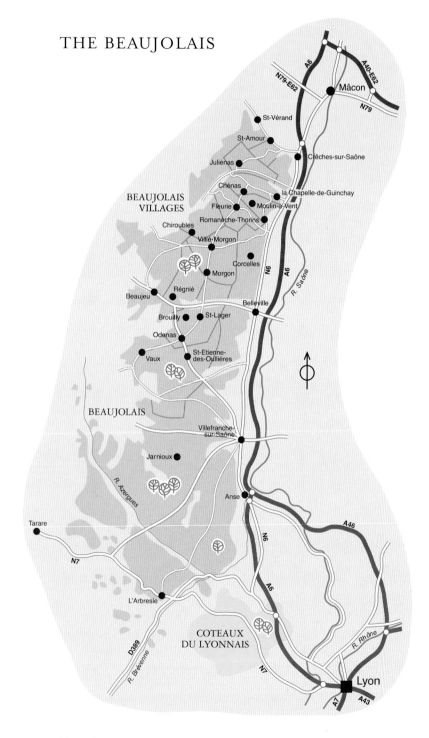

Mâcon

St-Vérand

St-Amour

Juliénas

Clêches-sur-Saône

Chénas

la Chapelle-de-Guinchay

BEAUJOLAIS
VILLAGES

Fleurie

Moulin-à-Vent

Romanèche-Thorins

Chiroubles

Villié-Morgon

Corcelles

Morgon

Régnié

Beaujeu

Belleville

Brouilly

St-Lager

Odenas

Vaux

St-Etienne-
des-Oullières

BEAUJOLAIS

Villefranche-
sur-Saône

Jarnioux

Anse

Tarare

COTEAUX
DU LYONNAIS

L'Arbresle

Lyon

Morning fog on the Beaujolais Valley. Photo by Jacques Croizer/Dreamstime.com

TO GET TO THE BEAUJOLAIS

Villefranche-sur-Saône is 439 km (274 miles) from Paris and 31 km (20 miles) from Lyon on the A6.

BEAUJEU

Domaine de Pavillon de Chavannes

69430 Quincié-en-Beaujolais.
Tel: 04 74 04 35 01.
Email: pauljambon@aol.com
Fax: 04 74 69 01 09.
T. Open daily 9AM–12PM and
2–6PM. WS. E.

BROUILLY

Château de la Chaize

Odenas, 69460
St-Etienne-des-Oullières.
Tel: 04 74 03 41 05.
Email: info@
chateaudelachaize.com
Fax: 04 74 03 52 73.
www.chateaudelachaize.com
Open weekdays 8:30AM–12PM
and 2–5PM; on Fridays, closes
at 3:30PM. AN for visits on
Sat. Closed in Aug and
during the grape harvest
(usually in Sept).

MORGON

Domaine des Pillets les Pillets

69910 Villié-Morgon.
Tel: 04 74 04 21 60.
Fax: 04 74 69 15 28.
Closed for the first two weeks
of August.

MOULIN−À−VENT

Château des Jacques

(of Maison Louis Jador)
71570 Romanèche-Thorins.
Tel: 03 85 35 51 64.
Email: contact@louisjador.com
www.louisjadot.com

Villefranche, while the third,
au pays des pierres dorées, meanders
round the southern part of the
region.

With the modern motorist in
mind there is also a "fast"
route, which turns off the N6 at
Crêches-sur-Saône, 8 km (5
miles) south of Mâcon, and
leads through the famous *crus*,
beginning with St-Amour and
then Juliénas.

Moulin-à-Vent, Fleurie, and Morgon

Within the boundaries of
Chénas is the sole windmill of
the Beaujolais, but perhaps
one of the best known in the
world, for it has given its name
to the wine Moulin-à-Vent.

From Fleurie the route goes
to Villié-Morgon and the
hamlet of Morgon, from
where it is worth making a
short diversion to the left to
visit the beautiful Château de
Pizay.

Brouilly

St-Lager lies at the foot of the
Mont de Brouilly, at the top of
which is a small chapel, Notre-
Dame du Raisin, the object of
a well-refreshed pilgrimage
each year on September 8.
There is a road to the top,
from where there is a
magnificent view of the
Beaujolais vineyards.

Odenas

At Odenas is the Château de la Chaize, built at the end of the 17th century by the nephew of the confessor of Louis XIV. Le Nôtre designed the gardens and the cellar is a national monument, the longest single-vaulted cellar in the Beaujolais. From there, the rapid route passes through St-Etienne-des-Oullières to Villefranche.

The route touristique

The *route touristique* follows largely the same outline, but with a number of diversions. The first takes in the Château de Corcelles, which is open to the public. The second is the former capital of the region, Beaujeu, which like Beaune has a hospital financed in part by its vineyard holdings.

The Château also owns La Grange Chartron at Régnié, which was built as an immense vineyard estate at the beginning of the last century. Régnié also has the distinction of being the last village to have its wines elevated to cru status. The final diversion takes in Vaux, the village that was the model for the Clochemerle books.

Les pierres dorées

The *pierres dorées* or "golden stones" circuit wanders vaguely for some 50 km (30 miles).

MOULIN-À-VENT

Château Portier Moulin-à-Vent
Romanèche-Thorins, 71570
La Chapelle-de-Guinchay.
Tel: 03 85 35 51 57.

ROMANECHE-THORINS

Georges Duboeuf
au Hameau en Beaujolais
71570 Romanèche-Thorins.
Tel: 03 85 35 34 20.
Email: gduboeuf@duboeuf.com
Fax: 03 85 35 34 25.
www.hameauenbeaujolais.com
or www.duboeuf.com
Open daily; in summer
(Apr–Oct) 9AM–7PM; in
winter (Nov–Mar) 10AM–6PM.
Closed January 2–15. Tours
(for a fee) through the theme-park-like Plaisirs en Beaujolais.

SAINT ETIENNE-LA-VARENNE

Château des Tours
69460 St-Etienne-la-Varenne.
Tel: 04 74 03 40 86.

SALLES-ARBUISSONAS-EN-BEAUJOLAIS

Domaine Christian Miolane
La Folie, 69460
Salles-Arbuissonnas.
Tel: 04 74 60 52 48.
Fax: 04 74 67 59 95.
Email: domainemiolane@wanadoo.fr

ARBOIS

Fruitière Vinicole d'Arbois

2, rue des Fossés,
39600 Arbois.
Tel: 03 84 66 11 67.
Email: contact@
chateau-bethanie.com.
www.chateau-bethanie.com
Also shops in Arbois:
40, rue Jean Jaures.
Tel: 03 84 66 21 78.
43, place de la Liberté.
Tel: 03 84 66 21 84.
TP. AN for 10+.
Open to the public free of
charge Jul 1–Aug 31,
10AM–7PM. WS. Bus tour of
vineyard available.

Henri Maire SA

Deux Tonneaux, place de la
Liberté, 39600 Arbois.
Tel: 03 84 66 15 27.
Email: info@henri-maire.fr
Fax: 03 84 66 22 87.
www.henri-maire.com
TF. Open daily; in winter,
9AM–12PM and 2–5:30PM; in
summer, 8AM–7PM. Visits to
vineyards and cellars and
informational video, all free
of charge. WS.

Domaine Rolet Père et Fils

Montesserin, Route de Dole,
39600 Arbois.
Tel: 03 84 66 00 05.
Email: rolet@wanadoo.fr
Fax: 03 84 37 47 41.
www.rolet-arbois.com

Domaine Jacques Tissot

39, rue de Courcelles
39600 Arbois.
Tel: 03 84 66 24 54.
Email: courrier@
domaine-jacques-tissot.fr
Fax: 03 84 66 25 15.
www.domaine-jacques-tissot.fr
T. WS. Also at 32, Grande
Rue (under the arcades),
Arbois, and at Winery Les
Bruyeres (Besancon's Road,
route Nationale 83).

Here the main attractions are
the beautiful scenery, the
castles at Jarnioux and
Châtillon d'Azergues, and a
liberal selection of tasting
cellars, many attached to
cooperatives.

Tasting cellars and restaurants

There is no shortage of
opportunity to taste the wines
of the Beaujolais. Around
every corner there seems to be
a tasting cellar. There are also
many fine restaurants specializing in the simple, but hearty,
food of the neighborhood.
Here the motto could be "Eat,
drink and be merry" with no
thought for tomorrow.

Food in Burgundy

The diversity of the wines of
Burgundy is matched by
the diversity of its foods, and
wine sauces form an essential
part of the cooking, be it the
white wines, for such dishes as
like *Jambon* (ham) *au Chablis*, or
the reds for *Coq au Chambertin* or
Oeufs en Meurette.

Close at hand, too, is the
city of Lyon, whose restaurants
are renowned throughout the
world of fine food. A local
saying has it that Lyon is
watered by three rivers: the
Rhône, the Saône, and the
Beaujolais!

Burgundy is rich in raw materials. The river Saône and its tributaries provide plenty of fish for such traditional dishes as the *Pochouse of Verdun sur le Doubs*. From beyond the river come Bresse chickens, with their distinctive yellowish flesh and rich texture, from their diet of maize. There are also the waterfowl of the Dombes. Charolais beef gives magnificent steaks, and the base for that dish that never seems to succeed so well elsewhere, *Boeuf Bourguignon*. The forests of the Morvan and the Châtillonnais offer venison and wild boar. The snails of Burgundy, too, are without rival, though their collection is now strictly limited.

Finally, Burgundy is proud of its cheeses. From northwest of Dijon comes Epoisses, often aged in the local brandy. The monks of Cîteaux make a tangy cow's-milk cheese. Goat's-milk cheeses are also made throughout the region, perhaps the best-known being the Chevreton de Mâcon. However, if you can find it, try the rare Claquebitou of the Hautes-Côtes.

The Jura

For what is a comparatively small vineyard area, the Jura produces a remarkably

CHÂTEAU-CHALON

Jean Berthet-Bondet
rue des Chèvres,
39210 Chateau-Chalon.
Tel: 03 84 44 60 48.
Email: domaine.berthet.
bondet@wanadoo.fr
Fax: 03 84 44 61 13.
www.berthet-bondet.net
TF for individuals; TP for groups (15+). Open Sat year round, 10AM–12PM and 2–5PM; in July and August, open daily, same hours. AN to visit other times. WS. E.

CÔTES DE JURA

Château d'Arlay
39140 Arlay.
Tel: 03 84 85 04 22.
Email: alaindelaguiche@
arlay.com
Fax: 33 84 48 17 96.
www.arlay.com
TF. AN for groups only, or on Sun, holidays. Open Mon–Sat 9AM–12PM and 2–6PM. WS. The estate, including the Château, is a listed historic monument; tours available mid-June to mid-Sept, 2–6PM.

L'ETOILE

Domaine de Montbourgeau
39570 L'Etoile.
Tel: 03 84 47 32 96.
Email: domaine.
montbourgeau@wanadoo.fr
www.jura-vins.com/
fichesvignerons/mont
bourgeau.htm

diverse selection of wines. The capital of the region is Arbois, a charming town whose architecture has been influenced by long-past Spanish occupation. It is particularly well known for its rosé wines, reputedly the best in France after Tavel.

More individual and expensive is the *vin jaune*, which tastes like a fino sherry and is produced in a similarly oxidative way. It is made from Savagnin, a local grape variety, and is aged for a minimum of six years in barrels that are not topped up, so it develops an oxidized character. *Vin jaune* can be kept for years—it is virtually immortal. Some of the best comes from the small and picturesque village of Château-Châlon as well as the similarly small appellation of l'Etoile. It is bottled in a traditional bottle called a *clavelin*, containing just 62 cl (21 oz) of wine.

Other local specialties are the rich *vin de paille* and the *aperitif macvin*, a blend of grape juice from Savagnin. *Vin de paille* is made by drying ripe grapes on trays for three or four months to concentrate to sugars before pressing them and starting a slow fermentation. Sparkling *Crémant de Jura* is also made.

The wines of the Jura are too often forgotten. In some ways they are among the most traditional in France, made in ways and from grapes that are not used elsewhere. The often dramatic vineyards are worth a visit in their own right, either on the way to Geneva and the ski resorts, or as a day off from the bustle of Burgundy.

FOR FURTHER INFORMATION

CIVJ BP
41 39602 Arbois.
Tel: 03 84 66 26 14.
www.jura-vins.com

Food

Naturally *vin jaune* plays a part in the local cuisine, being used in cooking crayfish, trout, and veal. Poulet de Bresse cooked in *vin jaune* and *morilles* is the classic dish and should be accompanied by a glass of *vin jaune*.

On the top of Pic de l'Aigle, Jura, France
Image by Olivier Deplus/Dreamstime.com

Where to stay and eat

ARBOIS
Jean-Paul Jeunet
9, rue de l'Hôtel-de-Ville, 39600 Arbois.
Tel: 03 84 66 05 67 (H/R). Email: reservation@ jeanpauljeneut.com
Fax: 03 84 66 24 20. www.jeanpauljeunet.com
Hotel and restaurant closed Tues and Wed, except in Jul and Aug.

CHABLIS—YONNE
Restaurant Jean-Luc Barnabet
14, quai de la République, 89000 Auxerre.
Tel: 03 86 51 68 88 (R). www.jlbarnabet.com/rterrasse.htm
Hostellerie des Clos
18, rue Jules-Rathier, 89800 Chablis.
Tel: 03 86 42 10 63 (H/R). www.hostellerie-des-clos.fr

CÔTE D'OR
Auberge Bourguignonne
4, place Madeleine, Beaune.
Tel: 00 33 3 80 22 23 53 (R).
Le Jardin des Remparts
10, rue de l'Hotel-Dieu, 21200 Beaune.
Tel: 03 80 24 79 41 (R).
Le Paradoxe
6, rue Faubourg, Madeleine, 21200 Beaune.
Tel: 03 80 22 63 94 (R).
Hôtel des Remparts
48, rue Thiers, 21200 Beaune.
Tel: 03 80 24 94 94 (H). www.hotel-remparts-beaune.com/
index.html
Hostellerie du Vieux Moulin
21420 Bouilland.
Tel: 03 80 21 51 16 (H/R). Fax: 03 80 21 59 90.
Closed Jan.
La Bouzerotte
21200 Bouze-les-Beaune.
Tel: 03 80 26 01 37 (R). www.labouzerette.com
Le Chassagne
4, Impasse des Chenevottes, Chassagne-Montrachet.
Tel: 03 80 21 94 94 (R).
Auberge du Vieux Vigneron
Route de Beaune, 21190 Corpeau.
Tel: 03 80 21 39 00 (R).
Aux Vendanges de Bourgogne
47, route de Beaune, 21200 Gevrey Chambertin.
Tel: 03 80 34 30 24 (R). Closed Sun.

Rôtisserie du Chambertin
21200 Gevrey Chambertin.
Tel: 03 80 34 33 20 (R). Closed Sun nights, Mon.
Domaine de Loisy
28, rue Général de Gaulle, 21700 Nuits-St-Georges.
Tel: 03 80 61 06 72 (H/R). Fax: 03 80 61 36 14.
www.domaine-de-loisy.com
Château de Gilly
Gilly-les-Cîteaux, 21640 Vougeot.
Tel: 03 80 62 89 98 (H/R). Email: contact@chateau-gilly.com
Fax: 03 80 62 82 34.

CÔTE CHALONNAISE—MACONNAIS
Aux Années Vins
2, Grande Rue, 71390 Buxy.
Tel: 03 85 92 15 76 (R). Email: contact@aux-annees-vins.com
www.bourgogne-restaurants.com/anneesvins/
AN for groups 10+. Open daily 12–1:15pm and 7:30–9:30pm
(closed Tues & Wed afternoons Apr 1–Nov 10; closed Tues &
Wed Nov 11–Mar 30).
Lameloise
36, place d'Armes, 71150 Chagny.
Tel: 03 85 87 65 65 (H/R). www.relaischateaux.com/lameloise
Open daily; closed in afternoon, Mon–Thurs. Annual closing
in July and Dec.
La Table de Chaintré
71570 Chaintré.
Tel: 03 85 32 90 95 (R). perso.wanadoo.fr/domaine-des-
vignes-oubliees/latabledechaintre.htm
Open Wed afternoon–Sun afternoon.
Hostellerie du Val d'Or
140, Grande Rue, 71640 Mercurey.
Tel: 03 85 45 13 70 (H/R). www.le-valdor.com

BEAUJOLAIS
Au Bon Cru
Route Romanèche, 69820 Fleurie.
Tel: 04 74 04 11 90 (R).
Le Cep
Place de l'Eglise, 69820 Fleurie.
Tel: 04 74 04 10 77 (R).
Château de Pizay
Hameau de Pizay, 69230 Saint-Jean d'Ardières.
Tel: 04 74 66 51 41 (H/R). Email: info@chateau-pizay.com
www.chateau-pizay.com
Le Coq à Julienas
Place du Marché, 69840 Julienas.
Tel: 04 74 04 41 98 (R).
www.julienas.fr/html/hebergement.htm

The Rhône

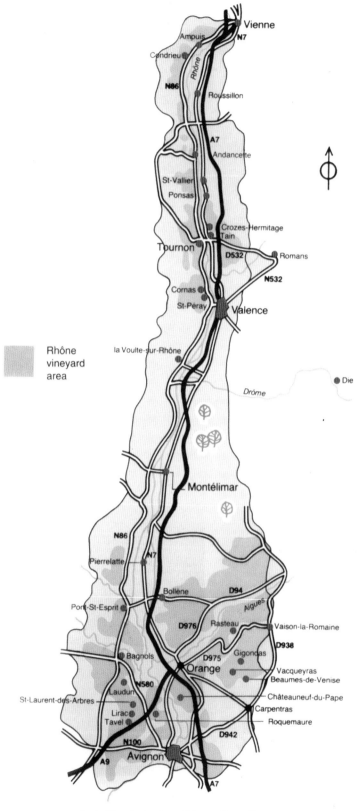

Vienne
Ampuis
Condrieu
N7
N86
Rhône
Roussillon
A7
Andancette
St-Vallier
Ponsas
Crozes-Hermitage
Tain
Tournon
D532
Romans
N532
Cornas
St-Péray
Valence
Rhône vineyard area
la Voulte-sur-Rhône
Drôme
Die
Montélimar
N86
N7
Pierrelatte
Bollène
D94
Aigues
Pont-St-Esprit
D976
Rasteau
Vaison-la-Romaine
D938
Bagnols
D975
Gigondas
Orange
Vacqueyras
Beaumes-de-Venise
N580
Laudun
Châteauneuf-du-Pape
St-Laurent-des-Arbres
Lirac
Carpentras
Tavel
Roquemaure
D942
N100
Avignon
A9
A7

THE RHÔNE

The Rhône is one of the greatest wine rivers of the world. Near its source, in Switzerland, are the wines of the Valais. After it leaves Lake Geneva and flows westward, it passes through Savoy, where the sparkling wines of Seyssel are made. At Lyon it joins the Saône, turning southward. Over the next 230 km (143 miles), as far as Avignon, some of the world's finest and best-known wines are made; wines such as Châteauneuf-du-Pape, Côte Rôtie, and Hermitage.

There are three main roads down the valley of the Rhône. On the west bank there is the N86, on the east the N7, and then the motorway, the A7. Of these three roads, the N86 is the route of the dedicated vineyard visitor. Driving south from Lyon, all the well-known vineyards are on this side as far as Tournon.

While the Rhône valley is best known for its full-bodied red wines, the area does produce a surprising selection and variety. As well as reds, there are also fine dry white wines (in the 19th century, white Hermitage was rated as one of the great wines of the world), good rosés such as Tavel and Lirac, sparkling wine from St-Péray, and luscious

TO GET TO THE RHÔNE

Vienne is 490 km (306 miles) from Paris and 92 km (57 miles) from Mâcon on the A6 and A7 motorways. Orange is 657 km (410 miles) from Paris and 259 km (162 miles) from Mâcon. The A46 bypasses Lyon. Alternatively, use A10, A71, A72, A47.

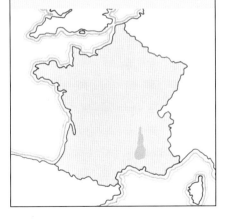

fortified sweet wines, such as the Muscats of Beaumes-de-Venise. It is also a source of soft, easy-drinking reds. Simple Côtes du Rhône, which can come in all three colors, is made virtually throughout the valley.

Côte Rôtie

The town of Vienne lies some 30 km (19 miles) south of Lyon, and it is just south of here that the Rhône vineyards begin. Vienne is one of the oldest cities of France, dating back to long before Roman times. Just south of Vienne, on the other bank of the river, are the vineyards of Côte Rôtie. These are among the steepest in France and the vines are planted in a unique fashion: three separate vines on individual poles that meet together at the top. As elsewhere in the Northern Rhône, Syrah is the red grape here.

The two main slopes are called the Côte Brune and the Côte Blonde, in memory of the two beautiful daughters of a local nobleman. Most Côte Rôtie is a blend from the two sources. However, the top wines are from individual vineyards. At the foot of the vineyards is the town of Ampuis, home to many of the growers and merchants.

Condrieu

Five km (3 miles) further along the road from Côte Rôtie comes the village of Condrieu, renowned for its white wine, made from the Viognier grape. At one time this variety was only found in this part of the Rhône. In recent years, however, it has been planted extensively in Languedoc and elsewhere in the world, with mixed success.

The little town of Condrieu beside the Rhône—famous for its perfumed whites made from the Viognier grape. Photo by Alain Gas.

Château Grillet

Viognier ought to reach its peak in the wines of Château Grillet, a vineyard that has its own microclimate and the smallest production of any single *appellation contrôlée* in France. The rarity of both Condrieu and Château Grillet means that they are not cheap, but are certainly worth it when on sale.

Hermitage

No one would claim that the twin towns of Tain and Tournon are attractive, but above them rises the stark

Domaine Gilles Barge
8, blvd des Allées,
69420 Ampuis.
Tel: 04 74 56 13 90.
Email: barge.gilles@wanadoo.fr
Fax: 04 74 56 10 98.
www.domainebarge.com
Open Mon–Sat 9AM–12PM
and 2–7PM. Sun by app't.
AN for groups (max 40).

Etienne Guigal
Château d'Ampuis,
69420 Ampuis.
Tel: 04 74 56 10 22.
Email: contact@guigal.com
Fax: 04 74 56 18 76.
www.guigal.com
AN. Open Mon–Fri
8AM–12PM and 2–6PM.
Closed holidays, all of Aug.

Yves Cuilleron
58 route Nationale, Verlieu,
42410 Chavannay.
Tel: 04 74 87 02 37.
Email: caves@cuilleron.com
Fax: 04 74 87 05 62.
www.isasite.net/cuilleron
Open Mon–Sat 8AM–12PM
and 2–6:30PM. Closed
holidays. E.

Neyrat-Guchet
Château Grillet,
42410 Vérin.
Tel: 04 74 59 51 56

Georges Vernay
1, route Nationale,
69420 Condrieu.
Tel: 04 74 56 81 81.
Email: pa@georges-vernay.fr
Fax: 04 74 56 60 98.
www.georges-vernay.fr
Open Mon–Fri 9AM–12PM
and 2–6:30PM. Sat PM AN.

hillside famous for Hermitage wine. There have been vines planted here for more than two thousand years. The hill gets its name, however, from Gaspard de Stérimberg, who retired to a cell on the summit, having been wounded fighting the Albigensian heretics in 1224.

There are two distinct types of soil on the hill: granite for the red grapes, and clay for the white. The exposure to the sun ensures exceptionally full-bodied wines, which are capable of lasting for decades.

Traditionally, there are a number of differently named sites on the hill, each giving a wine with its individual character. Occasionally, these can be found as individual wines, but more often they are blended together to produce the perfect whole. With only 131 hectares, Hermitage will never be cheap.

Crozes-Hermitage
Eleven villages surrounding the hill of Hermitage have the right to call their wine Crozes-Hermitage. While there is a relationship in style with its illustrious neighbor, it is not as close as the growers would have you believe; the reds might age well, but the whites are certainly best drunk young.

St-Joseph and the Ardèche

On the western bank of the river are the red wines of St-Joseph, made from the Syrah grape. There is a little white wine made from Marsanne and Roussanne, the two varieties used in white Hermitage. The rather elongated St-Joseph appellation runs southwards from just south of Condrieu to Cornas, just to the north of Valence. The wines are of variable quality but can offer good value compared to other northern Rhône wines, which are inevitably expensive because of their small production.

We are now in the Ardèche *département,* and it is here that many experimental plantings have been made with "foreign" grapes such as Gamay and Chardonnay. The famous Burgundy house of Louis Latour, for example, has planted in the region because of the comparative cheapness of the land and the favorable climate. The wines are sold as *vin de pays.*

Cornas

Opposite the important town of Valence, there are two small areas producing fine wines. The first of these is Cornas. Again, the vineyards are on steep slopes and the combination of soil and microclimate gives perhaps the biggest wine of the Rhône. As one

SAJ Vidal-Fleury
route Nationale,
69420 Ampuis.
Tel: 04 74 56 10 18.
Fax: 04 74 56 19 19.
Open year round,
Mon–Thurs 8AM–12PM and
and 2–5PM, Friday only until
4PM. Closed weekends and
holidays. AN for groups (up
to 25). E, G.

HERMITAGE

Maison M Chapoutier
18, ave du Dr. Paul-Durand,
26601 Tain-l'Hermitage.
Tel: 04 75 08 92 61.
Email: chapoutier@
chapoutier.com
Fax: 04 75 08 96 36.
www.chapoutier.com
Cellar open (T, WS)
Mon–Fri 9AM–12:30PM and
2–7PM; Sat 9:30AM–1PM and
2–6PM; Sun and holidays
10AM–1PM and 2–6PM. AN. E.

Paul Jaboulet Aîné
Les Jalets,
26600, La Roche-de-Glun.
Fax: 04 74 84 56 14.
www.jaboulet.com
T; AN. Open Mon–Thurs,
8–11:30AM and 2–5PM; Fri,
8–11:30AM and 2–4PM.
Caves, movie. Groups, Tues–
Sat (AN). E, G, S.

Cave de Tain-l'Hermitage
22 route de Larnage,
26601 Tain-l'Hermitage.
Tel: 04 75 08 20 87.
Fax: 04 75 07 15 16.
www.cave-tain-hermitage.com
Boutique open daily 9AM–12PM
and 2–6PM; open 9AM–12:30PM
and 1:30–7PM in June, July,
Aug. WS. E, G.

CROZES-HERMITAGE

Domaine du Colombier

2, rte de Chantemerle,
Mercurol,
26600 Tain-l'Hermitage.
Tel: 04 75 07 44 07.
Fax: 04 75 07 41 43.
Open year long. Groups up
to 12 welcome; AN.

Domaine des Entrefaux

Quartier des Baumes,
26600 Chanos-Curson.
Tel: 04 75 07 33 38.
Fax: 04 75 07 35 27
Open year long, Mon–Sat
9AM–12PM and 2–6PM.
Groups up to 20; AN. E.

Alain Graillot

Les Chênes Verts,
26600 Pont de l'Isère.
Tel: 04 75 84 67 52.
Email: graillot.alain@
wanadoo.fr
Fax: 04 75 84 79 33.
TF; AN. Open year round.
WS only in 1st 3 weeks in
December. E, S, I.

English writer has said, "A good Cornas one or two years old is a savage, dark wine that leaves the eye impressed and the palate colored." Modern techniques, however, have softened the savagery of the tannins, making some of the wines more approachable when young.

Two sparkling wine areas

The reputation of the wines of St-Péray goes back to classical times. Traditionally still and white, four-fifths are now sparkling, made in the same way as Champagne. The other sparkling wine area is around Die, some 65 km (40 miles)

away on the other side of the Rhône, on one of its tributaries, the Drôme. Here two styles of wine are made: a brut (Crémant de Die) using the traditional champagne method, and a sweeter variety (Clairette de Die), in which the sparkle in the bottle comes from a naturally delayed first fermentation.

Coteaux de Tricastin

After Valence, there is a break in the vineyards of the Rhône lasting some 70 km (43 miles). It is not until after Montélimar (renowned for its nougat) that, on the left bank of the Rhône, the vineyards begin again with the Coteaux de

ST–JOSEPH

Pierre Coursodon
Domaine Coursodon, place du Marche, 07300 Mauves.
Tel: 04 75 08 18 29.
Email: pierrecoursodon@ wanadoo.fr
Fax: 04 75 08 75 72.
Open Mon–Sat 8AM–12PM and 2–7PM. Closed holidays. E.

Domaine Bernard Gripa
5, ave Ozier, 07300 Mauves.
Tel: 04 75 08 14 96.
Fax: 04 75 07 06 81.
Open Mon–Sat 8AM–12PM and 2–7PM. Closed holidays. E.

Cave St Désirat
07340 St Désirat.
Tel: 04 75 34 22 05.
Email: info@ cave-saint-desirat.com
Fax: 04 75 34 30 10.
www.cave-saint-desirat.com
Open daily 8AM–12PM and 2–6PM, summer until 7PM.
Open Sun and holidays, 8AM–7PM. Two walking trails.

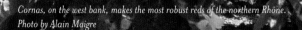

Cornas, on the west bank, makes the most robust reds of the northern Rhône. Photo by Alain Maigre

CORNAS

Auguste and Pierre Clape
Domaine Clape, 146 route
Nationale, 07130 Cornas.
Tel: 04 75 40 33 64.
Fax: 04 75 81 01 98.
Open Mon–Fri 8AM–12PM
and 2–6PM. E.

Vins Jean Luc Colombo
Croix Marais, 26600
La Roche de Glun.
Tel: 04 75 84 17 10.
Email: colombo@
vinsjlcolombo.com
www.vinsjlcolombo.3it.com

DIE

La Cave de Die Jaillance
ave de la Clairette,
26150 Die.
Tel: 04 75 22 30 15.
Email: info@jaillance.com
Fax: 04 75 22 21 06.
www.jaillance.com

ST–PÉRAY

**Stéphane Robert Domaine
du Tunnel**
20, rue de la République.
07130 St-Péray
Tel: 04 75 80 04 66.
Email: caveau@
domaine-du-tunnel.com
Fax: 04 75 80 06 50.
Open Mon–Fri 10AM–12:30PM
and 2–7:30PM, Sat until 6PM.
AN for weekends, groups;
groups up to 30 welcome.

Tricastin. This is the start of the southern Rhône with its Mediterranean climate. The steep-sided narrow valley opens out, and the palette of grape varieties is greatly expanded to include Grenache, Cinsault, Mourvèdre, and others.

At Tricastin the land is stony and poor, continually scoured by the Mistral, and it is only in the last 30 years that vines have been replanted after phylloxera destroyed them in the latter part of the 19th century. Much of the planting has been carried out by *pieds noirs* (ex-colonials from Algeria). The wines, mainly red, are very similar to Côtes du Rhône.

Côtes du Rhône

Although this appellation extends over the whole of the Rhône Valley, the vast majority of the wines come from the southern part. The bulk comes from the three *départements* of Drôme, Vaucluse, and Gard. At the center of the region is the town of Orange, the scene of an annual wine fair held in the Roman amphitheater.

To the east of Orange is the start of the Plan de Dieu—a flat plain that stretches southwards to Avignon. Hot in the summer months, and largely planted with vines, this is an important source of Côtes du Rhône. It is also open to the full force of the

Mistral, the cold wind that whistles down the Rhône Valley.

Northwest of Avignon are the Côtes du Rhône vineyards of the Gard *département*. These are particularly known for their rosé wines. The west bank of the Rhône here presents a totally different outlook to the east. Instead of a picture of rich greens, there is the drab gray aridity of the *garrigues* (areas of rough, stony countryside), baked by the sun and tormented by the wind. The soil is basically chalky, but is covered by layers of flat, flaking stones, which, as in Châteauneuf, reflect the heat.

Southern Rhône: Rhône Villages

Within the southern Côtes du Rhône, there are some communes that can add "Villages" to the appellation name. There are also sixteen

COTEAUX DE TRICASTIN

Michel Seroin
Château la Décelle,
route Pierrelatte, 26130
St-Paul-Trois-Châteaux.
Tel: 04 75 04 71 33.
Email: ladecelle@wanadoo.fr
Fax: 04 75 04 56 98.

Domaine de Grangeneuve
26230 Roussas.
Tel: 04 75 98 50 22.
Email: ohb@
domainesbour.com
Fax: 04 75 98 51 09.
www.domainesbour.com
Open daily 9AM–12:30PM
and 2–7PM.

Domaine de Vieux Micocoulier
Les Logis de Berre,
26290 Les Granges-Gontards.
Tel: 04 75 04 02 72.

Below: Sablet, with its houses clustered around the church, is a typical village in the southern Rhône.
Photo © Isabelle Desarzens

Château de Fontségugne
976, route de St-Saturnin,
le Vieux Moulin, 88470
Châteauneuf-de-Gadagne.
Tel: 04 90 22 58 91.
Email: gerenjm@aol.com
Fax: 04 90 22 42 40.
AN. Open daily 10AM–12PM
and 2–8PM. Closed Dec 25,
Jan 1. Groups up to 50
people. E, S.

Domaine des Girasols
84110 Rasteau.
Tel: 04 90 46 11 70.
Email: domaine@girasols.com
Fax: 04 90 46 16 82.
www.girasols.com
TF. Cellar open Mon–Sat
9AM–12PM and 2–7PM. AN
Sun and holidays. WS.
Patchwork art show, tasting
picnics arranged March
through to grape harvest. E.

Frédéric et François Alary
Domaine de l'Oratoire St-
Martin, route de St-Romain,
84290 Cairanne.
Tel: 04 90 30 82 07.
Email: caveau@
oratoiresaintmartin.fr
Fax: 04 90 30 74 27.
www.oratoiresaintmartin.fr
Open Mon–Sat 8AM–12PM
and 2–7PM. Closed holidays.
Groups up to 15; AN.

Domaine de la Présidente
route de Cairanne, 84290
Sainte-Cécile-les-Vignes.
Tel: 04 90 30 80 34.
Email: aubert@presidente.fr
www.presidente.fr

that can add the name of their
commune to the wine. So, for
instance, you can have Côtes
du Rhône Villages Cairanne.

Lirac and Tavel

Four villages have the right to
make Lirac wine. Of these, St-
Laurent-des-Arbres is perhaps
the most attractive, with a
Romanesque church that,
tradition has it, was fortified in
the 14th century by the Bishop
of Avignon, later Pope John
XXII. Roquemaure, too, has a
long history, claiming a supporting role in the Hannibal story.

Tavel has long had the
reputation of producing the
finest rosé wine in France. In
Britain and the United States,
where the consumption of rosé
represents only a small fraction

One of the Rhône villages, Tavel makes one of France's best-known rosés.
Photo © Isabelle Desarzens

Domaine la Remejeanne
Cadignac, 30200 Sabran.
Tel: 04 66 89 44 51.
Email: remejeanne@
wanadoo.fr
Fax: 04 66 89 64 22.
AN. Open Mon–Sat
9AM–12PM and 2–7PM.
Closed holidays. Groups
welcome.

Domaine Rigot
Les Hauts Débats,
84150 Jonquières.
Tel: 04 90 37 25 19.
Email: contact@
domaine-rigot.fr
Fax: 04 90 37 29 19.
www.domaine-rigot.fr
Open Mon–Sat 8AM–12PM
and 3–8PM. Open Sun in
summer, or by app't. E.

CÔTES DU RHÔNE VILLAGES

Caves des Vignerons de Chusclan
30200 Chusclan.
Tel: 04 66 90 11
Email:contact@
vigneronsdechusclan.com
Fax: 04 66 90 16 52.
www.vigneronsdechusclan.com
Cellar open daily 9AM–12PM
and 2–6:30PM, closed Dec 25
and Jan 1. WS. Guided tours
of vineyards and of nearby
Gicon Château (AN). Groups
up to 50; AN. Free parking
for camper vans. E.

of the total, this may not appear a very important title, but in France, where a lot is drunk, Tavel is held in high esteem. Some Tavel, however, can be heady and alcoholic.

Much of the vineyard area was allowed to return to scrubland after the phylloxera plague, and it is only during the last forty years or so that the vineyards of Tavel have taken on a new lease on life with extensive replanting.

Châteauneuf-du-Pape
Orange is one of the five communes that together produce perhaps the best-known wine of the Rhône valley,

Côtes du Rhône villages, cont.

Château la Courançonne

Le Plan de Dieu,
84150 Violès.
Tel: 04 90 70 92 16.
Email: info@ lacouraanconne.fr
Fax: 04 90 70 90 54.
www.lacouranconne.com
Open Mon–Fri
8:30AM–12PM and 2–5:30PM;
AN Sat and Sun.

Domaine Richaud

84290 Cairanne.
Tel: 04 90 30 85 25.
Fax: 04 90 30 71 12.
Open Mon–Sat 9AM–12PM
and 2–6PM. Groups up to 10;
AN. E, S.

André Roméro

La Soumade, 84110 Rasteau.
Tel: 04 90 46 11 26.
Fax: 04 90 46 11 69.
Open Mon–Sat 8–11:30AM
and 2–6PM. Groups up to 45;
AN.

Domaine Sainte-Anne

Les Cellettes, 30200
St-Gervais.
Tel: 04 66 82 77 57.
Fax: 04 66 82 74 58.
AN for tastings.

LIRAC

Christophe Delorme

Domaine de la Mordorée,
Chemin des Oliviers,
30126 Tavel.
Fax: 04 66 50 47 39.
www.domaine-mordoree.com
Open Mon–Fri 8AM–12PM
and 1:30–5:30PM.
Open Sat, Sun, and holidays,
10AM–12PM and 3–6PM.
Groups up to 50; AN.
E, S, G.

Châteauneuf-du-Pape. There is no doubt that much of the historic reputation of this wine is due to the fact that when the Popes left Rome and established themselves in nearby Avignon during the 14th century they did much to promote the local wines. It was at Châteauneuf that they built their summer palace, of which there are still some remains.

The complexity of the wine of Châteauneuf is due largely to the fact that up to 13 different grape varieties may be used in its production, each adding a touch of color to the final picture. Part of Châteauneuf is closely covered with large rounded stones (*galets roulets*) deposited by the Rhône. The closely pruned vines benefit from an inverted form of night storage heating: the stones retain much of the heat that they have picked up during the day throughout the night, and pass it on to the vines.

The local growers have been in the forefront of supporting legislation to protect the quality of their wines. Many of them, in a form of regional pride, have adopted a special bottle bearing the papal coat of arms on its shoulder.

Châteauneuf is best known for its red wines, which are full-bodied and capable of long aging, but it also produces small quantities of excellent white wine.

𝄢 123 𝄢

THE RHÔNE

Gigondas and Vacqueyras

Northeast of Avignon, and nestled in the foothills of the Dentelles de Montmirail, are Gigondas and Vacqueyras, which have been granted their own appellations. Gigondas, where there are the remains of a castle that belonged to

Cairanne is one of the best of the Rhône Villages. Photo by Alain Gas

TAVEL

Château Aqueria
30126 Tavel.
Tel: 04 66 50 04 56.
Email: contact@aqueria.com
Fax: 04 66 50 18 46.
www.aqueria.com
TF (TP for groups; up to 256 people). Open Mon–Thurs 8AM–12PM and 2–6PM; on Fri, open only until 5PM. Closed weekends. WS. E.

Jean-Claude Garcin
Domaine de la Genestière, Chemin de Cravailleux, 30126 Tavel.
Tel: 04 66 50 07 03.
Email: garcin-layouni@ domaine-genestiere.com
Fax: 04 66 50 27 03.
www.domaine-genestiere.com
Open Mon–Fri 8AM–12PM and 1:30–5:30PM. Closed holidays. Groups up to 15; AN. S.

Domaine Maby
rue St-Vincent, 30126 Tavel.
Tel: 04 66 50 03 40. Email: domaine-maby@wanadoo.fr
Fax: 04 66 50 43 12.
Open Mon–Fri 8AM–12PM and 1:30–6PM. Closed holidays. Groups up to 50; AN.

Les Vignerons de Tavel
30126 Tavel.
Tel: 04 66 50 03 57.
Email: tavel.cave@wanadoo.fr
Fax: 04 66 50 46 57.
www.tavel.tm.fr
Tasting caves open every day. Office open Mon–Fri 8AM–12PM and 2–6PM. E.

CHÂTEAUNEUF-DU-PAPE

Château de Beaucastel

84350 Courthézon.
Tel: 04 90 70 41 00.
Email: contact@beaucastel.com
Fax: 04 90 70 41 19.
www.beaucastel.com

Château Mont-Redon

84230 Châteauneuf-du-Pape.
Tel: 04 90 83 72 75.
Email: chateaumontredon@
wanadoo.fr
Fax: 04 90 83 77 20.
www.chateaumontredon.fr
T; AN. Cellar open daily
8AM–7PM, including weekends
and holidays. WS. Groups up
to 40. E.

Pierre Richard

Château la Nerthe,
route de Sorgues, 84230
Châteauneuf-du-Pape.
Tel: 04 90 83 70 11.
Email: alaindugas@
chateaulanerthe.fr
Fax: 04 90 83 00 15.
www.chateau-la-nerthe.com
AN for visit and tasting.
Open Sun.

Domaine-La-Roquette

2, ave Louis Pasteur, 84230
Châteauneuf-du-Pape.
Tel: 04 90 33 00 31.
Fax: 04 90 33 18 47.

Paul Avril Clos des Papes,

84230 Châteauneuf-du-Pape.
Tel: 04 90 83 70 13.
Email: clos-des-papes@
clos-des-papes.com
Fax: 04 90 83 50 87.
www.clos-des-papes.fr

the Princes of Orange, had the good fortune to be the home of two wine merchants intent on promoting the local wines, and in 1971 was rewarded with full *appellation contrôlée* status for its red wines. The same fate followed for Vacqueyras, its neighbor, in 1990.

Beaumes-de-Venise

Beaumes-de-Venise was a spa in Roman times, and has been well known for its wines for many centuries. No one for sure knows when the Muscat grape was first planted here. It is the only place where it can be

GIGONDAS

Dominique Ay
Domaine Raspail-Ay,
84190 Gigondas.
Tel: 04 90 65 83 01.
Fax: 04 90 65 89 55.
Open Mon–Sat
9AM–12:30PM and
1:30–5:30PM.

Jean-Pierre and Martine Meffre
Domaine St-Gayan,
84190 Gigondas.
Tel: 04 90 65 86 33.
Email: martine@
saintgayan.com
Fax: 04 90 65 85 10.
www.saintgayan.com

Gras Edmond et Fils
Domaine Santa Duc,
Quartier Hautes Garrigues,
route Violès,
84190 Gigondas.
Tel: 04 90 65 84 49.
Fax: 04 90 65 81 63.
Open year long, closed Sun.
Groups up to 50; AN.

Pascal Roux
Château de Trignon,
84190 Gigondas.
Tel: 04 90 46 90 27.
Email: trignon@
chateau-du-trignon.com
Fax: 04 90 46 98 63.
www.chateau-du-trignon.com
TF. AN for groups. Open
9AM–12PM and 2–7PM. WS.
E, J.

Top: The Dentelles de Monmirail.
Bottom: Gigondas, which makes rich,
full-bodied wines in the style of Châteauneuf-
du-Pape. Photos by Sopexa.

VACQUEYRAS

Roger Combe et Filles
Domaine de la Fourmone,
route de Bollène,
84190 Vacqueyras.
Tel: 04 90 65 86 05.
Email: contact@fourmone.com
Fax: 04 90 65 87 84.
www.domaine-la-
fourmone.com
T. Open Mon–Sat
9:30AM–12PM and 2–6PM.
Open Sun, Apr–Sept. WS. E.

Domaine le Sang des Cailloux
route de Vacqueyras,
84260 Sarrians.
Tel: 04 90 65 88 64.
Email: contact@
sangdescailloux.com
Fax: 04 90 65 88 75.
www.sangdescailloux.com
Open Mon–Sat 2–7PM, Sun
and holidays by app't.
Groups up to 30; AN. E.

BEAUMES–DE–VENISE

Vignerons de Beaumes de Venise Quartier Ravel
84190 Beaumes-de-Venise.
Tel: 04 90 12 41 00.
Email: contact@
beaumes-de-venise.com
Fax: 04 90 65 02 05.
www.beaumes-de-venise.com
Cellar open daily
8:30AM–12:30PM and 2–6PM,
7PM in summer. Groups up to
50; AN. E, G.

found in the entire Rhône Valley. However, there is every possibility that the Greeks, who settled along the Mediterr-anean coast before the Romans, also used Beaumes-de-Venise as a spa and brought the grape—a firm favorite of theirs—with them. Certainly its rich fruiti-ness seems to have had a wider appeal than most other wines of its type made in France. Nearby Rasteau has its own appellation for red fortified wine made from Grenache.

Beaumes-de-Venise is best-known for its fortified Muscat wines, although it also makes some good reds.
Photo by Isabelle Desarzens

Southern Rhône

Avignon

The bustling and historic city of Avignon is the central conurbation of the southern Rhône. The history of Avignon is closely linked to the period during which seven Popes, and three anti-Popes, lived there. When the Popes returned to Rome, Avignon remained part of their possessions, being governed by a Papal Legate. It did not finally become part of France until after the French Revolution.

There is much to see in Avignon, but be warned that driving in its center is a nightmare. It is still surrounded by 14th-century battlements with 39 watchtowers. The former Palace of the Popes has been, at various times, a military barracks and even a prison—a great come-down from the days of luxurious extravagance and debauchery that marked the times of the papal court.

Sur le pont

The opportunities for dancing on the bridge at Avignon, or at least on the 800-year-old Pont St Bénézet, are now strictly limited; only four out of the original nineteen arches remain.

Behind the church of St Didier, the narrow rue du Roi René has a number of beautiful old buildings.

The Pont du Gard

This is some 22 km (14 miles) west of the town, beyond Remoulins on the N100. The Pont is a magnificent Roman aqueduct, in three tiers, 48 meters (160 feet) above the valley of the river Gardon. The channel to carry the water is more than two meters (7 feet) deep and over a meter (4 feet) wide.

The Camargue

Where the river Rhône reaches the Mediterranean, the deposit it has carried down has created a vast sandy delta, the Camargue, noted for its bulls, horses, and flamingoes. Although the most unlikely place for a vineyard, it is here that you'll find one of the biggest vineyard companies in

Domaine des Anges
84570 Mormoiron.
Tel: 04 90 61 90 85.
Email: ciaranr@
club-internet.fr
Fax: 04 90 61 98 05.
www.domainedesanges.com
Open Sun, Apr–Oct. E.

Cave Canteperdrix
route de Caromb,
84380 Mazan.
Tel: 04 90 69 70 31.
Email: info@
cotes-du-ventoux.com
Fax: 04 90 69 87 41.
www.cotes-du-ventoux.com/fr
Open Sun.

Domaine des Hautes Roches
Roquefure, 84400 APT.
Tel: 04 90 74 19 65.

Gérard Marreau
Domaine de la Bastidonne,
84220 Cabrières-D'Avignon.
Tel: 04 90 76 70 00.
Email: domaine.bastidonne1@
tiscali.fr
Fax: 04 90 76 74 34.
www.vin-bastidonne.com
T. Cellar open May–Sept,
9AM–12PM and 3–7PM;
Oct–April, 9AM–12PM and
2–6PM. WS. AN for groups.

Château Pesquie
route de Flassan, 84570
Mormoiron.
Tel: 04 90 61 94 08.
Email: chateaupesquie@
yahoo.fr
Fax: 04 90 61 94 13.
www.chateaupesquie.com
Open daily 9AM–12PM and
2–6PM; open Sun Easter–
Sept 30, or by app't.

France, Les Salins du Midi
(Listel). The medieval walled
town of Aigues-Mortes is well
worth a visit.

Côtes du Ventoux

Overlooking the vineyards of
Gigondas and Vacqueyras is
Mont Ventoux. Along its
southern slopes run the
vineyards of Côtes du Ventoux.
Until fifteen years ago these
vineyards produced soft, easy-
drinking country wine. This
has changed dramatically, and
now the Ventoux makes some of
the most interesting wine of the
southern Rhône. Along with
neighboring Côtes du Luberon,
the vines here are at a much
higher altitude than those, such
as Châteauneuf-du-Pape, on
the floor of the Rhône Valley.
Although the same mix of
grapes are used, Syrah is
particularly suited to this cooler
climate. Many of the vineyards
are planted on the southern
slopes of the Ventoux and as far
as the town of Apt. Near
Bedoin some vineyards are
planted as high as 500 meters.
The bulk of the production is
red, although there is a little
rosé and white. From a top
producer the white can be very
good—the cooler summer
nights help to conserve the
grapes' aromas and acidity.

The area is also famous for its lavender, and in summer the hills are filled with its heady perfume.

Côtes du Luberon

The Luberon lies to the east and south of the Côtes du Ventoux. This hilly area is a world away from the floor of the Rhône Valley around Orange and Avignon. It is closer to the vineyards of Provence than to those of Châteauneuf-du-Pape. The Luberon is another up-and-coming wine area. There are now just over 4,000 hectares planted here.

The vineyards are planted on either side of the large and bleak block of the Montagne du Luberon that runs east to west. The summer heat is not so fierce here and the nights are much cooler. The whites are much fresher than others from the Rhône Valley and they account for about a quarter of the production. Like the Ventoux, the reds are fresher and less alcoholic than those of Châteauneuf and Gigondas. This beautiful and varied area has attracted a number of artists who have moved here and set up their workshops and studios.

Domaine de la Citadelle
route de Cavaillon,
84560 Ménerbes.
Tel: 04 90 72 41 58.
Email: domainedelacitadelle@wanadoo.fr
Fax: 04 90 72 41 59.
www.domaine-citadelle.com
Open daily April–Oct,
10AM–12PM and 2–7PM;
Nov–March, open Mon–Sat (closed holidays) 10AM–12PM and 2–5PM. AN for groups. Free parking. Corkscrew museum.

Cellier de Marrenon
84240 la Tour d'Aigues.
Tel: 04 90 07 40 65.
Email: marrenon@marrenon.com
Fax: 04 90 07 30 77.
www.cellier-de-marrenon.com
Open daily Mon–Sat
8AM–12PM and 3–5PM; in winter, 8AM–12PM and 2–6PM. Sun open 8AM–12PM.

FOR FURTHER INFORMATION ON ALL RHÔNE WINES:

Inter Rhône

6, rue des 3 Faucons, 84024 Avignon.
Tel: 04 90 27 24 00. Email: maison@inter-rhone.com
www.vins-rhone.com

Food in the Rhône

It is difficult to write about the food specialties of the Rhône, for gastronomically it is not one area. Indeed, while driving down it, you cross the great boundary in French gastronomy: on one side the cooking is done with butter, and on the other, with olive oil.

In the north, Lyon is one of the gastronomic centers of France, known for its sausages—including *rosette* and *judas*—its tripe, and such dishes as *quenelles* or *la poularde demi-deuil* (chicken in cream with truffles). Apart from Paris, it has the largest concentration of good restaurants in France.

Down the valley of the Rhône, there are a number of seasonal fruit markets for apricots, nectarines, and, near Carpentras, melons. The Ardèche is known for its chestnuts, and the Drôme for its herbs, honey, and thrush pâtés. The town of Nyons is famous for its olives. The food in the southern Rhône is closer to that of Provence.

For a sticky finale, the best nougat in the world comes from Montélimar, while Apt is known for its glacé fruit.

The ruins of the papal palace at Chateauneuf-du-Pape, which is famous for its full-bodied, powerful wines, are among the best-known landmarks of the south of France. Photo by Alain Gas.

Where to stay and eat

La Bastide de Marie
route de Bonnieux, Quartier de la Verrerie, 84560 Ménerbes.
Tel: 04 90 72 30 20 (R).
Open 12–2:30PM and 7:30–9:30PM.

Restaurant Beaugravière
route Nationale 7, 84430 Mondragon.
Tel: 04 90 40 82 54 (R).
Open lunch Tues–Sun, dinner Tues–Sat; closed Sept 15–30.

Auberge du Beaucet
84210 le Beaucet.
Tel: 04 90 66 10 82 (R). Closed Sun and Mon.
Annual holiday in winter.

Le Beau Rivage
2, rue du Beau Rivage, 69420 Condrieu.
Tel: 04 74 56 82 82 (H/R). Open year round.

Les Florets
route des Dentelles, 84190 Gigondas.
Tel: 04 90 65 85 01 (H/R).
Closed Jan 1–Mar 30. Restaurant closed Mon evening, Tues and
Thurs midday Nov–Mar; closed Wednesday April–Oct.

Restaurant Christian Etienne
10, rue de Mons, 84000 Avignon.
Tel: 04 90 86 16 50 (R). Closed Sun and Mon.

Château Fines Roches
route de Sorgues, 84230 Châteauneuf-du-Pape.
Tel: 04 90 83 70 23 (H/R).

Mère Germain
3, rue du Commandant Lemaitre, 84230 Châteauneuf-du-Pape.
Tel: 04 90 83 54 37 (H/R). Restaurant open for lunch and dinner
every day except Wed.

Pic
285, avenue Victor Hugo, 26000 Valence.
Tel: 04 75 44 15 32 (H/R).
Restaurant closed Sun evening, Mon and Tues Nov–Mar; Tues and
Wed noon April–Oct. Closed Jan 2–24.

La Pyramide
14, blvd Fernand-Point, 38200 Vienne.
Tel: 04 74 53 01 96 (R). Closed Tues and Wed. Closed Feb 15–Mar 10.

La Table du Comtat
Le Village, 84110 Séguret.
Tel: 04 90 46 91 49 (H/R).
Restaurant open 12:30–2PM and 7:30–9PM; closed Tues night and
Wed except in summer.

Provence

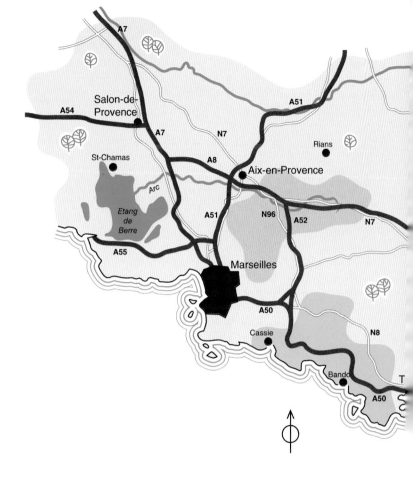

PROVENCE

There can be few happier memories than that of sitting outside a quayside bar in the south of France, watching the world go by, with a bottle of Côte de Provence rosé in an ice bucket, and a glass of it in your hand. Sadly, Provence wines are summer wines; they just do not taste the same in February in Flint, Michigan or Fulham, London.

As in many other parts of France, the wines of Provence have improved greatly in quality over the past decade. Not only has the quality of the rosé improved, but there are now more and more interesting reds being made. Indeed, the best wines from Provence are the reds. These are often being made from a blend of southern French varieties, such as Carignan, Mourvèdre, and Syrah, with

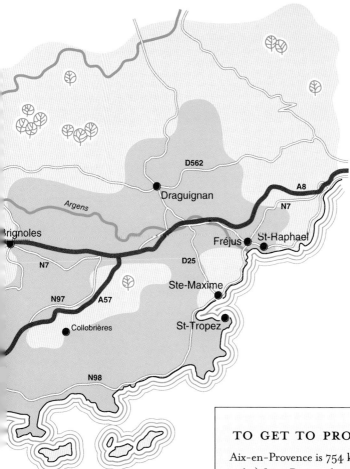

the addition of some Cabernet Sauvignon. The limited amount of white uses Clairette, Ugni Blanc, and Vermentino—also called Rollé. The whites are rarely exciting.

There are vineyards throughout Provence. However, because of the hilly, more fragmented landscape, they are quite scattered and it is rare to find swathes of vines as in Languedoc.

Most of the vineyards of Provence lie along the valleys of the rivers Arc and

TO GET TO PROVENCE

Aix-en-Provence is 754 km (471 miles) from Paris and 97 km (60 miles) from Orange on the A6, A7, and A8. It is 140 km (87 miles) from Montpellier on the A9, A54, N113, A54, A7, and A8. A number of budget airlines fly to Nice airport. Marseilles is three hours from Paris by high-speed train.

Argens, on the route of the A8 motorway. Much of the wine is made in cooperative cellars with emotive names like la Prévoyance, but there are also a number of high-quality individual estates. Although some over-alcoholic, traditional rosés still exist, quality has increased greatly over the last five years, and many Provence rosés have much more fruit and balance than they did.

Côtes de Provence

There is a second band of vineyards along the coast from Marseilles to Ste-Maxime and St-Tropez. From both these areas comes the ubiquitous Côtes de Provence, with the main zone stretching from Toulon to beyond Saint-Raphael. There are three smaller areas further west, close to Marseilles. There are more than 20,000 hectares of vines planted. As elsewhere, the reds are definitely the most exciting wines made here. A number of the most ambitious and high-quality estates are run by people who have moved into the area from elsewhere in France or from other parts of Europe.

Les Baux-de-Provence

The village from which the name of this appellation derives also gave its name to bauxite, the mineral ore used to produce aluminum. This is an area where organic vineyards develop naturally pure and harmonious wines, without the use of any manmade fertilizer. Once part of AC Coteaux d'Aix, Les Baux-de-Provence was given its own appellation in 1995 for reds and rosé, under stricter production regulation than that of Coteaux d'Aix. Although only a small appellation, the level of quality is high. Because of the rigidities of French wine law, the region's top estate, Domaine de Trévallon, no longer uses the appellation, but is labeled as a *vin de pays*.

The remarkable village of Les Baux is one of the must-see sights of the south of France. Inevitably, this means that it is very busy in the height of the tourist season.

Coteaux d'Aix-en-Provence

The reputation of the Coteaux d'Aix-en-Provence, which became an *appellation contrôlée* in 1985, has been growing steadily. Vines have been grown in the area since Roman times. Here a number of growers have built up the names of their properties by planting better grape varieties, usually a blend of Cabernet Sauvignon, along with more typical local varieties such as Syrah, Grenache, and Mourvèdre. In addition, growers have increased their investment in the vineyards and vinification, and have taken greater care in aging the wines.

A limited amount of white is made from Sauvignon and Sémillon, blended with local varieties such as Grenache Blanc and Vermentino.

One of the best-known properties is Château Calissanne. This is to the south of Salon de Provence, and close to the Etang de Berre. Calissanne is a very large and historic property of 1,000 hectares (2,420 acres), with 107 hectares (264 acres) of vines. The top red, Clos Victoire, is a blend of Syrah and Cabernet Sauvignon, and is aged for at least a year in new oak barrels.

Another well-known estate is Château de Fonscolombe, a 170-hectare (over 400-acre) estate on chalky clay soil on the south bank of the river Durance, north of

CÔTES DE PROVENCE

Mas de Cadenet
13530 Trets.
Tel: 04 42 29 21 59.
Email: mas-decadenet@wanadoo.fr
Fax: 04 42 61 32 09.
www.masdecadenet.fr
Open Mon–Sat; closed holidays. In winter, open 9AM–12PM and 2–7PM; in summer 8AM–12PM and 2–7PM. WS.

Domaine de la Cressonnière
route Nationale 97,
83790 Pignans.
Tel: 04 94 48 81 22.
Email: cressonniere@wanadoo.fr
Fax: 04 94 48 81 25.
www.cressonniere.com

Château du Galoupet
Saint Nicolas, 83250 La Londe les Maures.
Tel: 04 94 66 40 07.
Email: galoupet@galoupet.com
Fax: 04 94 66 42 40.
www.galoupet.com

Domaine du Grand Cros
83660 Carnoules.
Tel: 04 98 01 80 08.
Email: info@grandcros.fr
Fax: 04 98 01 80 09.
www.grandcros.fr
Open Mon–Fri 10AM–7PM; AN on weekends.

Les Maîtres Vignerons de la Presqu' ile de Saint-Tropez
La Foux, 83850 Gassin.
Tel: 04 94 56 32 04.
Email: info@mavigne.com
Fax: 04 94 43 42 57.
www.mavigne.com

Château Miraval
83570 Correns.
Tel: 04 94 86 39 33.
Email: miravalcom@
club-internet.fr
Fax: 04 94 86 46 79.
www.miraval.com

Château Minuty
Gassin, 83580 St-Tropez.
Tel: 04 94 56 12 09.
Fax: 04 94 56 18 38.
www.nice-art.com/vins/minuty

Domaine Rabiega
Clos d'Ière Méridional,
83300 Draguignan.
Tel: 04 94 68 44 22.
Email: vin@rabiega.com
Fax: 04 94 47 17 72.
www.rabiega.com
Vineyard open Mon–Fri
9AM–12PM and 2–5PM; closed
weekends and holidays.

Domaine de Rimauresq
route de Notre Dame des
Anges, 83790 Pignans.
Tel: 04 94 48 80 45.
Email: rimauresq@wanadoo.fr
Fax: 04 94 33 22 31.
www.rimauresq.fr
TF. Open Sept 16–May 31
9AM–12PM and 2–4:30PM;
open June 1–Sept 15
9AM–12PM and 2–6PM;
closed Sun and holidays. WS.
Cannot be reached by bus.

Château Roubine
route Départementale 562,
83510 Lorgues.
Tel: 04 94 85 94 94.
Email: riboud@
chateau-roubine.com
Fax: 04 94 85 94 95.
www.chateauroubine.com
T; AN. Open Mon–Fri
9am–6pm, Sat 10am–6pm,
Sun (summer only)
10am–6pm. Art exhibitions,
oenology classes.

Aix. There are 144 hectares of
vines planted. The imposing
château was built in 1720.

Palette

An enclave within the area of the
Coteaux d'Aix-en-Provence is
the small appellation of Palette,
with just 42 hectares (104
acres). The chalky soil gives
fuller-bodied wines (red, white,
and rosé are made) than the rest
of the region.

Coteaux-Varois

Broadly, this appellation lies
between the Coteaux d'Aix-en-
Provence and Côtes de Provence in the Var Department.
There are just over 2,000
hectares (4,942 acres) of vines,
with Brignoles as the chief town.
The wines come in three colors,
and are generally drunk young.

FOR FURTHER
INFORMATION

Caveau de la Maison des Vins
route Nationale 7,
83460 Les Arcs sur Argens.
Tel: 04 94 99 50 20.
Email: caveaucp@
wanadoo.fr
www.caveaucp.fr

LES BAUX-DE-PROVENCE

Mas de la Dame
13520 Les Baux-de-Provence.
Tel: 04 90 54 32 24.
Email: masdeladame@
masdeladame.com
Fax: 04 94 54 40 67.
www.masdeladame.com
Open daily 8:30AM–7PM;
closed Dec 25–Jan 1.

Château Romanin
13210 St-Rémy-de-Provence.
Tel: 04 90 92 45 87.
Email: contact@romanin.com
Fax: 04 90 92 24 36.
www.romanin.com

Domaine de Trevallon
13103 St-Etienne-du-Gres.
Tel: 04 90 49 06 00.
Email: info@trevallon.com
Fax: 04 90 49 02 17.
www.trevallon.com
T; AN. Open Mon–Fri. WS
with appointment. E, S.

COTEAUX D'AIX-EN-PROVENCE

Château de Calissanne
13680 Lançon de Provence.
Tel: 04 90 42 63 03.
Email: contact@calissanne.fr
Fax: 04 90 42 40 00.
www.calissanne.fr
AN for group visit.
Store open daily 9AM–7PM.
Open Sun and holidays
9AM–1PM. WS.

Château de Fonscolombe
route de Saint Canadet,
13610 Le Puy-Sainte-
Réparade.
Tel: 04 42 61 70 00.
Email: mail@fonscolombe.com
Fax: 04 42 61 70 01.
www.fonscolombe.com

Château Vignelaure
route de Jouques,
83560 Rians.
Tel: 04 94 37 21 10.
Email: info@vignelaure.com
Fax: 04 94 80 53 39.
www.vignelaure.com
T. Wine shop open Mon–Fri
9AM–6PM (summer),
9AM–5:30PM (winter);
Open Sat, Sun and holidays
10AM–6PM. WS. Tours
available of cellar and
vineyards. Groups 4–100
welcome.

PALETTE

Château Cremade
route de Langesse,
13100 Le Tholonet.
Tel: 04 42 66 76 80.
Fax: 04 42 66 76 81.

Château Simone
13590 Meyreuil.
Tel: 04 42 66 92 58.
Email: mail@
chateau-simone.fr
Fax: 04 94 66 80 77.
www.chateau-simone.fr

*Photo of Provence buildings at left provided
by Hiltrud Shultz.*

CASSIS

Château de Fontblanche
route de Carnoux,
13260 Cassis.
Tel: 04 42 01 00 11.
Fax: 04 42 01 32 11.
T; AN.

Château de Fontcreuse
13, route Pierre-Imbert,
13260 Cassis.
Tel: 04 42 01 71 09.
Email: contact@
fontcreuse.com
Fax: 04 42 0132 64.
www.fontcreuse.com
T and guided tour; AN.

BANDOL

Domaines Bunan
Moulin des Costes,
83740 La Cadière-d'Azur.
Tel: 04 94 98 58 98.
Email: bunan@bunan.com
Fax: 04 94 98 60 05.
www.bunan.com
TF; TP including 1-hour
guided tour. Open Mon–Sat
9AM–12PM and 2–7PM; open
Sun and holidays,
10AM–12PM and 4–7PM.

Château de Pibarnon
83740 La Cadière-d'Azur.
Tel: 04 94 90 12 73.
Email: contact@pibarnon.fr
Fax: 04 94 90 12 98.
www.pibarnon.fr
T. Open Mon–Sat
9AM–12PM and 2–6PM.
Closed Sun and holidays.

Cassis, Bandol, and Bellet

Apart from the wines that have already been mentioned, these are three long-standing AC wines, whose reputation—and price—have always stood out from the general mass of the wines of Provence. All three are coastal wines and are mainly drunk in the immediate neighborhood.

Cassis

Almost on the doorstep of Marseilles, Cassis is only 22 km (14 miles) away by the D559, which winds across the Col de la Gineste, from where there are beautiful views across to the islands of Calseraigne and Riou. Tucked away in a small bay, Cassis is a very popular fishing village with quayside restaurants. The steep slopes behind the village, once dominated by vines, are being steadily overrun with villas. Cassis makes red, white, and a little rosé wine, the most distinctive of the three being the white, which has a golden straw color and a vaguely nutty flavor.

Bandol

The vineyards of Bandol lie to the west of Toulon. This is easily the largest of these three appellations, with nearly 1,500 hectares (3,700 acres). It deservedly has the highest reputation. Most of the vineyard is on rocky, limestone soil. The chief grape variety is the Mourvèdre for the red wines and, by law, these must spend a minimum of 18 months in wood, generally large oak *foudres*. The result is a full, round, opulent wine that has an immediate appeal when young, but which will nevertheless age extremely well. A small amount of white and rosé is also made.

Bellet

Nice, especially the old town, has its own exotic feel that is quite different from other large towns on the coast, such as Cannes. Because of the pressure on land for building—even up into the hills—being so great, it is not surprising that only a little wine is made. Nevertheless, there is a tiny appellation— Bellet—in the hills above Nice. Bellet is produced in the three colors. By far the best is the white variety—but then rarity makes for a high price!

Domaine Tempier
83330 Le Plan du Castellet.
Tel: 04 94 98 70 21.
Email: info@
domainetempier.com
Fax: 04 94 90 21 65.
www.domainetempier.com
TF; AN for groups.
Open Mon–Fri 9AM–12PM
and 2–6PM. WS. Tour of
vineyard, cellars (AN). E.

Château Vannières
83740 La Cadière-d'Azur.
Tel: 04 94 90 08 08.
Email: info@
chateauvannieres.com
Fax: 04 94 90 15 98.
www.chateauvannieres.com

BELLET

Clos Saint-Vincent
Collet des Fourniers,
06200 St-Romain-de-Bellet.
Tel: 04 92 15 12 69.
Email: clos.st.vincent@
wanadoo.fr

Château de Crémat
442, Chemin de Crémat,
06200 Nice.
Tel: 04 92 15 12 15.
Email: chateaucremat@
wanadoo.fr
Fax: 04 92 15 12 13.
T. Groups welcome. Open
2–5PM. Guided tours. E.

FURTHER INFORMATION

Syndicat de Défense Viticole et de L'Appellation Contrôlée Bellet
Château de Bellet
440, route de Saquier, Saint Roman De Bellet, 06200 Nice.
Tel: 04 93 37 81 57.
www.vinsdebellet.com

Food in Provence

For me, the first thing that the word Provence conjures up is herbs. They seem to appear everywhere in the cooking: sprinkled on meat before it is grilled, in soups like *soupe au pistou*, even in the basic *provençal* sauce. Tomatoes, garlic, and of course, olive oil play major roles in the kitchen.

All of these are ingredients in that Mediterranean specialty, the *bouillabaisse*. To these must be added saffron and a selection of ten or more different fish plus shellfish. *Bourride* is another similar fish dish. But just as typical is a plate of grilled sardines.

Garlic is widely used. *Aioli* is a garlic mayonnaise whose preparation begins by pounding cloves of garlic to pulp. It is often served with boiled fish or vegetables. Often villages in Provence celebrate with a grand *aioli*—an enormous platter of fish, shellfish, and vegetables.

There are certain regional specialties. Aix is known for its sweets, particularly *calissons*, Cavaillon for its melons, and Arles for its sausages. The cooking around Nice is more exotic, and uses spices not often found elsewhere in France.

Perhaps the best cheeses are those made from goats' milk and then matured with herbs in olive oil. Because of the climate, this is a region of simple cooking. The freshest of raw materials are used. In this part of the world you eat outside: what could be better than a *salade niçoise*, grilled fish, fruit and cheese, washed down by a bottle of chilled wine.

WINE FESTIVALS

Brignoles Provence and Coteaux Varois Wine Festival,
mid-April.

Saint-Raphaël Côtes de Provence Wine Festival,
mid-June.

Nice Wine Festival,
1st Sunday in August.

Fréjus Wine Festival,
2nd weekend in August.

Sainte-Maxime Wine Festival,
4th weekend in August.

Saint-Tropez Harvest Festival,
mid-September.

Arles Corrida des Vendanges,
end of September.

Where to stay and eat

(Mainly away from the coast)

AIX–EN–PROVENCE AND SURROUNDINGS

Clos de la Violette
10, de la Violette, 13100 Aix-en-Provence.
Tel: 04 42 23 30 71 (R). Reservations required.
Open Tues–Sat 12–1:30PM and 8–9:30PM.
Closed two weeks in Aug.

Château de la Pioline
260, rue Guillaume-du-Var. Aix-en-Provence.
Tel: 04 42 52 27 27 (H/R).

Relais de la Sainte Victoire
D 46, 13100 Beaurecueil.
Tel: 04 42 66 94 98 (H/R). Closed Jan 2–8,
Feb vacation, and All Saints' Day vacation.

Villa Gallici
avenue de la Violette, 13100 Aix-en-Provence.
Tel: 04 42 23 29 23 (H/R).
Restaurant closed Tues and Wed, Feb–May and in Nov.
Closed Jan 2–Feb 3.

LES BAUX–DE–PROVENCE

La Cabro d'Or
Val d'Enfer, 13520 Les Baux-de-Provence.
Tel: 04 90 54 33 21 (H/R). Closed Mon, Nov 1–Mar 31;
restaurant closed Tues noon; closed Nov–Dec 22.

L'Oustau de Baumanière
val d'Enfer, 13520 Les Baux-de-Provence.
Tel: 04 90 54 33 07 (H/R).
Hotel closed Wed, Nov 1–Mar 31. Restaurant closed Wed,
Oct 1–April 30; Thursday lunch Nov 1–Mar 31.
Closed Jan–Feb.

BRIGNOLES AND SURROUNDINGS

Hostellerie de l'Abbaye de la Celle
place du Général-de-Gaulle, 83170 La Celle.
Tel: 04 98 05 14 14 (H/R).

LA CADIÈRE D'AZUR

Hostellerie Bérard
rue Gabriel Péri, 83740 La Cadière d'Azur.
Tel: 04 94 90 11 43.

CUERS

Le Lingousto
route de Pierrefeu, 83390 Cuers.
Tel: 04 94 28 69 10.

SAINT MARTIN DU VAR

Jean-François Issautier
route Nationale 202, route de Digne,
06670 Saint Martin du Var.
Tel: 04 93 08 10 65.

View of the famous lavender valley and Mt. Ventoux, taken from the town of Sault.
Image provided by Hiltrud Shultz

Corsica

CORSICA

A nineteenth-century French writer said of Corsica, "The vines of this island are remarkable as much for their quality as for the abundance of their fruit. There is very little land where excellent wine cannot be obtained, if only it were made with more care." Since that was written, phylloxera destroyed Corsica's vineyards at the end of the 19th century. Then for a period in the 1960s and 1970s that corresponded with Algeria's independence, the emphasis was on high production to make up for the loss of strong blending wine for French *vin de table*.

This situation could not last however; when the European Union was created, the way was open for large quantities of high-in-alcohol and low-in-price wine from Puglia, and other parts of Italy, to flow into France. As a result, many of the newly planted Corsican vineyards were grubbed up and replanted with better varieties.

The coast of Corsica at the Scandola Reserve. Image © Jean Schweitzer/Dreamstime.com

Traditionally, for red wines, these have been the local Sciacarello and the Niellucio. (The latter is a close relative of the Sangiovese of Tuscany.) It has strong tannins and is best planted on limestone soils. Sciacarello produces fruitier reds, which can be drunk young. Also from the mainland have come such southern grape varieties as the Grenache, the Syrah, and the Mourvèdre. White wines are made mainly from the Vermentino, the best white variety here, and the Ugni Blanc. There are now some very good Corsican wines available, with about 2,700 hectares (6,670 acres) having appellation status.

The dominant geographical feature of the island is the mountains, which come down steeply to the sea, except for one part of the eastern side where there is a plain up to 16 km (10 miles) wide. It was on this plain that many of the larger vineyard properties were created. The best wines, however, come from vineyards planted on the slopes.

AJACCIO

Vin de Corse Ajaccio
Comte Guy Tyrel de Poix
Domaine Peraldi
Chemin du Stiletto,
20167 Mezzavia.
Tel: 04 95 22 37 30.
Fax: 04 95 20 92 91.

CALENZANA

Vin de Corse Calvi
Tony Orsini Domaine
de Rochebelle
20214 Calenzana.
Tel: 04 95 62 81 01.
Email: info@
domaine-orsini.com
Fax: 04 95 62 79 70.
www.domaine-orsini.com

PATRIMONIO

Patrimonio
Domaine Pastricciola
route de St-Florent,
20253 St-Florent,
Patrimonio.
Tel: 04 95 37 18 31.
Fax: 04 95 37 08 83.

PORTO-VECCHIO

AOC Corse Porto-Vecchio
Christian Imbert Domaine
de Torraccia
Lecci, 20137 Porto-Vecchio.
Tel: 04 95 71 43 50.
Fax: 04 94 71 50 03.

ST-FLORENT

Patrimonio
Domaine Gentile
Olzo, 20217 St-Florent.
Tel: 04 95 37 01 54.
Fax: 04 95 37 16 69.
www.domaine-gentile.com

Much of the wine is sold as *vin de pays*—vin de pays de l'Ile de Beauté. The best wines, however, are entitled to the *appellation contrôlée* Vin de Corse, and there are a number of regional names that can be added to this. These are:

· *Coteaux du Cap Corse* (not to be confused with the local aperitif of the same name): here the most striking wine is a *vin doux naturel* made from Muscat grapes, often laid out on mats to gain extra sweetness.

· *Patrimonio*: the oldest AC on the island. Here the chalky soil gives deep purple wines with a great deal of complexity, perhaps the best on the island.

· *Porto-Vecchio*: from the southeast of the island. Generally the best white wines.

· *Figari*: the southern tip of Corsica is very rugged. Excellent red wines with much character are made here.

· *Sartène*: elegant red, white, and rosé wines, produced on granitic soil.

· *Coteaux d'Ajaccio*: similar wines to those of the southern Côtes du Rhône.

· *Calvi*: simple wines that should be drunk young. The whites, particularly, tend to lack acidity. Some medium-sweet wines are also made in the region.

Food in Corsica

Corsican food is the hottest and spiciest of the French regions, which overall tend to use limited herbs and spices. Being close to Italy, pasta is also part of the local cuisine. Naturally, fish is important, either from the sea, or fresh-water trout from inland, which is customarily grilled. *Ziminu* is the Corsican version of the *bouillabaisse* of Provence and uses red peppers and pimentos, so is hotter than the mainland version. Eels from the Etang de Biguglia are popular and are customarily grilled.

Lamb, mutton, pig, and kid are the main meats. Corsica also has a large amount of game of various sizes, including wild boar.

Corsica's most famous cheese is Brocciu and is made from goat or ewe's milk. It is similar to Italian ricotta and is generally eaten fresh, although some can be kept for up to a month. Brocciu is widely used in Corsican cuisine from soups to pastries. It is also used as a stuffing for ravioli, and is often served at breakfast.

The many chestnut trees on the island provide chestnut flour, which is used to make specialty cakes such as *brilliolo*. Because pigs are fed on them, chestnuts also flavor the local ham—*prizzutu*.

WHERE TO STAY AND EAT

La Corniche
20200 San Martino di Lota.
Tel: 04 95 31 40 98 (H/R).

Belvédère
route de Palombaggia, 20137 Porto Vecchio.
Tel: 04 95 70 54 13 (H/R).

Grand Hôtel de Cala-Rosa
route de Cala-Rosa, 20137 Porto Vecchio.
Tel: 04 95 71 61 51 (H/R).

Le Maquis
20166 Porticcio.
Tel: 04 95 25 05 55 (H/R).

FOR FURTHER INFORMATION

CIVC
Le Santa-Cruz Lupino
20600 Bastia.
Tel: 04 95 30 81 91.
Fax: 04 95 30 71 14.
www.vinsdecorse.com

Languedoc–
Roussillon

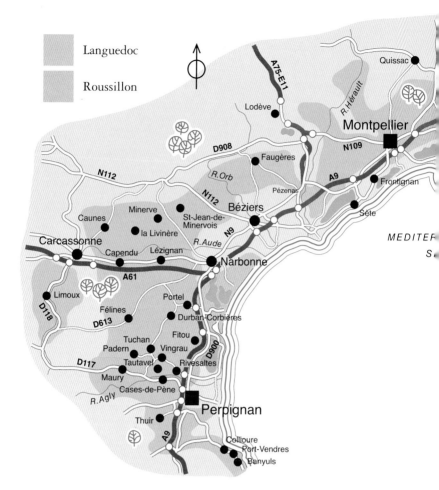

LANGUEDOC-ROUSSILLON

The vine has long been central to the economic life of the Midi—France's oldest wine-growing area. Along with Marseilles, Narbonne was one of the first places where the Greeks planted vines back in the 6th century BC. In parts of the Midi, the vine is the only viable crop, able to survive in the thin soils of the hills and the long dry summers.

Despite the recent explosion of plantings throughout the world, the swathe of vines that runs from the Rhône

Valley down to the Spanish border near Banyuls remains the largest vineyard area anywhere. It is now also one of the most dynamic in Europe.

Thirty years ago, when the average annual wine consumption in France was over 100 liters (25 gallons) a head,

the Midi produced oceans of cheap, thin red wine to supply the home thirst. Until Algerian independence these thin wines were bolstered by beefy wine from Algeria.

French drinking patterns are now radically different, and the Midi has changed beyond recognition; today it makes some of the most exciting and best value wines in France. The accent is now on quality.

International wine on the plains

In the vast plains of Languedoc, a new form of industrialized vine growing has replaced the old production of *gros rouge*. Instead of Aramon and Alicante Bouchet, which provided French workers with their *vin ordinaire*, now it is Chardonnay, Merlot,

TO GET TO LANGUEDOC–ROUSSILLON

There are now three motorway routes from Paris to choose from, depending upon which part of the region you are visiting. From Paris: Nîmes—take A6, A7, and A9. Montpellier is 759 km (472 miles) from Paris via the A10, A71, A75, and N109. It is 109 km (68 miles) from Orange by the A6, A7, and A9. Narbonne is 386 km (240 miles) from Bordeaux via A62 and A61. Perpignan is 854 km (530 miles) from Paris (A10, A71, A75, and A9). For Carcassonne, Corbières, and Minervois take A10, A71, A20 to Montauban and A62/61.

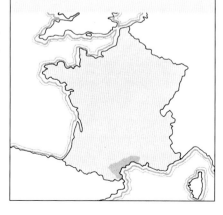

Domaine de Chevalière
route de Murviel,
34500 Béziers.
Tel: 04 67 49 88 30.
Email: info@
michellaroche.com
Fax: 04 67 49 88 59.
www.michellaroche.com

Noilly Prat
34340 Marseillan.
Tel: 04 67 77 20 15.
info@noillyprat.com
Fax: 04 67 77 32 22.
www.noillyprat.com
Guided tours of cellar (for
fee) every 30 minutes,
May–Sept 10–11AM and
2:30–6PM; Mar–April and
Oct–Nov 10–11AM and
2:30–4:30PM; AN for groups
only Dec and Feb; closed Jan.
WS; boutique open May–Sept
9:30AM–12PM and 2:30–7PM;
Mar–April and Oct–Nov
10AM–12PM and 2:30–5PM;
Dec 10AM–12PM and
2:30–4:30PM; AN for groups
only Feb; closed Jan.

Fanny Boyer
Château Beaubois,
30640 Franquevaux.
Tel: 04 66 73 30 59.
Email: fannyboyer@
chateau-beaubois.com
Fax: 04 66 73 33 02.
www.chateau-beaubois.com
T; open Mon–Sat 9AM–12PM
and 2–6PM. Groups 10–50.
E, S.

and Cabernet Sauvignon that are planted on the plain. During the last fifteen years there has been a lot of investment in these vineyards by French wine companies based in other parts of France, such as Bordeaux and Burgundy, and by companies from Australia and California.

Vins de Pays

Most of these wines from the plains are sold as *vin de pays*, usually as single varietal wines. Cabernet Sauvignon, Merlot, Syrah, and Chardonnay are the most popular varieties. The archaic French legislation now allows producers to name two varieties on the label, but under no circumstances are they allowed to mention three! The *vin de pays* denomination is also used by growers in *appellation contrôlée* areas who have grape varieties that do not fit into the overly rigid French appellation rules.

At the end of the 1980s, James Herrick raised eyebrows in the region by planting 170 hectares (420 acres) of Chardonnay a little to the northwest of Narbonne. He and his partners were among the first outside investors to spot the potential of the Languedoc. Penfolds bought the business in 1999.

A more recent investor in the region is the well-known Chablis grower and merchant, Michel Laroche. He has bought and renovated a property close to Béziers called Domaine la Chevalière and is making *vin de pays* varietal wines.

The Midi is also famous for the production of aperitifs such as Dubonnet, St Raphael, and Noilly Prat. The cellars of Noilly Prat in Marseillan are well worth a visit (see below for details). The Vermouth is aged outside in wooden barrels so that it matures in the heat. A number of producers in Languedoc make Cathagène, which is a local version of Pineau de Charentes. Eau de Vie de Marc is added to grape juice, often from Grenache Blanc, but other varieties can be used, and the blend is then aged in barrel.

Costières de Nîmes

This appellation marks the transition between the Rhône Valley and the vineyards of Languedoc.

Some 12,000 hectares of vines are currently planted between the city of Nimes, with its Roman remains and bustling center, and the north of the Camargue. Many of the vines are planted among rounded stones (*galets roulés*) that were once

Château de Campuget
30129 Manduel.
Tel: 04 66 20 20 15.
Email: campuget@wanadoo.fr
Fax: 04 66 20 60 57.
www.campuget.com
TF, WS. 17th-century château. E, S.

Les Vignerons Cave Co-operative de la Jonquières
30300 Jonquières-Saint-Vincent.
Tel: 04 66 74 50 07.
Email: cave.jonquieres@wanadoo.fr
Fax: 04 66 74 49 40.
www.cavejonquieres.com
Boutique open Tues–Sat 9AM–12:30PM and 2:30–6PM. WS. Groups up to 50. E, S.

Michel Gassier
Château de Nages,
30132 Caissargues.
Tel: 04 66 38 44 30.
Email: info@michelgassier.com
Fax: 04 66 38 44 39.
www.michelgassier.com
Open July–Aug, Tues–Sat 9AM–12PM and 3–7PM; Sept–June, Tues–Fri 3–7PM and Sat 9AM–12PM and 3–7PM. Groups up to 30. E.

Château Mourgues du Grès
30300 Beaucaire.
Tel: 04 66 59 46 10.

Hervé and Guilhem Durand
Château des Tourelles,
4294 route de Bellegarde,
30300 Beaucaire.
Tel: 04 66 59 19 72.
Email: contact@tourelles.com
Fax: 04 66 59 50 80.
www.tourelles.com
TF (without tour); AN by
phone. Cave open Mon–Fri
9AM–12PM and 2–5PM. WS.
For group visits (AN): T,
guided tour, film (E, French,
G), tastings. 1.5 hours long,
or 3 hours with lunch.
Lunch: 30 people min, AN.
For individual visits: T and
WS, April 1–Oct 31 daily
2–6PM; Nov 1–April 1 Sat
2–6PM; Jul–Aug daily
10AM–12PM and 2–7PM,
except Sun AM.

Chantal Comte
Château de la Tuilerie,
route de Saint-Gilles,
30900 Nîmes.
Tel: 04 66 70 07 52.
Email: vins@
chateautuilerie.com
Fax: 04 66 70 04 36.
www.chateautuilerie.com
Open summer Mon–Sat
9AM–12PM and 3–7PM; winter
Mon–Sat 9AM–12PM and
2–6PM; closed holidays.
Groups up to 60. E, S.

deposited by the Rhône. Some of the vineyards are extraordinarily stony, with hardly a trace of soil. The vineyards are relatively low lying—80 meters (263 feet) above sea level is a high-altitude vineyard here. This is one of the hottest and driest parts of France.

Wines of all three colors are made here, although the quantity of white made is tiny. Quality has improved markedly over the past fifteen years, and the best reds are capable of aging for five to eight years depending on the vintage. Costières de Nîmes are full bodied and richly fruited wines.

Hervé Durand, who also has a vineyard in Ontario, Canada, has been involved in fascinating experiments in replicating the way that the ancient Romans made wine.

Head for the hills—the Coteaux

Although it is interesting to see the developments on the plain, the visitor will find the real excitement in the hills that lie between the plain and the Cevennes mountains. Head for the Haut-Corbières, Minervois, Faugères, St-Chinian, Montpeyroux, or Pic St Loup.

Here much of the scenery is spectacular, with patches of vines interspersed by *garrigue*,

the local name for the dry, scrubby bush that covers the hills. You find small villages either perched on the side of steep hillsides or wedged in between ravines. These hills are a world away from the busy beaches that fringe the Mediterranean, and are well worth exploring.

Most of the wine is red and it is usually made from a blend of Mediteranean varieties. Carignan is the traditional grape of the hills. From low-yielding, old vines it produces full-bodied, tannic wine. Grenache is used to give soft body and alcohol. Syrah and Mourvedre have been planted to improve the quality of the wines.

Coteaux de Languedoc

This is the general appellation for the eastern part of Languedoc. It covers wine in all three colors. A number of specific areas can add their local names to the appellation, such as Pic St Loup, Monteyroux, and La Clape. In time, many of these areas will probably have their own separate appellations, as Faugères and St-Chinian have since 1982.

Pic St Loup

The Pic is an impressive limestone rock some 20 km (12 miles) north of Montpellier.

COTEAUX DU LANGUEDOC

Includes Pic St Loup and Picpoul de Pinet.

Sylvain Fadat
Domaine d'Aupilhac,
28, rue du Plô,
34150 Montpeyroux.
Tel: 04 67 96 61 19.
Email: aupilhac@wanadoo.fr
Fax: 04 67 96 67 24.
www.aupilhac.net
Groups up to 12. E, S.

André Leenhardt
Domaine de Cazeneuve,
34720 Lauret.
Tel: 04 67 59 07 49.
Email: andre.leenhardt@
wanadoo.fr
Fax: 04 67 59 06 91.
www.cazeneuve.net
T. Open Sat. AN Mon–Fri.
WS. E, G.

Pierre Clavel
Domaine Clavel, Mas de Périé, route de Sainte Croix 34820 Assas.
Tel: 04 99 62 06 13.
Email: info@vins-clavel.fr
Fax: 04 99 62 06 14.
www.vins-clavel.fr
WS, Mon–Sat 2–7PM; closed holidays. Tasting hall available to rent.

Cave Co-operative de Montagnac
15, route de Aumes,
34530 Montagnac.
Tel: 04 67 24 03 74.
Email: info@
cave-picpoul-de-pinet.com
Fax: 04 67 24 14 78.
www.cave-picpoul-de-
pinet.com
Boutique open Mon–Fri
10AM–12PM and 3:30–6PM;
in summer, open also Sat
9:30AM–12:30PM.

Luc and Elizabeth Moynier
Domaine de la Coste,
34400 Saint-Christol.
Tel: 04 67 86 02 10.
Email: luc.moynier@
wanadoo.fr
Fax: 04 67 86 07 71.

Ermitage du Pic St Loup
34720 St-Mathieu.
Tel: 04 67 55 20 15.

Jean Orliac
Domaine de l'Hortus,
34720 Valflaunès.
Tel: 04 67 55 31 20.
Email: domaine.hortus@
wanadoo.fr
Fax: 04 67 55 38 03.
www.vignobles-orliac.com
TF. Open Mon–Fri
8AM–12PM and 1–6PM; open
Sat 10AM–12PM and 3–5PM.
WS. E.

Simone Arnaud-Gaujal
Château de Pinet,
34850 Pinet.
Tel: 04 68 32 16 67.
Fax: 04 68 32 16 39.

Because of the height, the distance from the sea, and the cooling influence of the Cevennes Mountains, the wines here have more finesse and elegance than those of the plains. Over the past ten years, Pic St Loup has established a reputation as one of the best areas for red wine in the Languedoc and, more recently, has been making some very impressive whites as well. The reds are chiefly made from Syrah, which particularly likes the cooler climate and makes wines that are closest to those of the Northern Rhône, though always with the herbal spice of the local *garrigue*.

Picpoul de Pinet

Close to to the Bassin de Thau, famous for its oysters and other shellfish, is Picpoul de Pinet—another area that can add its name to Coteaux du Languedoc. Picpoul de Pinet is a dry, lemony white that is paired with the local fish.

Faugères

This elongated appellation is in the hills to the north of Béziers. AC Faugères runs east to west and encompasses a number of pretty little villages, including Fos, Roquessels, Lenthéric, and La Liquière. The soil is schist, and vines share this hilly area with the *garrigue*. Some of the best wines from the Midi come from here, often with a high proportion of Syrah, which grows very successfully. These are attractive hillside vineyards and it is worth taking the time to explore this area and to enjoy the landscape.

St-Chinian

The St-Chinian appellation follows directly to the west from Faugères. Like Faugères, the appellation is for red and rosé only. Whites come under the Coteaux du Languedoc. However, both are likely to be allowed to have their own ACs for whites in the future.

The first small town of any consequence is the very picturesque Roquebrun, the center of which is built on a steep hillside overlooking the river Orb. A few miles west of Roquebrun is the cooperative of Berlou, which is among the best run in the Midi.

In the center of St-Chinian, on the ave de la Promenade, is the Maison des Vins. Here you can taste and buy wines from St-Chinian, as well as obtain information about the appellation and its producers.

Minervois

Driving southwest from St-Chinian, you come to St-Jean-

Jean-Benoit Cavalier
Château de Lascaux, 34270 Vacquières.
Tel: 04 67 59 00 08.
Email: jb.cavalier@wanadoo.fr
Fax: 04 67 59 06 06.
www.chateau-lascaux.com
TF. Open Mon–Sat 10AM–12PM and 2–7PM. AN on Sun. WS. E, S.

Abbaye de Valmagne
34560 Villeveyrac.
Tel: 04 67 78 06 09.
Email: info@valmagne.com
Fax: 04 67 78 02 50.
www.valmagne.com
TP. Open year round; April 1–June 15 2–5:40PM; June 15–Sept 15, 10–11:45AM and 2–5:40PM; closed Dec 25, Jan 1, and Tues between Dec 15–Feb 15. Gothic church, gardens open to visit; church and cloister available to rent for events.

FAUGÈRES

Jean-Michel Alquier
Domaine Alquier, 4, route Pezènes les Mines 34600 Faugères.
Tel: 04 67 23 07 89.
Fax: 04 67 23 98 28.

Michel Louison
Château des Estanilles, 34480 Caberolles.
Tel: 04 67 90 29 25.
Email: earl.louison@ worldonline.fr
Fax: 04 67 90 10 99.

Château Grézan
D909, 34480 Laurens.
Tel: 04 67 90 27 46.
Email: contact@
chateau-grezan.fr
Fax: 04 67 90 29 01.
www.chateau-grezan.com
T; groups (20–45) AN.
Open May–Sept daily
8AM–7PM, closed Sun AM;
Oct–April, Mon–Sat
8AM–12PM and 2–6PM.
Guided tours of cellar.
E, S.

Alain Ollier Fils et Fille
Domaine Ollier-Taillefer,
route de Gabian, 34320 Fos.
Tel: 04 67 90 24 59.
Fax: 04 67 90 12 15.
Groups up to 15. E.

ST-CHINIAN

Château Cazal-Viel
34460 Cessenon-sur-Orb.
Tel: 04 67 89 63 15.
Email: info@cazal-viel.com
Fax: 04 67 89 65 17.
www.laurent-miquel.com
Groups 10+. E.

Les Coteaux de Rieu-Berlou
34360 Berlou.
Tel: 04 67 89 58 58.
Email: contact@berloup.com
Fax: 04 67 89 59 21. Open
Mon–Sat 9AM–12PM and
2–6PM; open Sun and
holidays, 10AM–12PM and
3–6PM. Free guided tours of
vineyard and cellar.
Mountain biking, hiking,
seasonal festivities.

de-Minervois, well known for
its fortified Muscat, and then to
the extraordinary town of
Minerve—built in a canyon
where two gorges meet. It has a
bloody past. In 1210, during
the religious wars against the
Cathars, Simon de Montfort
besieged the town and slaugh-
tered most of the population.

Nowadays the area is more
peaceful and is the highest part
of AC Minervois, which became
an appellation in 1985. Minervois can come in all three
colors, but most are red. The
Minervois is shaped like an
enormous amphitheater facing
south toward the flat valley of
the Aude.

Recently the area around La
Livinière has been recognized
as having some of the best
vineyards, so La Livinière can
now append its village name to
the Minervois appellation. A
number of producers are
making a sweet late-harvest
wine here.

Corbières and Fitou

This is an extraordinarily
varied area. AC Corbières
runs from the flat vineyards
around Narbonne, close to the
Mediterranean and the valley
of the Aude, to the remote
hills in the southern Corbières
around the village of Cucug-
nan and the Château de Peyre-

pertuse, on the border with Roussillon. Although the Haut-Corbières is very attractive, some of the best wine comes from the lower land in the north, around the village of Boutenac.

Fitou, which became an AC in 1948, is the oldest red wine appellation in the Midi. It is formed of two separate enclaves within Corbières. The coastal enclave is around the village of Fitou by the Etang de Leucate, while the largest part is well inland, around Tuchan and Mont Tauch. Fitou should be round and generous.

La Clape

The coast between Agde and Narbonne is very flat except for the fascinating lump of lime-stone that is La Clape. This is a very dry, rocky area of scrub and vines. There are a number of quality producers here, among them Châteaux Hospitalet, Pech-Celeyran, and Pech-Redon.

Limoux

Limoux is south of the medieval city of Carcassonne, toward the Pyrénées. With its Blanquette, Limoux claims to be the original producer of sparkling wines. In the Middle Ages, locals used to bottle the wine before fermentation had finished. The cold of winter would have temporarily stopped

Château La Dournie
route de St Pons,
34360 St-Chinian.
Tel: 04 67 38 19 43.
Email: chateau.ladournie@wanadoo.fr
Fax: 04 67 38 00 37. TF; TP for groups of 15+. Open Mon–Sat 9AM–12PM and 2–6PM; AN on Sun. WS. Botanic walk. E.

Domaine des Jougla
le Village, 34360 Prades-sur-Vernazobre.
Tel: 04 67 38 06 02.
Email: alex@domainedesjougla.com
Fax: 04 67 38 17 74.
www.domainedesjougla.com
Open Mon–Sat 9AM–12PM and 3:30–6PM. Groups up to 20. E, S.

MINERVOIS

Patricia and Daniel Domergue
Clos Centeilles, Campagne de Centeilles, 34210 Siran.
Tel: 04 68 91 52 18.
Email: clos.centeilles@libertysurf.fr
Fax: 04 68 91 65 92.
www.clos-centeilles.fr.st
TF; AN. Groups up to 20. WS. Rooms for 2 or cottages for 4 to rent; can also visit the Centeilles chapel. E.

Les Coteaux du Haut Minervois
34210 La Livinière.
Tel: 04 68 91 42 67.
Email: info@lesvigneronsdelanrous.com
www.lesvigneronsdelanrous.com

Jean-Louis Poudou
Domaine la Tour-Boisée,
11800 Laure-Minervois.
Tel: 04 68 78 10 04.
Fax: 04 68 78 10 98.
www.domainelatourboisee.com

CAUNES-MINERVOIS

Abbaye de Caunes
11160 Caunes-Minervois.
Tel: 04 68 78 09 44.
Email: otsi@
caunesminervois.com
www.caunesminervois.com
TP. Open Nov–Mar
10AM–12PM and 2–5PM;
Apr–Oct 10AM–12PM and
2–6PM, except July–Aug,
when open 10AM–7PM.
Closed Dec 24–Jan 1. Cellars
in 16th-century abbey. WS.

SCV Castelmaure
4, route des Cannelles,
11360 Embres et Castelmaure.
Tel: 04 68 45 91 83.
Email: castelmaure@wanadoo.fr
Fax: 04 68 45 83 56.
AN by email or phone.

Château de Lastours
11490 Portel-des-Corbières.
Tel: 04 68 48 29 17.
Email: chateaudelastours@
wanadoo.fr
Fax: 04 68 48 29 14.
Open April 1–Oct 31.

Guido Jansegers
Château Mansenoble,
11700 Moux.
Tel: 04 68 43 93 39.
Email: mansenoble@
mansenoble.com
Fax: 04 68 43 97 21.
www.mansenoble.com
Groups up to 25. E, G, S, D.

Les Producteurs du Mont Tauch
11350 Tuchan.
Tel: 04 68 45 41 08.
Email: contact@
mont-tauch.com
Fax: 04 68 45 45 29.
Open summer Mon–Sat
9AM–1PM and 2–7PM; winter
Mon–Fri 9AM–12PM and
2–6PM. Animals OK.
E, S.

Louis Panis
Château du Vieux Parc,
avenue des Vignerons,
11200 Conhilac-Corbières.
Tel: 04 68 27 47 44.
Email: louis.panis@
wanadoo.fr
Fax: 04 68 27 38 29.
TF. Open daily. AN to visit
cellar. Groups up to 35.
E, S.

Patrick Reverdy
Château La Voulte-
Gasparets, 11200 Boutenac.
Tel: 04 68 27 07 86.
Email: chateau-la-voulte@
wanadoo.fr
Fax: 04 68 27 41 33.
Open 9AM–12PM and 2–6PM.

Gérard Bertrand
Château Hospitalet,
oute de Narbonne-Plage,
11100 Narbonne-Plage.
Tel: 04 68 45 36 00.
Email: vins@
gerard-bertrand.com
Fax: 04 68 45 27 17.
www.gerard-bertrand.com
Cellar open daily, July 1–Aug
31 9AM–8PM; Sept 1–June 31,
9AM–12PM and 2–7PM.

View of the River Orb at Béziers
© Nicholas Mosienko/Dreamstime.com

Jacques de Saint-Exupèry
Château Pech-Celeyran,
11110 Salles-d'Aude.
Tel: 04 68 33 50 04.
Email: saint-exupery@
pech-celeyran.com
Fax: 04 68 33 36 12.
www.pech-celeyran.com
Open daily 9AM–6PM, except
Sun in the off-season. E.

Christophe Bousquet
Château Pech Redon, route
Gruissan, 11100 Narbonne.
Tel: 04 68 90 41 22.
Email: chateaupechredon@
wanadoo.fr
Fax: 04 68 65 11 48.

LIMOUX

Aimery Sieur d'Arques
ave de Carcassonne,
11300 Limoux.
Tel: 04 68 74 63 00.
Fax: 04 68 74 63 13.
www.sieurdarques.com

NARBONNE

James Herrick
Domaine de la Motte,
chemin de Bougna,
11100 Narbonne.
Tel: 04 68 42 38 92.
Email: info@
jamesherrick.com
Fax: 04 68 42 38 84.
www.jamesherrick.com

the process. Once the warmer days of spring arrived, the fermentation started again, trapping the resulting bubbles in the bottle. Now most Blanquette de Limoux, and all of the more recently created Crémant de Limoux, are made by the champagne method.

Limoux is also an important producer of Chardonnay, both VDP Haute Vallée de l'Aude and AC Limoux. The cooler climate of this area gives more intensity of flavor to white grapes, so the whites produced here have more flavor and acidity than those of the Languedoc plain.

The Caves de Sieur d'Arques is one of the most dynamic cooperatives, and is responsible for a large part of the production of still and sparkling wine around Limoux.

Roussillon

Although linked administratively with Languedoc, Roussillon has its own distinct identity. This is Catalan France with strong links to neighboring Spanish Catalonia. Many road signs are in both Catalan and French.

The table wines of Roussillon are broadly similar to those of Languedoc. The grape varieties used are the same. The emphasis is on reds, with some rosés, and an increasing amount of white wine. But, as in Languedoc, the heat of the summer means that it is difficult to make really interesting white wines. Modern refrigeration allows producers to make perfectly drinkable whites, but they are rarely exciting. The problem is whether to pick the grapes when they are still a little green, so preserving freshness and acidity but giving the wines a green, sometimes thin finish, or to wait until they are fully ripe, in which case the wines will often be heavy and over-alcoholic.

Harsh climate

As well as the hot summers, rainfall here can be very erratic. Long periods of drought are often ended by violent storms that can be very destructive, dumping a couple months of rain on the vineyards in just a few hours.

Valley of the Agly

Supposedly the best red wines come from the area in the north of Roussillon chiefly around the River Agly, which is entitled to the appellation Côtes du Roussillon Villages. Château de Jau and Mas Crémat are two of the leading properties here. The Villages appellation, however, is for the reds only.

Vineyards to the south of Perpignan have to content themselves with being plain Côtes du Roussillon. However, whatever the French wine legislation may believe, the quality of the wine produced south of Perpignan can be just as good as that of its neighbors to the north.

Vin Doux Naturel (VDN)

It is the fortified wines that make the Roussillon really different.

MAURY

Domaine Mas Amiel
66460 Maury.
Tel: 04 68 29 01 02.
Email: mas.amiel@
wanadoo.fr
Fax: 04 68 29 17 82.
Groups up to 40. E.

BANYULS–SUR–MER

Domaine du Mas Blanc
9, ave Général de Gaulle,
66650 Banyuls-sur-Mer.
Tel: 04 68 88 32 12.
Email: info@
domaine-du-mas-blanc.com
Fax: 04 68 88 72 24.
www.domaine-du-mas-
blanc.com.
AN.

CÔTES DU ROUSSILLON AND CÔTES DU ROUSSILLON VILLAGES

(Most of these producers also make Rivesaltes and Muscat de Rivesaltes.)

Etienne Montes
Château La Casenove,
66300 Trouillas.
Tel: 04 68 21 66 33.

Domaine Cazes
4, rue Francisco-Ferrier,
BP 61, 66602 Rivesaltes.
Tel: 04 68 64 08 26.
Fax: 04 68 64 69 79.
www.cazes-rivesaltes.com
Groups up to 15.
G, E, S.

Gérard Gauby
Domaine Gauby, Lieu-dit
Darré Pla Roque Nord,
66600 Calce.
Tel: 04 68 64 35 19.
Fax: 04 68 64 41 77. AN.

Château de Jau
66600 Cases-de-Pène.
Tel: 04 68 38 90 10.
TP. Open June 15–Sept 30
10AM–7PM; Oct 1–June 14
8AM–5PM. Tours. Entrance
fee includes admittance to
modern art museum.
Restaurant open
June 15–Sept 28.

They are little appreciated outside France, but the best are some of the most interesting fortified wines in the world.

Misleadingly called *vin doux naturel*, they are not really naturally sweet because pure alcohol is used to stop the fermentation, so the wine is usually left sweet. The strength of the spirit used is much higher than that used for port, for example. For a VDN, the spirit is over 96fl, so it is flavorless. With port, the spirit added is 77fl, so it adds flavor to the wine. Also the proportion added is much lower: a minimum of five percent and a maximum of ten percent compared to twenty percent for port. This is because the wine is allowed to ferment to around 13fl, whereas port only reaches 8fl before the spirit is added.

Muscat de Rivesaltes has become popular outside France over the past 20 years. The other fortified wines, especially Banyuls, Maury, and Rivesaltes, are little known outside France, but they count among the world's most fascinating fortified wines. Domaine Cazes in Rivesaltes, just north of Perpignan, make some of the most complex, especially their Aimé Cazes, which is made from Grenache Blanc. They also make a very good range of table wines, both *vin de pays* and AC.

Maury

This small town, in the lee of the vertiginous Château de Queribus, has its own appellation for fortified wines. Grenache, which becomes very ripe with a high potential of alcohol, is the chief variety used. Mas Amiel, the leading property, has one of the most extraordinary sights in the wine world—a "park" of over 3,000 carboys. Filled with Maury, these are left outside for a year. Exposure to heat and rain gives an oxidized taste, known locally as *rancio*.

Côte Vermeille

The vineyards of Collioure and Banyuls are some of the most dramatic in France. The very steep, terraced vineyards stretch up the coastal hills of the Pyrénées where they meet the deep blue Mediterranean.

In mid-summer these vineyards are searingly hot, as the heat reflects off the schisteous soil. Grenache is the main variety here. AC Collioure is a powerful still wine, mainly red though a little rosé is made, while AC Banyuls is for fortified.

Les Maîtres Vignerons de Tautavel
24, ave Jean Badia,
66720 Tautavel.
Tel: 04 68 29 12 03.
Email: vignerons.tautavel@wanadoo.fr
Fax: 04 68 29 41 81.
www.vignerons-tautavel.com
Open Mon–Sat 8AM–12PM and 2–6PM, Sun 10AM–12PM and 3–6PM. AN for groups. Free visit to exhibition on winemakers.

Domaine Mas Crémat
66600 Espir-de-Agly.
Tel: 04 68 38 92 06.
Email: mascremat@mascremat.com
Fax: 04 68 38 92 23.
www.mascremat.com
AN. Open Mon–Sat 10AM–12PM and 2–6PM; closed Thurs AM and holidays. Groups up to 45. E.

Les Vignobles du Rivesaltes
1, rue de la Roussillonaise,
66602 Rivesaltes.
Tel: 04 68 64 06 63.
Email: vignobles.rivesaltes@wandoo.fr
Fax: 04 68 64 64 69.
www.rivesaltes.com
Cellar open Mon–Sat 9AM–7PM.

Food in Languedoc-Roussillon

As one would expect, the cooking of this region has considerable similarities to the cuisine of neighboring Provence. Both are Mediterranean. Roussillon, in particular,

BANYULS

(These producers also make unfortified wines.)

Cellier des Templiers

route du Mas-Reig,
66650 Banyuls-sur-Mer.
Tel: 04 68 98 36 70.
Email: accueil-visite@
templiers.com
Fax: 04 68 88 00 84.
www.banyuls.com/banyuls
T. Open Mar 27–Oct 31 daily
10AM–7PM; visit and tasting in
E every hour, 10:30AM–
12:30PM and 3–6PM. Open
Nov 1–Mar 26: during school
holidays (Dec 17–Jan 3),
Mon–Sat 10AM–1PM and
2:30–6:30PM; outside school
holidays, only Mon–Fri,
2:30–6PM. WS. G. AN.
Underground cellar open
July 1–Aug 31, 11AM–7PM, or
by app't. 1-hour free guided
tour of cellar, film, and
tasting. Groups 10–50
people. Guided tours of
vineyards (AN) every Thurs,
May 1–Oct 30, lasts from
8:45AM–4PM.

Domaine la Tour Vieille

3, ave du Mirador,
66190 Collioure.
Tel: 04 68 82 42 20.

Vial Magnères

14, rue Eduoard–Herriot,
66650 Banyuls-sur-Mer.
Tel: 04 68 88 31 04.
Email: al.tragou@wanadoo.fr
Fax: 04 68 88 02 43. AN.

has its own cuisine, which reflects a time when this region was part of Catalonia. As in other parts of the Mediterranean, the food is based on good ingredients treated simply. For much of the year it is possible to eat outside, so fish and meat are often plainly grilled.

Oysters from the Bassin de Thau near Sété are a speciality, especially those from the oyster farms near the village of Bouzigues. Mussels and other shellfish are also farmed in the Bassin. *Brandade de morue* (a salt cod mayonnaise) is a blend of salt cod, olive oil, a little garlic, and either cream or milk. This is a speciality of Nîmes.

In Roussillon, sweet red peppers are widely used. Grilled, skinned, and mixed with olive oil, they make a delicious and simple salad. Collioure is famous for its anchovies, although these days many of them are caught in the Atlantic. In the eastern Pyrenées, *ouillade de cerdagne*—a filling dish similar to *pot au feu* but based on a knuckle of pork, local blood pudding, and cabbage—is more a winter dish or for mountain walkers.

A street in the French medieval walled village of Castelnou, Roussillon.
Image provided by Dreamstime.com

Where to stay and eat

Arranged from east to west.

Wine bar Chez Michel
11, square de la Couronne, 30000 Nîmes.
Tel: 04 66 76 19 59 (R).

Le Jardin des Sens
11, ave Saint-Lazare, 34000 Montpellier.
Tel: 04 99 58 38 38 (H/R). Restaurant open Mon–Sat 12–2PM
and 7:30–10PM; closed July–Aug, Mon & Wed lunch; closed
Sept–June, Mon all day, Tues & Wed lunch; closed two weeks Jan.

Le Mimosa
34725 Saint Guiraud.
Tel: 04 67 96 67 96 (R). Open Tues–Sat, dinner only, Sun
lunch. Closed early Nov–mid Mar.

Château de Hospitalet
route de Narbonne-Plage, 11100 Narbonne.
Tel: 04 68 45 28 50 (H/R). Restaurant open 7–10AM, 12–2PM,
and 7:30–10PM.

Auberge du Vieux Puits
ave Saint-Victor, 11360 Fontjoncouse.
Tel: 04 68 44 07 37 (H/R). Hotel and restaurant closed Jan
1–Mar 3. Restaurant closed Sun night, Mon, & Tues, except
from June 15–Sept 15 when only closed Mon lunch.

Park Hotel and Restaurant Chapon Fin
18, boulevard Jean-Bourrat, 66000 Perpignan.
Tel: 04 68 35 14 14 (H/R). Restaurant open 10AM–7PM.

Château de Jau le Grill
66600 Cazes de Pene.
Tel: 04 68 38 91 38 (R).

Auberge Saint-Paul
7, place de l'Eglise, 66500 Villefranche de Conflent.
Tel: 04 68 96 30 95 (R). Open 12–2:30PM & 7:30–9:30PM.
Closed Sun night and Mon, also closed Tues from Nov 1–
Easter; closed Jan 3–27, June 13–19, Nov 1, & Nov 20–28.

Le Domaine d'Auriac
route de Saint-Hilaire, 11000 Carcassonne.
Tel: 04 68 25 72 22 (H/R). Hotel & restaurant closed Sun
night and Mon from Feb 12–April 3 and Oct 31–Dec 31, except
holidays. Restaurant closed Mon, Tues, & Wed lunch from May
2–Sept 30. Closed Jan 3–Feb 7, April 23–May 1, & Nov 12–20.

WINE FESTIVALS

Faugères Fête du Grand St Jean:
1st Sunday in July

Narbonne spring wine fair:
end April

*Trausse–Minervois wine
festival:*
1st two weeks of July

Minerve wine festival:
last two weeks of July

Rivesaltes Muscat Festival:
August

*Lézignan–Corbières wine
festival:*
1st two weeks of August

Béziers Feria:
mid-August

*Sweet wine and French sunset © Jean
Schweitzer/Dreamstime.com*

For further information:

ROUSSILLON

GIP Côtes du Roussillon
19, ave de Grande Bretagne, 66000 Perpignan.
Tel: 04 68 51 31 81. Fax: 04 68 34 88 88. G.S.
www.vins-du-roussillon.com

LANGUEDOC

Conseil Interprofessionnel des Vins du Languedoc
9, Cours Mirabeau, 11100 Narbonne.
Tel: 04 68 90 38 30. Fax: 04 68 32 38 00.

Syndicat des Vignerons Coteaux du Languedoc
Domaine de Maurin, Mas de Saporta, 34970 Lattes.
Tel: 04 67 06 04 44. Fax: 04 67 58 05 15.

Southwest France

SOUTHWEST FRANCE

Some of the most distinctive and interesting French wines come from Southwest France. The vineyards are widely scattered from close to the Atlantic coast eastward across to the hills around Albi. From the north they stretch southward from Bergerac in the valley of the Dordogne south to the Pyrenees and the Spanish border. Because of the distances involved it is difficult to tour the whole region at one time.

Many of the wines are made from varieties indigenous to the Southwest. This becomes more marked the further you move away from Bordeaux. Madiran and Pacherenc de Vic Bihl are mainly made from local varieties. Some have names that are very difficult to pronounce. The Len de l'El or Loin de l'Oeil, a white variety from Gaillac, is one tongue-straining example.

Closer to Bordeaux, the classic Bordelais varieties are used: Cabernet Sauvignon, Cabernet Franc, Merlot for the reds, and Sauvignon Blanc and Sémillon along with some Muscadelle for the whites. Before the establishment of the appellation system from 1935–1936, vineyards such as Bergerac could sell their wines as Bordeaux.

Irouléguy

This small Basque appellation is right on the Spanish border on the western end of the Pyrenees. It centers on the small and historic town of St-Jean-Pied-de-Port at the northern end of the Pass of Ronceveaux. These wines came close to disappearing after World War II. Lately they have staged a modest revival. Being in the foothills of the Pyrenees, the region is naturally hilly, punctuated by deep valleys. Some of the vineyards are planted on vertiginous slopes with spectacular views across to the Pyrenees. The wines are mainly red and rosé and made from Tannat and Fer Severadou, as well as Cabernets Franc and Sauvignon. A small amount of white is made from Courbu, Gros, and Petit Manseng.

This beautiful region is also known for its cheese made from ewes' milk.

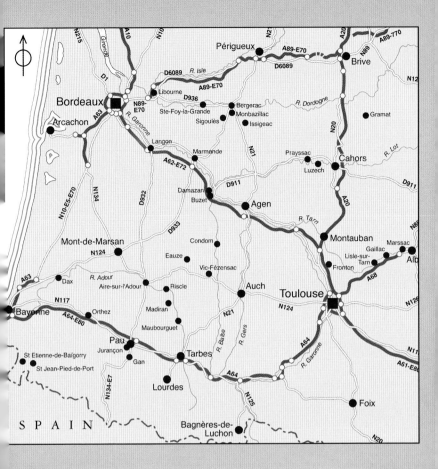

HOW TO GET TO THE SOUTHWEST

With the completion of the A20 from Paris to Montauban there are now two quick routes to the Southwest. For the western part of the region, take A10 from Paris to Bordeaux, then either A63 or N10 toward Bayonne. For the eastern part, take the A10 to Orléans, A71 to Vierzon, then A20. This route passes through the Cahors appellation. Much of the cross-country A89 autoroute from Clermont–Ferrand to Bordeaux is now open.

IROULÉGUY

Etienne Brana
3, bis ave du Jai-Alai,
64220 St-Jean-Pied-de-Port.
Tel: 05 59 37 00 44.
Fax: 05 59 37 14 28.
www.brana.fr

Les Vignerons de Pays Basque
route de St-Jean-Pied-de-Port,
64430 St-Etienne-de-Baigorry.
Tel: 05 59 37 41 33.

JURANÇON

Charles Hours
Quartier Trouilh,
64360 Monein.
Tel: 05 59 21 46 19.
contact@uroulat.com
Fax: 05 59 21 46 90.
www.uroulat.com

Pascal Labasse
Domaine de Bellegarde,
Quartier Coos,
64360 Monien.
Tel: 05 59 21 33 17.
Email: domaine.bellegarde@
wanadoo.fr
Fax: 05 59 21 44 40.
www.domainebellegarde-
jurancon.com

Jean-Bernard Larrieu
Clos Lapeyre, La Chapelle-
de-Rousse, 64110 Jurançon.
Tel: 05 59 21 50 80.
Email: contact@
lapeyreenjurancon.com
Fax: 05 59 21 51 83.
www.lapeyreenjurancon.com

Jurançon

These white wines have been famous since the time of Henry of Navarre, when they were used for his baptism. The wines have traditionally been sweet, and those labeled Jurançon still are, ranging from slightly to intensely sweet. The sweetness is balanced by relatively high acidity, which prevents the wines from being cloying. This comes from sun-drying on the vine rather than noble rot. The generally long, dry autumns are not conducive to developing botrytis. An increasing amount of dry white is made and is labeled Jurançon Sec. The grape varieties used are the Gros and Petit Manseng and the Petit Courbu. The Petit Manseng is particularly favored for the sweet wine because of its low yield and widely spaced grapes.

The Jurançon vineyard is divided into two separate areas. One is just to the south of the elegant town of Pau, between Jurançon and the small town of Gan, especially on the amphitheater of hills at Chapelle-de-Rousse. The other area of vineyards is around the small town of Monein, some 25 km west of Pau. Again, many of the vines are planted on steeply undulating land.

The wines are attractive young but gain complexity as

they age. They have a great potential to age, but it is unfortunately very difficult to find old bottles.

Madiran & Pacherenc du Vic-Bilh

Madiran is as beefy as the rugby players who come from the region. The main variety is Tannat, which is as tannic as its name suggests. The vineyards are some 30 km northeast of Pau in hills just to the west of the valley of the Adour. Tannat can be blended with Fer Servadou, a local variety, or Cabernets Franc and Sauvignon. However, many of the

Henry Ramonteau
Domaine de Cauhapé,
Quartier Castet,
64360 Monein.
Tel: 05 59 21 33 02.
Email: contact@cauhape.com
Fax: 05 59 21 41 82.
www.cauhape.com
Cellar open Mon–Fri
8AM–6PM, Sat 10AM–6PM.

Cave des Producteurs de Jurançon
53, avenue Henri-IV,
64390 Gan.
Tel: 05 59 21 57 03.
Fax: 05 59 21 72 06.
www.cavedejurancon.com

Jurançon grape vines grow in neat rows in the Pau region.
Image: Alison Cornford-Matheson/Dreamstime.com

MADIRAN AND PACHERENC DU VIC-BILH

Alain Brumont
Château Bouscassé,
32400 Maumusson-Laguian.
Tel: 05 62 69 74 67.
Email: brumont.alain@
wanadoo.fr

Patrick Ducourneau
Chapelle Lenclos, Domaine
Mouréou, 32400
Maumusson-Laguian.
Tel: 05 62 69 7811.

Vignobles Laplace
Château d'Aydie,
64330 Aydie.
Tel: 05 59 04 08 00.
Email: pierre.laplace@
wanadoo.fr

Producteurs Plaimont
32400 Saint-Mont.
Tel: 05 62 69 62 87.
Fax: 05 62 69 61 68.
www.plaimont.com
Also the leading producers of
VDQS Côtes de Saint-Mont
and Ciotes de Gascogne.

ARMAGNAC

Francis Darroze
ave de l'Armagnac,
40120 Roquefort, France.
Tel: 05 58 45 51 22.
Email: delphine@
darroze-armagnacs.com
Fax: 05 58 45 57 12.
www.darroze-armagnacs.com

top producers prefer to make their top *cuvées* from 100 percent Tannat. Pacherenc du Vic-Bilh is a white wine that can be dry or sweet and is produced in the same zone as Madiran. Some of the sweet wines, especially those that are picked as late as December, can be very fine.

Alain Brumont has been a very significant force behind the current fame of the region's wines. The wineries that he has built at Bouscassé and Montus would not be out of place in Bordeaux or the Napa Valley.

Armagnac

The brandy of the Southwest epitomizes the region—the Gascon spirit. Single distilled, it has more flavor but is more rustic than Cognac, which is double distilled and comes from the Charente, north of Bordeaux. The Armagnac area is divided into three zones: Bas Armagnac, Tenareze, and Haut Armagnac. The best area is the most westerly—the Bas Armagnac close to the sandy pine-clad area of Les Landes. The chief towns for Armagnac are Labastide d'Armagnac, Condom, and Eauze.

Unlike Cognac, Armagnac has long been allowed to come from a single year and there are vintage specialists, such as Francis Darroze in Roquefort.

It is often possible to find Armagnacs from your birth or wedding year.

The mainly white *vin de pays,* Côtes de Gascogne, also comes from the Armagnac area.

Gaillac

As in many of the vineyards of the Southwest, there is a long tradition of vine growing here, with the first traces dating back to Roman times.

In addition to Albi with its cathedral and Toulouse Lautrec Museum, there are a number of sites worth visiting, including the remarkable medieval town of Cordes—the town in the sky.

Côtes du Frontonnais

Closer to Toulouse are the vineyards of Fronton, where the chief grape variety is the local Negrette. This can also be blended with Cabernet Franc, Cabernet Sauvignon, Gamay, Syrah, and other varieties.

Château de Larressingle
Ets Papelorey SA, Château de Larressingle,
32100 Condom.
Tel: 05 62 28 15 33.
Email: papelorey@
armagnac-larressingle.com
Fax: 05 62 28 36 99.
www.armagnac-larressingle.com
TF; AN on Sat, for groups of 8+, Aug 1–15. Open Mon–Fri 8:30–11:30AM and 1–4PM.
WS. E, S.

Château de Laubade
32110 Sorbets.
Tel: 05 62 09 06 02.

GAILLAC

Cave de Labastidede-Lèvis
81150 Marssac-sur-Tarn.
Tel: 05 63 53 73 73.

Domaine de Larroque
81150 Cestayrols.
Tel: 05 63 56 87 63.

Robert et Bernard Plageoles
Domaine des Très Cantous,
81140 Cabuzac-sur-Vère.
Tel: 05 63 33 90 40.

Buzet

There are just under 2,000 hectares (4,942 acres) planted in the gentle hills to the south of the River Garonne centered on Buzet. The well-run cooperative dominates production and has its own cooperage.

Cahors

Long famous for its "black wine," Cahors can produce some of the best and most age-worthy red wines of the region. The black wine is no more. Historically, it was probably the result of boiling down and concentrating

CÔTES DU FRONTONNAIS

Château Bellevue

La Foret, 4500,
ave de Grisottes,
31620 Fronton.
Tel: 05 34 27 91 91.
Email: contact@
chateaubellevuelaforet.com
Fax: 05 61 82 39 70.
www.chateaubellevuelaforet.com
T. Mon–Sat 9AM–12PM and
2–6PM; closed holidays. WS.
Tours (AN).

Château Montauriol

route des Châteaux,
31340 Villematier.
Tel: 05 61 35 30 58.
Email: contact@
chateau-montauriol.com
Fax: 33 5 61 35 30 59.
www.chateau-
montauriol.com
No tastings; WS. Open
Mon–Fri 8AM–12PM and
2–6PM. E, G, S.

BUZET

Les Vignerons de Buzet

47160 Buzet-sur-Baise.
Tel: 05 53 84 74 30.
Email: buzet@
vignerons-buzet.fr

must so as to produce a powerful wine that could travel and was supplied to the French Navy. The vineyards are planted both in the Lot Valley and up on the limestone *causse*.

The major grape here is the powerful Auxerrois. This is the local name for Malbec, which plays a minor role in Bordeaux but a major one in Argentina. A proportion of Merlot is often used to soften the wine. Most of the reds need time in the bottle, but there is also a new fruity style of Cahors being made that is ready to drink young.

The Lot Valley, and its river with tortuously snaking curves, is quite attractive, with the old town of Cahors as the center-piece. The famous Pont Valentré across the Lot was opened in 1308.

Upper Lot Valley

Further up the Lot Valley are two tiny curiosities—the VDQS of Estaing and Entraygues as well as the small nearby appellation of Marcillac.

Bergerac & associated appellations

However much the producers of Bergerac and its associated appellations try to assert their independence, these vineyards remain an extension of the right bank of Bordeaux—St-Émilion and Côtes de Castillon. They are also in the valley of the Dordogne and use identical grapes and blends. The landscape is more rural, however, and less dominated by vineyards. This is an area of mixed agriculture. In addition to Bergerac, there are also a rather confusing number of small appellations in the Dordogne, such as Côtes de Bergerac, Pécharmant for reds, Montravel, Côtes de Montravel (sweet), Haut-Montravel, Rosette, and Saussignac (sweet).

In poor years it can difficult to get the Cabernets properly ripe, giving some rather green reds.

CAHORS

Baldes et Fils
Clos Triguedina,
46700 Puy-l'Evèque.
Tel: 05 65 21 30 81.
Fax: 05 65 21 39 28.

Château la Caminade
46140 Parnac.
Tel: 05 65 30 73 05.
Email: resses@wanadoo.fr
Fax: 05 65 20 17 04.
www.chateau-caminade.com
Open Mon–Fri 8AM–12PM and 2–6PM; AN on Sat; Sun and holidays closed.

Château Saint-Didier-Parnac
46140 Parnac.
Tel: 05 65 30 70 10.

Verhaeghe
Château du Cèdre, Bru,
46700 Vire-sur-Lot.
Tel: 05 65 36 53 87.
Email: chateauducedre@wanadoo.fr
TF; AN for groups. Open Mon–Sat 9AM–12PM and 2–6PM. WS. E.

UPPER LOT VALLEY

Jean-Marc Viguier
Les Buis,
12140 Entraygues.
Tel: 05 65 44 50 45.

Côtes de Duras

Bordeaux varieties grow in undulating countryside around the town of Duras, to the east of the Entre Deux Mers. Affordable dry whites from Sauvignon Blanc dominate.

A view of the River Lot © David Hughes/Dreamstime.com

BERGERAC

Comte de Bosredon

Château Belingard,
24240 Pomport.
Tel: 05 53 58 28 03.
Email: contact@
belingard.com
Fax: 05 53 58 38 39.
www.chateaubelingard.com
Open Mon–Fri 8AM–6PM, Sat
10:30AM–6PM; also by app't.

Château de Fayolle

24240 Saussignac.
Tel 05 53 74 32 02.
Email: chateau.de.fayolle@
wanadoo.fr
Fax: 00 33 553 74 51 35.
www.fayolle.co.uk
AN; open Mon–Fri 2–6PM.

Château Masburel

Fougueyrolles,
33220 Ste-Foy-la-Grande.
Tel: 05 53 24 77 73.
Email: Olivia@
chateau-masburel.com
www.chateau-masburel.com
Open Mon–Fri 9AM–12PM
and 2–6PM; AN on weekends,
holidays.

Château de Panisseau

24240 Thénac.
Tel: 05 53 58 40 03.

Thierry Dauilhiac

Château le Payral,
24240 Razac-de-Saussignac.
Tel: 05 53 22 38 07.
www.pays-de-bergerac.com/
english/wine/chateau-payral

De Conti

Château Tour des Gendrees,
24240 Ribagnac.
Tel: 05 53 57 12 43.

Monbazillac & other sweet wines

Using the same grapes as Sauternes and Barsac—Sémillon, Sauvignon Blanc, and Muscadelle—Monbazillac has a long reputation for its botrytis-affected sweet wines. They are often sweetened with notes of honeycomb, and well-made Monbazillacs will last for decades. There has recently been a revival in the quality of these wines due to the efforts of producers such as Château Tirecul la Gravière.

The impressive Château of Monbazillac dominates the slopes that overlook the pretty old town of Bergerac on the banks of the Dordogne. The château is owned by the local cooperative.

Food in the Southwest

The food here is hearty and typically French. Duck and goose play an important role—the Department of Gers is the largest producer of *foie gras* in France. *Confit de canard* is a widely available classic. Agen is famous for its prunes. The Basque region has its own cuisine, in which sweet red peppers play an important part in dishes such as *piperade*. The town of Bayonne is celebrated for its ham and chocolate.

Where to stay and eat

Les Pyrénées
19, place du Géneral-de-Gaulle,
12230 St-Jean-Pied-de-Port.
Tel: 05 59 37 01 01 (H/R).

Le Grand Ecuyer
Haut de la Cité,
81170 Cordes-sur-Ciel.
Tel: 05 63 53 79 50 (H/R).

Hotel Terminus and Restaurant
Le Balandre,
5, ave Charles-de-Freycinet,
46000 Cahors.
Tel: 05 65 53 32 00 (H/R).

Château de Mercuès
46090 Mercuès.
Tel: 05 65 20 00 01 (H/R).
www.chateaudemercues.com

Le Gindreau
46150 St-Medard.
Tel: 05 65 36 22 27 (R).
21 km from Cahors.

Pain Adour et Fantaisie
14-16, place des Tilleuls,
Grenade-sur-Adour.
Tel: 05 58 45 18 80 (H/R).

Patricia Atkinson
Clos d'Yvigne, Le Bourg,
24240 Gageac-et-Rouillac.
Tel: 05 53 22 94 40.
Email: patricia.atkinson@
wanadoo.fr
Fax: 05 53 23 47 67.
www.cdywine.com
AN.

CÔTES DE DURAS

Prodiffu
17-19, route des Vignerons,
33790 Landerrouat.
Tel: 05 56 61 33 73.
Email: prodiffu@
prodiffu.com
Fax: 05 56 61 40 57.
www.prodiffu.com
Specializes in kosher wine.

MONBAZILLAC

**Cave Cooperative de
Monbazillac**
route de Monbazillac,
24240 Monbazillac.
Tel: 05 53 63 65 60.

**Claudie and Bruno
Bilancini**
Château Tirecula la Gravière,
24240 Monbazillac.
Tel: 05 53 57 44 75.

Christian Roche
Domaine de l'Ancienne Cure,
24560 Colombier.
Tel: 05 53 58 27 90.

A peaceful scene in the Basque town of St-Jean-Pied-de-Port, in the foothills of the Pyrenees, close to the border with Spain. The robust local wine is called Irouléguy.

Bordeaux

BORDEAUX

There are many reasons why the favorite French wines among English-speaking people have traditionally been those from Bordeaux. First of all, the province of Aquitaine belonged to the English Crown for more than 300 years. Secondly, the situation of Bordeaux as a port has made it ideal for the shipment of wine to Britain, and the United States. Even during the German occupation in World War II, in order to secure more arms from Britain, local resistance fighters would load a few casks of their best wine on to a boat and sail for England. Another reason can be seen in the names within the trade. Among the merchants there are Lawtons and Bartons, and the vineyard names include Cantenac-Brown, Clarke, and Boyd. These are good historical reasons for our interest. The vineyards of Bordeaux cover a vast area along both banks of the Gironde, and of the two rivers whose estuary this is: the Dordogne and the Garonne. Within this area is a broad range of styles of wine, ranging from the classic red wines of the Haut-Médoc (based on the Cabernet Sauvignon grape) and of St-Émilion (on the Merlot), to the dry white wines of the Graves and the luscious sweet wines of Sauternes. However, the great wines with famous names form only a minute proportion of the total production. It has been claimed that there are over 3,000 château names in Bordeaux, but of these only a handful are known to even the most devoted wine lover.

The City of Bordeaux

Coming into Bordeaux from the north, across the Pont de Pierre, the city unfolds in a vast semi-circle to the right, presenting one of the most attractive waterfronts anywhere in the world. Many of the finest buildings surrounding the Place de la Bourse were built in the middle of the 18th century. Further to the right is the Esplanade des Quinconces and further still, the Quai des Chartrons, the former center of the Bordeaux wine trade.

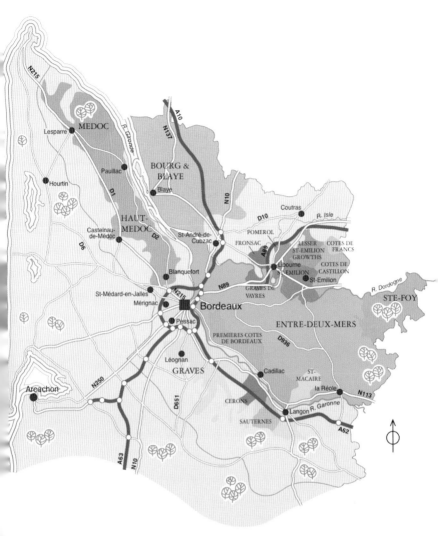

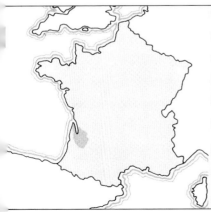

TO GET TO BORDEAUX

Bordeaux is 579 km (360 miles) from Paris by the A10 and 610 km (379 miles) by the D732 and A10. Bordeaux is three hours from Paris by fast train (TGV). There is also the international airport of Bordeaux Merignac. Now that the A89 is largely complete, the journey across from central France is considerably easier.

Image on previous page of tree in Sauterne, Bordeaux © Frank Farrell/ Dreamstime.com

Just behind all these are such wonderful buildings as the Grand Theater and the narrow streets of the old city.

On these quays, from which ships sailed all over the world, the wealthy merchants had their warehouses. With the coming of long-distance trucks and container-ports, little wine now leaves Bordeaux by boat. However, the quays continue to be used by cruise ships, mainly carrying passengers from the US.

The warehouses

Most of the merchants have moved to specially made temperature-controlled warehouses outside the city. Only a few retain their token presence on the Chartrons. In their day, these warehouses, too, were custom-built, running back in narrow strips for a quarter of a mile or more behind the offices at the front. Their thick walls kept them cool, and the barrels could be rolled along the narrow railways provided. The office boy would often ride from one end of the cellar to the other on a bicycle.

There are a few remains from the time when Bordeaux was a Roman city, and among other monuments the Tour du Prince Noir (the Tower of the Black Prince) bears witness to the time of English occupation.

The meaning of château

Having "château" on a wine label is not necessarily grand. In Bordeaux, the word "château" may mean that the wine comes from a castle or an imposing country house. But that can mean anywhere from the most impressive of palaces to a country cottage, or even a barn. There may not even be a building. The word has come to be synonymous with a vineyard, and not necessarily a distinct vineyard at that, for now many properties sell their second wine under a separate château name. However, to use a château name, the grapes must come from particular vineyards. They cannot just be a blend from wherever.

There are around 13,000 producers in Bordeaux—ranging from the extremely wealthy with world famous estates to unknown producers barely scratching a living. Bordeaux is like an enormous pyramid with famous

Margaux, Yquem, and Cheval Blanc at the top and representing only about two percent of the production. It is, of course, the famous properties that visitors will want to see. Unfortunately, some of the most famous are closed to the public.

Classifications

Bordeaux has a number of classifications. The 1855 classification, drawn up at the request of Napoleon III for the Universal Exhibition of that year, is the best known and most durable. It covers the top properties of the Médoc and Sauternes, plus Haut-Brion. The only change has been the elevation of Mouton-Rothschild to the top rank in 1973. St-Émilion is reclassified every ten years. The *cru bourgeois* classification has been recently revised, with arguments still continuing. Pomerol does not have a classification.

To get to the vineyards
St-Émilion/Pomerol, etc: Exit A10 at St André de Cubzac,
taking D670 to Libourne
The Médoc: A10, A63, D1 (Junction 7)
Pessac: A630 (Junction 13), N250
Léognan: A630 (Junction 18), D651
Sauternes: A62 Langon

MARGAUX

Château d'Angludet
33460 Cantenac.
Tel: 05 57 88 71 41.
Email: contact@
chateau-angludet.fr
Fax: 05 57 88 72 52.
www.chateau-angludet.fr

Château Lascombes
1, cours de Verdun, BP 4,
33460 Margaux.
Tel: 05 57 88 97 43.
Email: visite.lascombes@
chateau-lascombes.fr
Fax: 05 57 88 33 28.
www.chateau-lascombes.com/fr
AN (contact Nathalie
Siraud). Multilingual guides.

Château Margaux
33460 Margaux.
Tel: 05 57 88 83 83.
Email: chateau-margaux@
chateau-margaux.com
Fax: 05 57 88 31 32.
www.chateau-margaux.com
AN; closed weekends,
holidays, and in Aug during
harvest. Tastings only for
professionals; no direct sales.

Château Prieuré-Lichine
33460 Cantenac.
Tel: 05 57 88 36 28.

Château Siran
33460 Margaux.
Tel: 05 57 88 34 04.
Fax: 05 57 88 70 05.
www.chateausiran.com
Open daily year round
10AM–6PM.

The Haut-Médoc

The Haut-Médoc is the image of Bordeaux that most of us have in mind: noble châteaux fronted by broad sweeps of gravel and then the vines. It is the most famous region because it is from here that many of the best wines come—not always the most expensive, for Pétrus and Le Pin in Pomerol have recently had that distinction. Without the famous names and their châteaux, however, this would be a flat, rather featureless area.

Temples of wine

Over the last twenty-five years the top châteaux have enjoyed a remarkable boom due to the success of *en primeur* (selling their wines before they are bottled) and the current global demand for top Bordeaux. Many of the properties have been transformed, with glittering arrays of fermentation equipment and impressive barrel chais. Often world-class architects have been employed and some of the châteaux really are like temples to wine.

Alternative routes

There are two roads through the Médoc. One is the D2, which winds through the succession of wine villages and seems designed to drop you almost at the front door of every château. The other is a peculiar, but much faster, road, which starts as the N215, becomes the D1, and then turns back into the N215 once again. This passes to the west of the vineyards, but there are a series of connecting crossroads to the D2, so you can drive as far as you want up the one and then return by the other.

Normally, beside the imposing château, there will also be the *chais*, or barrel cellars. The word "cellar" is misleading however; with the single exception of Château Margaux, the *chais* are built above ground.

Margaux

On arriving in the hamlets of Labarde and Cantenac, you enter the area entitled to call itself Margaux. It is here that the châteaux begin to come thick and fast. Between the two

The elegant classical façade of Château Margaux reflects its wines' first-growth status.

ST-JULIEN

Château Beychevelle

33250 St-Julien-Beychevelle.
Tel: 05 56 73 20 70.
Email: beychevelle@
beychevelle.com
www.beychevelle.com
AN; open Mon–Fri
10AM–12PM and 1:30–5PM;
open Sat in July and Aug.

Château Lagrange

33250 St-Julien-Beychevelle.
Tel: 05 56 73 38 38.
Email: chateau-lagrange@
chateau-lagrange.com
Fax: 05 56 59 26 09.
www.chateau-lagrange.com
Visit free; AN. Mon–Thurs
9–11AM and 4–4:30PM; Fri
9–11AM; closed weekends,
holidays, harvest. E.

Château Léoville-Barton

33250 St-Julien-Beychevelle.
Tel: 05 56 59 08 30.
Email: chateau@
leoville-barton.com
Fax: 05 56 59 14 29.
www.leoville-barton.com
AN; TF (only last vintage).
Mon–Thurs 8:45–11AM and
1:30–4PM; Fri 8:45–11AM;
closed weekends, holidays. E.

PAUILLAC

Château Lafite-Rothschild

33250 Pauillac.
Tel: 05 56 73 18 18. AN.
Tel: 01 53 89 78 00.
Fax: 01 53 89 78 01.
App't through Paris office.
www.lafite.com

hamlets, you also cross the railway line that leads all the way up the Médoc, from Bordeaux to Pointe de Grave, where there is a ferry across the Gironde to Royan.

The current Château Margaux was built in a classical style at the beginning of the 19th century. On the same site there had been a fortress where Edward III of England lived. The wines of Château Margaux were classified as a first growth in 1855. They went through a bad period between 1970 and 1976, but since then they have once again climbed back into the first rank.

Château Palmer

Among the other well-known vineyards with the Margaux appellation is the attractive Château Palmer, which stands just on the right of the road as you go north. Officially only classified as a third growth, the reputation and price of its wines are much higher.

After the cluster of classified growths at Margaux, there is something of a lull on the D2. At Arcins, there is an important cooperative cellar for wines from the Haut-Médoc, and one can turn left to see the group of châteaux with the appellation of Moulis around the village of Grand Poujeaux.

Back on the D2, you come to the village of Lamarque. Parts of its château date back to the 11th century, though most of the present structure is from the 14th. To continue the royal English tradition, it was occupied by Henry V.

St-Julien

Beyond Cussac, the most concentrated group of fine vineyards in the world begins at Beychevelle. Châteaux Lagrange and Beychevelle have the appellation St-Julien—one that they share with many of the finest wines of Bordeaux, though none of them are classified as first growths.

Château Beychevelle

This château used to belong to a French high admiral, and as a token of respect all the boats sailing past on the Gironde used to lower their sails (*baisse-voile*). This became corrupted to the present name.

Off to the left is Château Lagrange, which, though classified in 1855, had fallen on hard times until it was purchased in 1983 by the Japanese whisky group, Suntory. They spent millions of francs in restoring the vineyards, the press house and cellars, and the château.

Other châteaux of note in St-Julien include Ducru-Beaucaillou,

Château Lynch-Bages
33250 Pauillac.
Tel: 05 56 73 19 33.
Email: accueil@lynchbages.com
Fax: 05 56 59 26 42.
www.lynchbages.com
AN. Open May 1–Sept 30, 9AM–12PM and 2–6PM; Oct 1–Apr 30, 9AM–12PM and 2–5PM.

Château Mouton Rothschild
33250 Pauillac.
Tel: 05 56 73 21 29.
Email: webmaster@bpdr.com
www.bpdr.com
TP; AN. Open Mon–Thurs 9:30–11AM and 2–4PM; on Fri, open until 5PM; Apr–Oct open on holidays, closed weekends. Guided tours. Visit cellars, vat room, barrel hall, and Museum of Wine in Art. E, G.

Château Pichon-Longueville Baron
33250 Pauillac.
Tel: 05 56 73 17 17.
Email: contact@pichonlongueville.com or infochato@pichonlongueville.com
www.pichonlongueville.com

Château Pichon-Longueville
Comtesse de Lalande
33250 Pauillac.
Tel: 05 56 59 19 40.
Email: pichon@pichon-lalande.com
www.pichon-lalande.com

ST–ESTÈPHE

Château Cos d'Estournel
33180 St-Estèphe.
Tel: 05 56 73 15 50.
www.cosestournel.com
AN. Tour and tasting; groups
up to 15. Open Mon–Fri
9AM–12:30PM and 2–5:30PM;
closed weekends, holidays. E.

Château Lafon-Rochet
33180 St-Estèphe.
Tel: 05 56 59 32 06.
Email: lafon@lafon-rochet.com
www.lafon-rochet.com

Château Montrose
33180 St-Estèphe.
Tel: 05 56 59 30 12
www.chateaumontrose-
charmolue.com

Château Ormes de Pez
33180 St-Estèphe.
Tel: 05 56 73 24 00.
Email: infochato@
ormesdepez.com
www.ormesdepez.com

Château Phelan-Ségur
33180 St-Estèphe
Tel: 05 56 59 74 00.
Email: phelan.segur@
wanadoo.fr

CISSAC

Château Hanteillan
33250 Cissac.
Tel: 05 56 59 35 31.
Email: chateau.hantellan@
wanadoo.fr
www.chateau-hanteillan.com
TF. Open year round, Mon
AM–Fri until noon. Contact
for hours. WS.

Gruaud-Larose, Langoa Barton,
Léoville-Barton, and Léoville
Las Cas.

Pauillac

The town of Pauillac has three
first growths: Mouton-Rothschild, Latour, and Lafite-
Rothschild.

In the 1855 classification,
Mouton was only rated as a
second growth. For more than a
century it was in a rather ambi-
valent position because it considered itself to be a first growth
in all but name. In a bid to
strengthen its position it used
to charge as much as, and
sometimes more than, the first
growths. This led to an unfor-
tunate leap-frogging situation
and a price spiral. In fact, it
took a ministerial decree, in
1973, to confirm its status as a
premier cru. This is the only
change that has been made to
the 1855 classification.

Château Latour, which has
a reputation for producing the
firmest wine of the first
growths, stands on a low hill to
the south of the village. It has a
highly rated second wine called
Les Forts de Latour. The
vineyard takes its name from a
19th century tower standing by
the château, which is reputed
to have been built from a fort
that previously stood on the
site.

Château Lafite-Rothschild is a beautiful château standing in a lovely park on the northern boundaries of Pauillac. (Note that visits should be arranged through the château's Paris office.) Beyond lies the last of the village appellations of the Haut-Médoc, St-Estèphe.

St-Estèphe

While Pauillac may give the fullest wines, Margaux the most delicate, and St-Julien the richest, those of St-Estèphe have the tendency to be the most austere, and they take some time to soften out and become great wines.

Perhaps the best-known wine of the village is Château Cos d'Estournel, which has a striking position on a small hill on the right-hand side of the road. The architecture is certainly striking; there is no other château quite like this in all Bordeaux. To build one's cowsheds in the form of an oriental folly must have taken some imagination—and a lot of money. This is exactly what Louis Gaspard d'Estournel, the then-owner, did almost two centuries ago.

Château Montrose is the other top property in St-Estèphe. It makes very long-lived wines.

Château Lamothe-Cissac
33250 Cissac.
Tel: 05 56 59 58 16.
Email: domaines.fabre@
enfrance.com

Château La Tonnelle
33250 Cissac.
Tel: 05 56 59 58 16.
Email: domaines.fabre@
enfrance.com

LAMARQUE

Château de Lamarque
33460 Lamarque.
Tel: 05 56 58 90 03 or
05 56 58 97 55.
Email: chdelamarq@aol.com
www.chateaudelamarque.com.
Also accommodation.

MOULIS EN MÉDOC

Château Chasse-Spleen
Moulis en Médoc
33480 Castelnau en Médoc.
Tel: 05 56 58 02 37.
Email: info@chasse-spleen.com
www.chasse-spleen.com

ST-YZANS-DE-MÉDOC

Château Loudenne
33340 St-Yzans-de-Médoc.
Tel: 05 56 73 17 97.
Email: visite@lafragette.com

Maison du Vin de Margaux
place la Trémoille,
33460 Margaux.
Tel: 05 57 88 70 82.

Maison du Vin de St-Estèphe
place de l'Eglise,
33180 St-Estèphe.
Tel: 05 56 59 30 59.

FOR FURTHER INFORMATION

Conseil des Vins du Médoc
1, Cours du 30 Juillet,
33000 Bordeaux.
Tel: 05 56 48 18 62.
Email: medoc@
medoc-bordeaux.com
www.medoc-bordeaux.com

Maison du Tourisme et du Vin de Pauillac
la Verrerie
33250 Pauillac.
Tel: 05 56 59 03 08.

Haut-Médoc and Médoc

If you turn left, just beyond Cos d'Estournel, you come to the small village of Cissac. While it has no classified growths in the 1855 table, there is little doubt that when a new table is created, Cissac will have some candidates for the lower ranks.

The Haut-Médoc finishes at the northern boundary of St-Estèphe. To the north, the wines only have a right to the appellation Médoc. Many of these are very sound wines. One vineyard that is of particular note is Château Loudenne, which was set up as a model estate during the last century by the Gilbey family. The property even had its own quay, so that the wine could be shipped direct to Britain.

Bourg and Blaye

Few would claim that the vineyards of Bordeaux are beautiful. There are beautiful châteaux and there is some agreeable countryside, but if it were not for the wines, there are few places one would drive just for the view. One of the exceptions is in the region of Bourg and Blaye. Bourg is a pleasant town that, for nearly a year during the siege of Bordeaux in the 17th century, was the seat of the French court. The road from Bourg leads along the bank of the river at the foot of chalky cliffs, with wonderful views across the flat islands in the river to the Haut-Médoc and its châteaux.

The town of Blaye is dominated by the citadel, which was built by Vauban to command the approaches to the Gironde, together with Fort Médoc at Cussac and Fort Pâté on a small island in the middle of the river. The strategic importance of Blaye was recognized by the Romans, who built a fort there. Gastronomically, it has some importance as the center of a limited caviar industry.

To the north of Blaye, the vineyards finish where the land turns into a sandy marsh. Here there is a nuclear power station looking across the river to St-Estèphe.

Before there were vineyards in the Médoc, the vineyards of Bourg and Blaye made the reputation of the wines of Bordeaux. Now they concentrate on producing light, early-maturing red wines, with a lot of fruit, as well as clean, dry white wines. Much of the latter is turned into sparkling wine. From Blaye, the wines (white and red) are mainly called Côtes de Blaye and Premières Côtes de Blayes, while those from Bourg are called Côtes de Bourg. The Côtes de Bourg are mainly red, with a high percentage of Merlot, which makes them soft and approachable when young.

The countryside is very pretty, much hillier than most of Bordeaux, consisting largely of a series of rolling ridges, running parallel to the river and topped with attractive little châteaux—the better wines seem to come from those closer to the river. This is a good area to explore; the chances of tasting and buying wine here are much greater than in some of the more famous parts of Bordeaux. For the lover of churches, there are a number in the area that date back to before the time of the English occupation.

BLAYE

Château Peybonhomme-les-Tours
33390 Cars.
Tel: 05 57 42 11 95.
Email: peybonhomme@
terre-net.fr
www.peybonhomme.com
TF; AN. Open 10AM–5PM.
WS. E, G.

Château Segonzac
39, Segonzac,
33390 St-Génés-de-Blaye.
Tel: 05 57 42 18 16.
Email: segonzac@
chateau-segonzac.com
www.chateau-segonzac.com

Château Tayat
2, Tayat, 33620 Cézac.
Tel: 05 57 68 62 10.
www.chateau-tayat.com

BOURG

Château de Barbe
33710 Villeneuve.
Tel: 05 57 42 64 00.

Château Fougas
33710 Lansac.
Tel: 05 57 68 42 15.
Email: jeanyvesbechet@
wandadoo.fr
www.vignoblesbechet.com/ach
ateau_fougas2.htm

Château Tayac
St-Seurin-de-Bourg,
33710 Bourg-sur-Gironde.
Tel: 05 57 68 40 60.
Email: tayac-saturny@
wanadoo.fr
www.chateau-tayac.fr
TF. Open Mon–Fri
9AM–12:30PM and 2–7PM;
AN on weekends. E, S.

Pomerol

POMEROL

Château la Croix de Gay/
Château la Fleur de Gay
33500 Pomerol.
Tel: 05 57 51 19 05.
Email: contact@
chateau-lacroixdegay.com
www.wine-journal.com/
croixgay.html

Château Gazin
33500 Pomerol.
Tel: 05 57 51 07 05.
Email: contact@gazin.com
www.chateau-gazin.com
TF; AN. Open 9AM–12PM and
2–5PM. Tour. E.

Château Petit Village
33500 Pomerol.
Tel: 05 57 51 21 08.
www.petit-village.com

CANON–FRONSAC

Château Belloy
33126 Fronsac.
Tel: 05 57 24 98 05.
Email: helene.texier-
travers@wanadoo.fr
www.vignobles-
travers.com/belloy.htm

Château Cassagne Haut-Canon
33126 St-Michel-de-Fronsac.
Tel: 05 57 51 63 98.
Email: jjdubois@club-internet.fr
www.expression-de-
fronsac.com/gb/chateau-
cassagne-haut-canon.htm
AN.

The vineyards of Pomerol form an angled square, with the western corner in the center of the old wine port of Libourne (today better known for its excellent food market). Each side of the square measures no more than 3 km (2 miles), so the area is small.

There were vineyards here in Roman times, and the viticultural tradition was maintained by the Knights of St John of Jerusalem, who built a manor house, a hospital, and a church in the neighborhood.

The Pomerol vineyards

The small village of Pomerol has no real center, only quite an austere church and a small clutch of buildings. The individual vineyards are scattered around all over the area—many of the "châteaux" are only unassuming farmhouses.

Pomerol's vineyards are split in two by the N89, which follows the route of an old Roman road. To the west of this road, the soil has a sandy base, and this gives wines that are lighter and rather lacking in character. All the finest wines come from the eastern side of the road, where the gravelly soil gives them much more "backbone."

Here, the Merlot is the dominant grape variety, and it gives a wine that is believed by some to resemble the wines of Burgundy, with a rich, velvety taste not found elsewhere in Bordeaux.

Pétrus

The small scale of the vineyard properties, taken together with increasing demand from around the world, means that certain wines from Pomerol are now the most expensive in all Bordeaux.

Even the most famous, Pétrus (for some reason the word "château" is usually dropped from its name) produces no more than 160 casks in an average vintage, less than a sixth of Château Latour, for example.

These two lesser-known areas can offer good value in comparison to the high prices that the Pomerol name can command. Fonsac and Canon-Fronsac lie to the west of Libourne, while Lalande de Pomerol is to the north of the Pomerol appellation. Two hundred years ago, the wines of Fronsac used to be better known and more expensive than those of St-Émilion. Around 255 of the wines in the Fronsac area use the Canon-Fronsac appellation.

St-Émilion

If I were asked to nominate the three most complete wine

FOR FURTHER INFORMATION

Bourg:

Maison du Vin de Bourg
place de l'Eperon,
33710 Bourg.
Tel: 05 57 94 80 20.
www.bourg.cotes-bordeaux.alienor.fr
www.cotes-de-bourg.com

Blaye:

Syndicat des Vins de Premières Côtes de Blaye
www.clictoutdev.com/syndicat-blaye

Fronosac:

Maison des Vins de Fronsac
Plaisance,
33126 Fronsac.
Tel: 05 57 51 80 51.

Lalande-de-Pomerol:

Château Grand Ormeau
33500
Lalande-de-Pomerol.
Tel: 05 57 25 30 20.
Email: grand.ormeau@wanadoo.fr

Château La Sergue
Haut-Chaigneau,
33500 Néac.
Tel: 05 57 51 31 31.
www.cerclerivedroite.com/lasergue.html

FRONSAC

Château Dalem

33141 Saillans.

Tel: 05 57 84 34 18.

Email: chateau-dalem@
wanadoo.fr

www.expression-de-
fronsac.com/
fr/chateau-dalem.htm

Château Mayne-Vieil

33133 Galgon.

Tel: 05 57 74 30 06.

Email: maynevieil@aol.com

Fax: 05 57 84 39 33.

TF. Open Mon–Fri
9AM–12PM and 2–6:30PM.
WS. E.

Château de la Rivière

33126 La Rivière.

Tel: 05 57 55 56 56.

Email: info@
chateau-de-la-riviere.com

www.chateau-de-la-riviere.com

June–Aug, guided tours
Mon–Sat at 10:30am,
2:30pm, and 4:30pm.
Sept–May, guided tours
Mon–Fri leaving 10–11:30am
and 2:30–4:30pm.

ST-ÉMILION

Château Belair

33300 St-Émilion.

Tel: 05 57 24 70 94.

Fax: 05 57 24 67 11.

www.chateaubelair.com

AN. Open Apr–Oct,
Mon–Sat 10AM–12PM and
2–5PM; Nov–Mar same
hours, but closed Wed.

towns in France, they would be
Beaune, in Burgundy; Riquewihr, in Alsace; and St-
Emilion. Coincidentally, each
of them has a compactness
given by town walls. Perhaps it
is these that have helped to
preserve, and concentrate, the
character in each case.

Much of St-Émilion's history
is recalled in the names of many
of the châteaux. The vineyards
were first planted by the
Romans, and the poet
Ausonius (who also appre-
ciated the wines of the Moselle)
is supposed to have found his
wife in Bordeaux and to have
lived in St-Émilion. His name
is remembered in the great
wines of Château Ausone.

For a time, the region was
occupied by the Moors
(Château Villemaurine) and
then became an important
ecclesiastical center, as
indicated by such names as
Château le Couvent, which is
actually within the town walls,
Clos la Madeleine, and Clos de
l'Oratoire.

There is much to see in the
town: the underground church
and the catacombs, the Couvent
des Jacobins, the Collegiate
Church, with its beautiful
cloisters, the town walls, and the
cave retreat of the 8th-century St
Aemilianus, who gave his name
to the town. There are regular
guided tours on foot from the

tourist office in the Place des Créneaux throughout the year.

The appellation St-Émilion includes a host of châteaux, with vineyards, in eight communes, on three distinct types of soil, and, therefore, of three distinct qualities. Perhaps surprisingly, the final decision as to which villages could call their wine St-Émilion came as late as 1929 and was based on rights granted in 1289.

The first of the vineyard types is the continuation of the plateau with its chalky soil, rich in iron, of the vineyards of Pomerol. Here the two outstanding châteaux are Cheval Blanc and Figeac.

Around the town itself, the plateau falls away to the plain. On the slopes, where the soil is similar, are the vineyards of the Côtes, with ideal exposure to the southeast. Here, the château with the highest reputation is Ausone, followed by Belair, Pavie, and La Gaffelière.

Down on the plain, where the soil is a mixture of sand and gravel, the quality of the wine can be distinctly inferior, yet it still benefits from the name St-Émilion. Perhaps because of this weakness, there has developed an immensely complicated system of classification. The two top classifications are *St-Émilion*

Château Canon la Gaffelière
SCEV Comtes de Neipperg,
BP 34, 33330 St-Émilion.
Tel: 05 57 24 71 33.
Email: info@neipperg.com
Fax: 05 57 24 67 95.
www.canon-la-gaffeliere.com

Château Cheval Blanc
33300 St-Émilion.
Tel: 05 57 55 55 55.
Email: contact@
chateau-chevalblanc.com
www.chateau-cheval-blanc.com
Tours for wine professionals only.

Château Dassault
33330 St-Émilion.
Tel: 05 57 55 10 00.
Email: lbv@chateaudassault.com
Fax: 05 57 55 10 01.
www.chateaudassault.com
TF; AN. Mon–Fri 9AM–5PM.
E.

Château Pavie
33330 St-Émilion.
Tel: 05 57 55 43 43.
www.chateaupavie.com

Château de Valandraud
SARL des Etablissements
Thunevin, 6 rue Guadet,
33330 St-Émilion.
Tel: 05 57 55 09 13.
Email: info@thunevin.com
www.thunevin.com

Château Yon-Figeac
33330 St-Émilion.
Tel: 05 57 42 66 66.
Email: bordeaux@vgas.com

premier grand cru classé and *St-Émilion grand cru classé*. Unlike the 1855 classification of the Médoc, which appears to be immutable, *St-Émilion classé* properties are reassessed every ten years. At present there are thirteen within the first category—with two of them, Ausone and Cheval Blanc, given a higher rating within the category—and 55 in the second.

FOR FURTHER INFORMATION

Maison du Vin de St-Émilion
place Pierre Meyrat,
33330 St-Émilion.
Tel: 05 57 55 50 55.

In addition, each year any vineyard can send its wine to be sampled and, if it is found worthy, it is given the status of *grand cru* for that particular vintage. This means that in any given year, there may be hundreds of such wines, some scarcely of a quality that their classification would suggest.

Most St-Émilion is made from the Merlot and Cabernet Franc grapes. At its best it is one of the most satisfying wines of Bordeaux, having a rich fruitiness that appeals to those put off by the austerity of many Médoc wines. Generally, they can be drunk much sooner than those of the Médoc, while the top wines from the best properties can age for many years. The 1947 Cheval Blanc is still legendary.

Garagistes

Over the last fifteen years a number of small, previously unknown St-Émilion properties and producers have controversially shot to stardom, although they are often not on what is considered the best land. Their attraction is down as a result of very low yields and a huge proportion of new oak barrels allied to a high mark from American wine critic, Robert Parker. The name *garagiste* comes from the fact that some of the original production was so small that the wine was made in people's garages. Valandraud was the archetypal *garagiste* when it first appeared in 1991. Success means that Château de Valandraud has now outgrown the garage.

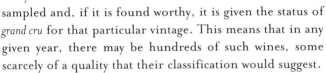

A narrow, cobbled street in St-Émilion. This ancient small town is easily the most attractive in the Bordeaux region. Photo © Greg Boiarsky/Dreamstime.com

LUSSAC-ST-ÉMILION

Château de Bellevue
33570 Lussac.
Tel: 06 72 83 18 04.
Email: andrechatenoud@
wanadoo.fr

Château de la Grenière
14, La Grenière,
33570 Lussac.
Tel: 05 57 74 64 96.
Email: earl.dubreuil@
wanadoo.fr

Château Jamard Belcour
3, Bonneau, Montagne.
Tel: 05 57 74 60 72.
Email: despagne@tiscali.fr

Château Mayne-Blanc
33570 Lussac.
Tel: 05 57 74 60 56.
Email: mayne.blanc@
wanadoo.fr

**Cave de Puisseguin/
Lussac St-Émilion**
33570 Lussac.
Tel: 05 57 55 50 40.

MONTAGNE-ST-ÉMILION

Château de Beaulieu
Château Haut-Piquat,
33570 Lussac.
Tel: 05 57 55 59 59.

Château Maison Blanche
33570 Montagne.
Tel: 05 57 74 62 18.

St-Émilion satellites

Surrounding the vineyards of St-Émilion are a number of areas producing similar wines. Indeed, before the coming of *appellation contrôlée*, much of the wine used to be sold under the vineyards' names, and these areas have since gained reflected glory by adding St-Émilion to their own name. The St-Émilion satellites are to the north of the appellation. They are Lussac-St-Émilion, St Georges-St-Émilion, Puisseguin-St-Émilion, and Montagne-St-Émilion. Of these, Lussac and Montagne are the most important, while little wine is produced under the St-Georges appellation. Some of the estates here are considerably larger than those found in St-Émilion and Pomerol. Like the wines of Lalande de Pomerol and Fronsac, those from the satellite appellations of St-Émilion can be worth searching out because they can offer better value. Also, being less famous they attract fewer visitors, so you may well receive a warmer welcome.

Entre-Deux-Mers

The vast area between the Garonne and Dordogne rivers is known as the Entre-Deux-Mers, "between two seas."

It stretches from Libourne in the north to Saint Macaire in the south, and from Bordeaux in the west to Sainte-Foy-la-Grande in the east. There are some 23,000 hectares (56,800 acres). The appellation of Entre-Deux-Mers is much more limited because various appellations along the north bank of the Garonne and south bank of the Dordogne are not included. It is also for dry white wine only. Increasingly, it is pure Sauvignon Blanc; the other permitted varieties are Sémillon and Muscadelle. The region's red has to be called Bordeaux or Bordeaux Supérieur.

This is a region of rolling countryside with small villages. In the south there are a number of fortified mills. There are also market towns established by the English, such as Sauveterre de Guyenne. This is a gentle area off the normal routes—an area of mixed farming where the vine does not always dominate.

In the northwest part of the Entre-Deux-Mers, opposite Libourne, is the small appellation of Graves de Vayres. Mainly red wine comes from the appellation's 600 hectares (1,482 acres). The region around the attractive medieval town of Sainte-Foy-la-Grande has the appellation Sainte-Foy-Bordeaux. Again mainly red wine is made. Generally all of these wines are best drunk young.

Château Vieux Bonneau
3, Bonneau,
33570 Montagne.
Tel: 05 57 74 60 72.
Email: despagne@tiscali.fr

Vieux Château Saint-André
1, Samion, 33570 Montagne.
Tel: 05 57 74 59 80.

PUISSEGUIN-ST-ÉMILION

Château Bel-Air
33570 Puisseguin.
Tel: 05 57 74 51 82.

Château Rigaud
33570 Puisseguin.
Tel: 05 57 74 54 07.

ST-GEORGES-ST-ÉMILION

Château St-Georges
33570 Montagne.
Tel: 05 57 74 62 11.
Email: contact@
chateau-saint-georges.com
Fax: 05 57 74 58 62.
www.chateau-saint-
georges.com

ENTRE-DEUX-MERS

Château Bonnet
33420 Grézillac.
Tel: 05 56 64 75 87 or
05 56 64 71 76.
Email: andrelurton@
andrelurton.com
Fax: 05 57 74 98 59.
www.andrelurton.com
TP; AN. Mon–Fri
10AM–5PM; some Sat by app't.
WS. Tours. E.

Château de Vaure
Les Chais de Vaure,
33350 Ruch.
Tel: 05 57 40 54 09.
Email: chais-de-vaure@
wanadoo.fr

Château Turcaud
33670 La Sauve.
Tel: 05 56 29 04 41.
Email: chateau-turcaud@
wanadoo.fr
Fax: 05 56 23 35 85.
www.chateauturcaud.com
WS. Open Mon–Fri
8:30AM–12PM and 2–6PM; AN
on Sat, closed Sun.

GRAVES DE VAYRES

Château Haut-Gayat
La Souloire,
33750 St-Germain-du-Puch.
Tel: 05 57 24 52 32.

STE-FOY-BORDEAUX

Château des Chapelains
Les Chapelains,
33220 St-André-et-Appelles.
Tel: 05 57 41 21 74.
Email: contact@
chateaudeschapelains.com
Fax: 05 57 41 27 42.
www.chateaudeschapelains.com

Château Pichaud Solignac
La Niolaise
33790 Pellegrue.
Tel: 05 56 61 43 55.
Email: contact@
chateaupichaudsolignac.com
Fax: 05 56 61 43 55.

Graves and Pessac-Léognan

The vineyards of Graves come right to the door of Bordeaux. Many have disappeared in the face of rising land prices, but there are still four notable vineyards, even within the motorway corset that now restricts Bordeaux on the southern side.

Of these, the most famous is Château Haut-Brion, which can be reached by taking the N250 road in the direction of Arcachon, from the center of the city. Haut-Brion was classified in 1855 as a *premier grand cru*, the only vineyard from outside the Haut-Médoc to be so honored.

The château was built in 1550 and its first written mention is by the British diarist, Samuel Pepys, in April 1663. In 1787, Thomas Jefferson tried to buy a hogshead of the famous 1784 vintage, through the local honorary American consul, but was refused. He ultimately managed to buy a few cases of "Obrion," which he shared with a friend. In 1934, the owner offered the vineyard to the city of Bordeaux, but the gesture was rejected and it was bought by the Dillons, an American banking family, in whose hands it has since remained.

The other châteaux close to the city are La Mission Haut-Brion, La Tour Haut-Brion and, in neighboring Pessac, Pape-Clément. All these vineyards are particularly known for their red wines, and this is true of all the vineyards of the northern part of the Graves, closest to Bordeaux. A new appellation, Pessac Léognan, was created in 1987 for this northerly, and more famous, part of the Graves, which also includes such famous properties as Châteaux Haut-Bailly and Smith-Haut-Lafitte and Domaine de Chevalier.

The rest of the Graves

The rest of the Graves runs for about 25 km down from the southern end of the Pessac-Leognan appellation at La Prade to the sweet-wine-producing areas of Barsac and Sauternes, close to the small market town of Langon. The appellation actually finishes just beyond Langon at St-Pardon-de-Conques. There are around 3,700 hectares (9,139 acres) of vines planted on gravel terraces laid down by the River Garonne. The vineyards are often interspersed with woods. Around 75 percent of the wine is red. Graves was once a byword for poorly made, over-sulphured, sweetish whites almost guaranteed to give you a hangover the next day.

PESSAC-LÉOGNAN

Château Carbonnieux
33850 Léognan.
Tel: 05 57 96 56 20.
Email: info@
carbonnieux.com

Domaine de Chevalier
33850 Léognan.
Tel: 05 56 64 16 16.
Email: domainedechevalier@
domainedechevalier.com
Fax: 05 56 64 18 18.
www.domainedechevalier.com

Château Pape-Clément
216, ave du Dr Nancel Pénard,
33600 Pessac.
Tel: 05 57 26 38 38.
Email: chateau@
pape-clement.com
Fax: 05 57 26 38 39.
www.pape-clement.com

Château Smith-Haut-Lafitte
33650 Martillac.
Tel: 05 57 83 11 22.
Email: visites@
smith-haut-lafitte.com
Fax: 05 57 83 11 21.
www.smith-haut-lafitte.com

FOR FURTHER INFORMATION

CIVB
3, cours du XXX Juillet,
33000 Bordeaux.
Tel: 05 56 00 22 66.
Email: civbevins-bordeaux.fr
Fax: 05 56 00 22 82. List of all châteaux welcoming visitors. G, D, S.

GRAVES

Château de Castres
33640 Castres-sur-Gironde.
Tel: 05 56 67 51 51.

Château de Chantegrive
33720 Podensac.
Tel: 05 56 27 17 38.
Email: courrier@
chateau-chantegrive.com
Fax: 05 56 27 29 42.
www.chantegrive.com

Clos Floridene
Château Reynon,
33410 Béguey
Tel: 05 56 62 96 51.
Email: reynon@
mail.quaternet.fr

Château Rahoul
4, route du Courneau,
33460 Portets.
Tel: 05 56 67 01 12.
Email: chateau-rahoul@
alain-thienot.fr

Château du Seuil
33720 Cérons.
Tel: 05 56 27 28 79.
Email: mailing@
chateauduseuil.com
www.chateauduseuil.com
Email to request a visit.

Fortunately, this situation has changed—over the past fifteen years there has been considerable investment in this region because vineyards here are much cheaper than more fashionable parts of Bordeaux.

The White Wines of Bordeaux

It was not very long ago that the white wines of Bordeaux were not being treated very seriously, but now all that has changed. The great sweet white wines have made a comeback, although with the exception of Château d' Yquem, they sell for a fraction of the top reds—quite unlike their hey-day in the mid-19th century, when they were far more expensive. Modern wine-making techniques, and the Sauvignon grape, have created a new generation of crisp white wines. In the past, few of the wines could truly have been described as dry, but this is no longer the case.

FOR FURTHER INFORMATION

Conseil des Vins de Graves
61, cours du Maréchal Foch,
33720 Podensac.
Tel: 05 56 27 09 25.
Email: contact@
vins-graves.com

There is some white wine made in most of the Bordeaux regions—even Château Margaux produces a little called Pavillon Blanc de Château Margaux—but the finest are produced upstream from Bordeaux on both banks of the Garonne. The vineyards of the Graves close to Bordeaux are best known for their red wines, but as you drive southwest, parallel to the motorway on the N113, you move into white wine country.

Sweet white wines

To make a great sweet wine in Bordeaux is not an easy, or a cheap, process. It is also much riskier than making either red or dry white wine. However, great sweet Bordeaux can last almost forever. Sweet wines are made by picking the grapes late in the autumn, when they have been attacked by what is known as the noble rot, Botrytis cinerea. This feeds on the water in the grapes but leaves the sugar. The resulting grape is shriveled like a raisin, but extremely sweet.

Noble rot

Naturally, the yields are very low, for there is little juice in the grapes. The noble rot is encouraged by autumn mists, and thus the greatest vineyards making this type of wine are nearly always close to water, in this case the Ciron or the Garonne rivers.

Botrytis is usually looked upon as an enemy to winemaking, because it is normally caused by rain.

BARSAC & SAUTERNES

Château d'Arche
33210 Sauternes.
Tel: 05 56 76 66 55.
Email: chateaudarche@
wanadoo.fr
www.chateaudarche-sauternes.com
Offers accommodation.
Email to arrange a visit or a
stay at the hotel.

Château Climens
33720 Barsac.
Tel: 05 56 27 15 33.
Email: contact@
chateau-climens.fr
Fax: 05 56 27 21 04.
www.chateau-climens.fr

Château Filhot
33210 Sauternes.
Tel: 05 56 76 61 09.
Email: filhot@filhot.com
Fax: 05 56 76 67 91.
www.filhot.com
Open Mon–Fri 9AM–12PM and
2–6PM; AN on weekends.
Tours; up to 35 people. E.

Château Gilette
33210 Preignac.
Tel: 05 56 76 28 44.
Email: christian.medeville@
wanadoo.fr

Château Guiraud
33210 Sauternes.
Tel: 05 56 76 61 01.
Email: xplanty@
chateau-guiraud.fr
Fax: 05 56 76 67 52.
www.chateau-guiraud.fr
AN. Open Mon–Fri 9–11AM
and 2–5PM. Tours; up to 35
people. E.

It is this particular combination of moisture from the mists and the autumn sun that results in the greatest sweet white wines in the world. In all of these, the intense sweetness will be balanced by a certain acidity. It is this factor that enables these wines to age for 50 years or more.

At vintage time, the pickers will pass through the vineyards three or four times, just picking those grapes that have been affected by the rot. There are three reasons, therefore, for the high cost of these wines: perfect, long warm falls are needed; yields are very low; and the vintages are labor intensive.

Sauternes

The finest of these sweet wines are called Sauternes, and they come from the vineyards of five small villages to the right of the main road. The first of these is Sauternes itself (from which comes the noble, and expensive, Château d'Yquem), Bommes, Fargues, Preignac, and Barsac.

The wines from this last village can call themselves Barsac, rather than Sauternes. Barsac wines are generally considered to have less intense sweetness than the normal Sauternes, but more finesse.

Three varieties of grape can be used in sweet Bordeaux: Sémillon, normally about three quarters of the whole; Sauvignon, about a quarter; and sometimes traces of Muscadelle.

Château d'Yquem

The white wines of the Château d'Yquem are generally considered the finest. As with the wines of the Haut-Médoc, those of the Sauternes were classified in 1855, and this was the only one to be rated *premier cru supérieur*.

The château passed by marriage to the Lur-Saluces family in 1785. In 1999, it was bought by Moët Hennessy Louis Vuitton (LVMH). However, Count Alexandre de Lur-Saluces, the sixth generation of the family at d'Yquem, remained in charge until 2004, when he retired.

In poor years no wine will be sold as Château d'Yquem, but in some years a dry white wine is made called "Y" (pronounced "ygrec"). This is produced from 50 percent Sauvignon grapes and 50 percent Sémillon—at Yquem there is no Muscadelle planted. The yields for their Sauternes are so small that they claim that each year they produce one glassful per vine!

There are a number of other great wines made, including Coutet and Climens from Barsac, Rieussec at Fargues, Suduiraut at Preignac, and La Tour-Blanche at Bommes. This last belongs to the French

Château Rieussec
33210 Fargues-de-Langon.
Tel: 01 53 89 78 00.
Email: rieussec@lafite.com
Fax: 05 57 98 14 10.
www.lafite.com
TF; AN, 2 weeks' advanced notice min; 15 person max.
Tours at 9AM, 10:30AM, 2PM, 3:30PM. Closed holidays, Aug–Oct. WS. E.

Château Suduiraut
33210 Preignac.
Tel: 05 56 63 61 90.
Email: contact@suduiraut.com
Fax: 05 56 63 61 93.
www.suduiraut.com

CADILLAC

Château Fayau
33410 Cadillac.
Tel: 05 57 98 08.
Email: medeville-jeanetfils@wanadoo.fr

CÉRONS

Château de Cérons
33720 Cérons.
Tel: 05 56 27 01 13.
Email: perromat@chateaudecerons.com

LOUPIAC

Château de Ricaud
33410 Loupiac.
Tel: 05 56 62 66 16.

Château les Roques
33410 Ste-Croix-du-Mont.
Tel: 05 56 62 01 04.
Email: a.v.fertal@wanadoo.fr
Tel: 05 56 62 00 92.
www.chateau-du-pavillon.com

STE-CROIX-DU-MONT

Château des Arroucats
33410 Ste-Croix-du-Mont.
Tel: 05 56 62 07 37.

Château Lousteau-Vieil
33410 Ste-Croix-du-Mont.
Tel: 05 56 62 01 68.
Email: m.sessacq@wanadoo.fr

Domaine du Barrail
Château la Rame, 33410
Ste-Croix-du-Mont.
Tel: 05 56 62 01 50.
Email: chateau.larame@
wanadoo.fr
TF; AN. Open 8:30AM–12PM
and 1:30–6PM. WS. E.

Château Brethous
33360 Camblanes.
Tel: 05 56 20 77 76.
Email: brethous@libertysurf.fr
Fax: 05 56 20 08 45.
www.brethous.com

Château Carsin
33410 Rions.
Tel: 05 56 76 93 06.
Email: chateau@carsin.com
Fax: 05 56 62 64 80.
www.carsin.com
TF: AN. WS. E, Finnish.

Château Langoiran
Le Pied du Château,
33550 Langoiran.
Tel: 05 56 67 08 55.
Email: infos@
chateaulangoiran.com
Tel: 05 56 67 32 87.
www.chateaulangoiran.com

Château Memories
33490 St-Maixant.
Tel: 05 56 62 06 43.

Château Roquebert
34, Chemin Bécut,
33360 Quinsac.
Tel: 05 56 20 88 98.

Ministry of Agriculture and is run as a form of wine school for local, and other, growers.

People often wonder what is the best accompaniment for Sauternes. The French like to drink it at the beginning of a meal and suggest it is the ideal accompaniment for *foie gras*. For most of us that would certainly restrict the consumption! I feel that it is better at the end of a meal—it can go well with nuts or even certain strong cheeses, such as Roquefort. It is also wonderful with crème brulée and strawberries.

Other sweet wines

There are several other sweet wine appellations close to Sauternes, on both sides of the River Garonne. To the west of Barsac is Cérons, where producers can also use the Graves appellation. On the opposite and hillier bank of the Garonne you'll find Cadillac, Loupiac, and Ste-Croix-du-Mont. Although they have a long history, these wines are not as famous and consequently not as expensive as Sauternes. They can offer very good value—a good example is certainly far better than a poor Sauternes.

Ste-Croix-du-Mont

The sweet wines of Ste-Croix-du-Mont were once as highly prized as those of Sauternes, which lies on the opposite bank of the Garonne. The hill of Ste-Croix is made up of fossilized oyster shells and provides fine views over the Graves and Sauternes.

Langon

The capital of the white wine district is Langon. Here, Claude Darroze has an excellent restaurant, which also has reasonably priced rooms. One can then either return to Bordeaux directly by the highway, or cross over the Garonne and return via the vineyard areas on the other bank. A third possibility is to drive south on the D932 to the vineyards of Armagnac.

Premières Côtes de Bordeaux

This appellation, which is now mainly for red wines, is on the east bank of the Garonne. It runs for about 60 km from Bordeaux down to the town of St-Macaire. There are some 4,000 hectares (9,880 acres) planted. Follow the D10, along the east bank of the Garonne, a pretty route between the river and vineyard slopes. This side of the river is much more hilly than the rather flat Graves, and the vines are often planted on quite steep slopes facing the Garonne. This is certainly one of the prettier parts of the Bordeaux region. Red Premières Côtes de Bordeaux is made with an increasing proportion of Merlot to give softer wines and is often a good value. The small amount of sweet Premières Côtes de Bordeaux made can also be a good value.

Some wines here, especially dry whites, are marketed under the basic Bordeaux appellation. The soils are quite varied: alluvial by the river, gravel and limestone on the slopes, with an increased proportion of clay as

FOR FURTHER INFORMATION

Maison du Vin de Sauternes
place de la Mairie,
33210 Sauternes.
Tel: 05 56 76 69 83.

Maison du Vin de Cadillac
104, rue Cazeaux,
33410 Cadillac.
Tel/Fax: 05 56 62 15 27.

you move inland. The best wines tend to come from the well-exposed slopes.

Food in Bordeaux

Bordeaux is fortunate to have access to prime ingredients: young salt-marsh lamb from Pauillac, seafood (especially oysters) from the Atlantic coast, and lampreys that look like eels but are in fact large leeches from the river estuaries. Oysters from Arcachon are often served with small sausages. Eels are grilled with garlic and breadcrumbs.

Naturally, wine, especially red, plays an important part in the local cooking. Once they have been drained of blood, lampreys are usually stewed with leeks and red wine for several hours. *Entrecôte à la Bordelaise* is a grilled *entrecôte* steak topped with a sauce made from red wine, beef stock, and shallots. Meat is often simply grilled and served without complicated sauces, so that the wines show to best advantage. Saltmarsh lamb tends to be either plain roasted to pink or slow cooked for several hours.

Foie gras also features widely. Although some is produced locally, most comes from a little further south, from the Armagnac region. Prunes from Agen, further up the River Garonne, also feature in a number of recipes.

Where to stay and eat

Le Chapon Fin
5, rue Montesquieu, 33000 Bordeaux.
Tel: 05 56 79 10 10 (R). www.chapon-fin.com

Le Pavillon des Boulevards
120, rue Croix-de-Seguey, 33000 Bordeaux.
Tel: 05 56 81 51 02 (R).

Le Saint-James
3, place Camille-Hosten, 33270 Bouiliac.
Tel: 05 57 97 06 00 (H/R).

Restaurant Claude Darroze
95, Cours du General-Leclerc, 33210 Langon.
Tel: 05 56 63 00 48 (H/R). www.darroze.com

Relais de Margaux
Chemin l'Ile Vincent, 33460 Margaux.
Tel: 05 57 88 38 30 (H/R). www.relais-margaux.fr

Les Sources de Caudalie
Château Smith-Haut-Lafitte, 33650 Martillac.
Tel: 05 57 83 83 83 (H/R). www.sources-caudalie.com

Château Cordeillan-Bages
route des Châteaux, 33250 Pauillac.
Tel: 05 56 59 24 24 (H/R). www.cordeillanbages.com

Thierry Arbeau
pavillon St-Aubin, route de Picot, 33160 St-Aubin-de-Médoc.
Tel: 05 56 95 98 68 (R).

Au Logis des Remparts
18, rue Guadet, 33330 St-Émilion.
Tel: 05 57 24 70 43 (H).

Château Grand-Barrail
route de Libourne, 33330 St-Émilion.
Tel: 05 57 55 37 00 (H/R). www.grand-barrail.com

Hostellerie de Plaisance
place du Clocher, 33330 St-Émilion.
Tel: 05 57 55 07 55 (H/R). www.hostellerie-plaisance.com

Le Saprien
14, rue Principale, 33210 Sauternes.
Tel: 05 56 76 60 87 (R).

Cognac

COGNAC

Cognac is one of the greatest spirits in the world. It is a brandy, the distillation of wine. As there are many whiskies, so are there many brandies—but only two of them, Cognac and Armagnac, have reputations based firmly on the source of their wines and the method of distillation.

The fertile, chalky countryside around the town of Cognac, on the river Charente, gives thin, acidic wines with a low alcoholic degree. It is such wines that produce the finest brandies, and since distillation began in the region at the beginning of the 15th century, it has built up for itself a proud reputation for quality. The nature of the product lends itself to brand promotion, and there are a few companies that dominate world markets. They may not, however, actually own vineyards, or even distill the Cognacs they sell, so there is a broad range of places for the interested tourist to visit.

TO GET TO COGNAC

Cognac is 476 km (297 miles) from Paris and 242 km (151 miles) from Tours by the A10, D939, D650, and D731.

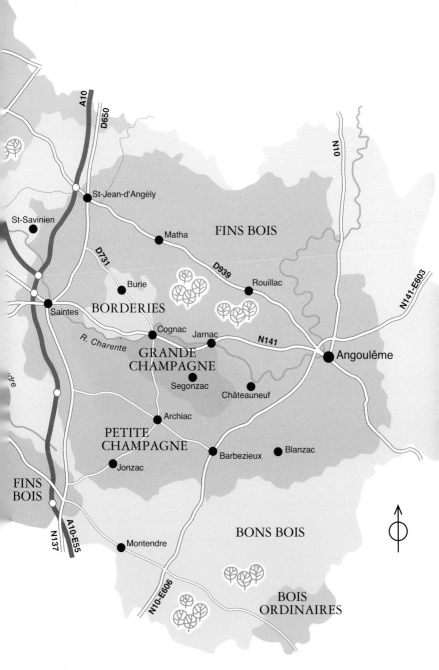

The regions

There are four basic factors that go into the production of a Cognac: the soil, the grapes, the distillation, and the aging.

The area within which Cognac may be produced is quite large, most of the two *départements* of the Charentes. There are vineyards on the Ile de Ré and the Ile d'Oléron in the Atlantic; on the north bank of the Gironde estuary; and around the three towns in the heart of the region: Cognac itself, Jarnac, and Saintes. In each of these areas, different soils produce different qualities of wine, giving different qualities of spirit. For example, a Cognac from the sandy soil of the Ile de Ré may have a hint of iodine in its flavor from its proximity to the sea. A Cognac from the chalky soil to the south of Cognac itself will have the most finesse and bouquet.

Because of these factors, there is an elaborate hierarchy within the vineyard areas, and the price of the resultant spirit will vary considerably. The finest region is the Grande Champagne to the south of Cognac, then the Petite Champagne, and through the Borderies, Fins Bois, Bons Bois, and the fringe Bois Ordinaires, and Bois à Terroir.

You can find a Cognac labeled Grande Champagne, which means that it has been distilled solely from wines from that region. A Fine Champagne will be a blend of Grande and Petite Champagne. Most Cognacs, however, will be a blend created to a standard by the various companies from several regions.

Cognac production

St-Émilion, Colombard, and Folle Blanche are the chief grapes grown, and are picked before full ripeness to give thin, acidic wines—ideal for distillation. As soon as fermentation is finished, the wine is double distilled in a copper pot still. Double distillation ensures that the spirit is as pure as possible.

"The angels' share"

The new spirit is harsh and fiery, so it is put to age in casks of local, Tronçais, or Limousin oak. The length of time it is allowed to age depends on the individual company. As the spirit mellows, there is heavy evaporation—up to the equivalent of 20 million bottles each year. This evaporation, called "the angels' share," blackens the roofs of the warehouses and gives a grimy, industrial air to many buildings in Cognac. Most companies will have small stocks of exceptionally old Cognacs, which they store in a warehouse called "paradise." This spirit may no longer be stored in casks, but in glass carboys.

Pineau des Charentes

Pineau des Charentes is another local specialty. It can be white or rosé, and is made by mixing sweet, unfermented grape juice with one-year-old brandy, and then leaving them to marry for eighteen months or more in oak barrels.

Scenery and historic towns

The Cognac region is pleasant and varied. It is not a region of intensive viticulture; it is just as renowned for its dairy products.

There are beautiful beaches at Royan and on the Ile d' Oléron. You can hire a boat on the languid river Charente— until recently the brandy boats used to come up it to the little port of Tonnay-Charente to load.

There are a number of beautiful historic towns. In Cognac, the 10th-century castle now belongs to Cognac Otard. Like many of the other important companies in the region, Otard was founded by a British family: the Martells were from the Channel Islands; the Hines from Dorset; and the Hennessys and the Exshaws from Ireland.

Saintes

Historically, the capital of the region was Saintes, some 26 km (16 miles) to the west. This was an important Roman town and there are still a number of remains, including an amphitheater and a triumphal arch.

The arch originally stood on the Roman bridge over the Charente. It was erected during the reign of Nero by Caius Julius Rufus to the memory of Germanicus, Tiberius, and Drusus. In 1844, it was dismantled and re-erected where it now stands. Nearby Jonzac has a fine 15th-century castle.

COGNAC LABELS

On Cognac labels, there can be a bewildering variety of quality symbols. These are the minimum legal aging requirements:

· 3 star/VS: youngest spirit in the blend must have aged for at least two years from April 1st following vintage.
· VSOP/Reserve: minimum of four years.
· Napoleon, XO, Hors d'Age: minimum of six years.

In many cases the bulk of the Cognac may be much older.

COGNAC

Hennessy
Les Quais Hennessy,
Quai Richard Hennessy,
16100 Cognac.
Tel: 05 45 35 72 68.
Email: quais@hennessy.fr
Tel: 05 45 35 79 49.
www.hennessy-cognac.com
Tours can be booked online.
Open daily Mar–Dec;
June–Sept 10AM–6PM (start
of last tour); Mar–May and
Oct–Dec 10AM–5PM (start of
last tour); open for groups
only, with reservation, in Jan
and Feb. Closed Jan 1, May 1,
Dec 25.

Martell & Co.
place Edouard Martell,
16100 Cognac.
Tel: 05 45 36 33 33.
www.martell.com
Tours can be booked online.
Tours: June–Sept, Mon–Fri
anytime from 10AM–5PM,
weekends 11AM–5PM; in Apr,
May, Oct: Mon–Fri tours at
10AM, 11AM, 2:30PM, 3:45PM,
5PM, and weekends anytime
from 12–5PM; Jan–Mar and
Nov–Dec AN.

Philippe Naud le Buisson
St-Laurent-de-Cognac
16100 Cognac.
Tel: 05 45 82 74 70.

Rémy-Martin
Domaine de Merpins
16100 Cognac.
Tel: 05 45 35 76 66.
Email: visites.remymartin@
remy-cointreau.com
www.remy.com
Tours available.

Cognac Otard SA
Château de Cognac
16101 Cognac.
Tel: 05 45 36 88 86.
Email: infovisite@otard.com
Tel: 05 45 36 88 87.
www.otard.com
Tours can be booked online.
Tours: AN Jan 1–Mar 31;
open daily Apr 1–June 30
and Aug 31–Oct 1, 11AM-
–noon, 2–6PM (last tour
5PM); open daily July and
Aug, 11AM–noon and
1:30–7PM (last tour 6PM).
Nov 1–Dec 31, tours
Mon–Thurs at 11AM, 2:30PM,
3:45PM; Fri 11AM, 2:30PM,
4PM. Open holidays except
May 1.

JARNAC

Courvoisier SA
2, place du Château
16200 Jarnac. (Museum).
Tel: 05 45 35 55 55.
www.courvoisier.com
Open daily May–Sept
10AM–6PM, except closed Sat
in May and Sept. Rest of year
AN. WS.

Delamain
7, rue Jacques & Robert
Delamain, 16200 Jarnac.
Tel: 05 45 81 08 24.
Email: delamain@
delamain-cognac.com
www.delamain-cognac.com
AN; groups up to 6. Open
Mon–Thurs 9AM–12PM and
2–4PM; Fri 9AM–12PM. WS. E.

Vineyards of Cognac after grape-gathering.
Image © Maksim Esin/Dreamstime.com

ST-JEAN-D'ANGELY

Cognac Louis Bouron SA
La Grange,
17416 St-Jean-d'Angély.
Tel: 05 46 32 00 12.
Email: monique.parias@
wanadoo.fr
Fax: 05 46 32 06 11.
www.swfrance.com/
louisbouron.htm
TF; open daily 10AM–12PM
and 2–6PM.

ST-MEME-LES-CARRIERES

Cognac Ménard
16720 St-Même-les-Carrières.
Tel: 05 45 81 90 26.
Fax: 05 45 81 98 22.
www.cognac-menard.com

FOR FURTHER INFORMATION

BNIC
23, allées du Champ de
Mars, 16101 Cognac.
Tel: 05 45 35 60 00.
Email:
contact@cognac.fr
www.bnic.fr

Pineau des Charentes
Comité National du
Pineau des Charentes
112, ave Victor Hugo,
16100 Cognac.
Tel: 05 45 32 09 27.
Email: pineau@pineau.fr
www.pineaõ.fr

La Rochelle

Make time to visit the pretty port of La Rochelle in the northwest corner of the Cognac region. The inner harbor is protected by the twin towers of La Chaîne and St-Nicolas. Angoulême, in the extreme east of the area, has an impressive girdle of fortifications.

Where to stay and eat

Hotel François Ier
3, place Francois Ier, 16100 Cognac.
Tel: 05 45 32 07 18 (H).

Domaine de l'Echassier
70–72, rue de Bellevue,
16100 Châteaubenard.
Tel: 05 45 35 01 09 (H/R).
www.echassier.com

Château de l'Yeuse
66, rue de Bellevue,
16100 Châteaubenard.
Tel: 05 45 36 82 60 (H/R).
www.yeuse.fr

Le Château
15, place du Château, 16200 Jarnac.
Tel: 05 48 51 81 07 17 (R).

La Ribaudière
place du Port, 16200
Bourg Charente.
Tel: 05 45 81 30 54 (R).
www.laribaudiere.com

Richard Coutanceau
Plage de la Concurrence,
17000 La Rochelle.
Tel: 05 46 41 48 19 (R).

Relais du Bois Saint-Georges
cours Genêt, 17100 Saintes.
Tel: 05 46 93 50 99 (H/R).
www.relaisdubois.com

The Loire Valley

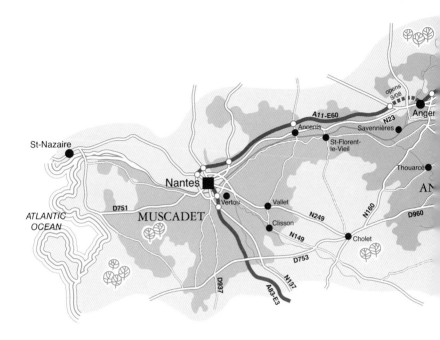

THE LOIRE VALLEY

I t is easy to see why the French kings treated the Loire
Valley as their playground: the climate is temperate, the
landscape soft and beguiling, and much of the land is
fertile. There was also plenty of honey-colored limestone
with which to build the famous châteaux, such as Azay-le-
Rideau, Chambord, and Chenonceau. The valley remains
a wonderful region for visitors to explore, with its rich
historical heritage and the diversity of its wines. The Loire
is the climatic border between the frequently cold and wet
northern France and the warmer south.

Although they are by no means continuous, the Loire
vineyards extend over nearly 850 km (530 miles), and so it
is far too ambitious to try to visit them all at once. It is best
to concentrate on a section at a time, for instance
Touraine or Anjou-Saumur or the Pays Nantais.

At 1,000 km (about 600 miles) long, the Loire is easily
the longest river in France. The source is high up in the massif
Central, only 100 km (60 miles) from the Mediterranean.
Although the Loire appears a gentle river, it is prone to
flooding and its currents and sandbanks can be treacherous.

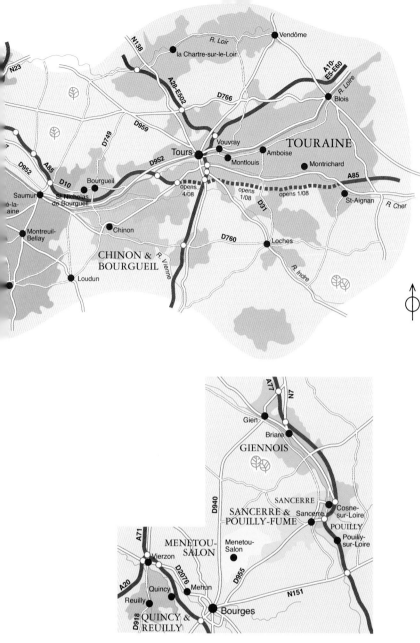

The Upper Loire

The first Loire vineyards are those of the Côtes de Forez and the Côte Roannaise, which are just to the north of St-Etienne. Gamay is the chief variety, and the wines are similar to those of the Beaujolais.

Next come those of St-Pourçain-sur-Sioule, which are made in three colors from Chardonnay, Tressalier, Gamay, and Pinot Noir.

TO GET TO THE LOIRE

From Paris: Tours is 234 km (146 miles) by the A10; Angers is 296 km (185 miles) and Nantes 380 km (237 miles) by the A11. From Calais and Boulogne, Paris can now be avoided by taking the A16, A28 to Rouen, and then A13 and A28 to Tours. Tours is 234 km (146 miles) from Caen by D514, N158, N138, and A28, while Nantes is 155 km (97 miles) from Saint-Malo by the N137. Train: by TGV Tours is just less than an hour from Paris; Angers about 90 minutes; and Nantes two hours. There are regular budget flights to Nantes and Tours.

All of these vineyards were much more important in the 19th century, as were the Côtes d'Auvergne on the Allier, a tributary to the Loire. They are worth visiting if you are in the area, but do not warrant a special journey.

Central Vineyards

The sleepy little town of Pouilly-sur-Loire marks the halfway point of the river Loire and the first appellation with an international reputation. Pouilly-Fumé and Sancerre are the best known appellations in the central region. Sauvignon Blanc and Pinot Noir are the dominant grape varieties here.

Pouilly-Fumé & Sancerre

Pouilly, on the east side of the Loire, grows only white grapes, largely Sauvignon but with a small quantity of Chasselas. Of these two, the Sauvignon makes the classic wine Pouilly-Fumé, which is a similar wine to Sancerre, though lacking some of its aggression. The Chasselas, on the other hand, is an historical anomaly. Originally grown as a table grape for the Parisian market, it now makes an agreeable, uncomplicated wine labeled as Pouilly-sur-Loire.

The Pouilly vineyards run either side of the busy N7 road. The largest producer of Pouilly Blanc Fumé is Patrick de Ladoucette, who owns the Château de Nozet, just north of the town of Pouilly. As well as making wine from his own vineyards, he buys both juice and wine from other growers. The finest wines from his own vines he sells under a luxury presentation with the name of Baron de L.

Another attractive property producing full-bodied wines is the Château de Tracy, by the Loire just across from Sancerre.

Two hamlets whose names often appear on wine labels are Les Loges and Les Berthiers. At Les Loges, the vineyards rise steeply above the Loire. A natural sun-trap, it produces perhaps the most full-bodied wines in the area.

Prominent among the local growers are a number of members of the Dagueneau family.

Sancerre

Planted on steeply rolling hills, the vineyards of Sancerre are the most spectacular in the Loire. Wine is produced in Sancerre itself and thirteen other surrounding villages. As far as reputation is concerned, perhaps the most important are Bué, Chavignol, and Verdigny. In Bué, the best-known vineyards are the Chêne Marchand and the Clos de la Poussie.

With 2,700 hectares (6,534 acres) planted, it is easily the

Domaine Dagueneau et Filles
Les Berthiers,
58150 St-Andelain.
Tel: 03 86 39 11 18.
Email: dagueneau@
s-dagueneau-filles.fr
Fax: 03 86 39 05 32.
www.s-dagueneau-filles.fr
TF. Open Mon–Sat 9AM–12PM
and 2–6PM.

Masson-Blondelet
1, rue de Paris,
Pouilly-sur-Loire.
Tel: 03 86 39 00 34.
Email: info@
masson-blondelet.com
Fax: 03 86 39 04 61.
www.masson-blondelet.com
Email to arrange a tour.

Michel Redde et Fils
"La Moynerie," rte. Nationale 7,
Pouilly-sur-Loire.
Tel: 03 86 39 14 72.
Email: thierry-redde@
michel-redde.fr
Fax: 03 86 39 04 36.
www.michel-redde.fr
TF; TP/AN for groups larger
than 5. Open Mon–Fri
8AM–6:30PM, Sat
9:30AM–6:30PM. WS.

Domaine Guy Saget
La Castille, Pouilly-sur-Loire.
Tel: 03 86 39 57 75.
Email: guy.saget@wanadoo.fr
Tel: 03 86 39 08 30.
www.guy-saget.com

Château de Tracy
Tracy-sur-Loire.
Tel: 03 86 26 15 12.
Email: tracy@wanadoo.fr

SANCERRE

Henri Bourgeois
Chavignol, Sancerre.
Tel: 02 48 78 53 20.
Fax: 02 48 54 14 24.
www.bourgeois-sancerre.com

Lucien Crochet
place de l'Eglise, Bué.
Tel: 02 48 54 08 10.
Email: lcrochet@terre-net.fr

Alphonse Mellot
3, porte César, Sancerre.
Tel: 02 48 54 07 41.
Email: alphonse.mellot@
wanadoo.fr
Fax: 02 48 54 07 62.
www.mellot.com
TF for groups of 10 or fewer;
for 10+ TP/AN. Shop open:
Nov–Mar, Mon–Fri
10AM–12:30PM and
2:30–7PM; Apr–Oct daily
10AM–12:30PM and
2:30–7PM. Office hours:
Mon–Fri 8:30AM–12PM and
2–5PM. E, S.

Jean-Max Roger
11, place du Carrou,
18300 Bué.
Tel: 02 48 54 32 20.
Email jean-max.roger@
wanadoo.fr
Fax: 02 48 54 10 29.
TF. Open Mon–Sat
8AM–12PM and 1:30–6:30PM.
AN only on Sun, in late Aug,
and Christmas holidays. WS. E.

largest appellation in the central zone. White wines from Sauvignon Blanc make up about 75 percent of the production, while Pinot Noir is used to make red and a small amount of rather expensive rosé.

It is perhaps in Sancerre that the Sauvignon best shows its characteristics—gooseberry and grapefruit. Aggressively vegetal aromas are a sign of unripe Sauvignon. In a good vintage the best wines can be safely kept for up to ten years. Once the reds of Sancerre were decidedly thin, but over the past ten years top producers have been making more concentrated and full-bodied reds. In good vintages they can be surprisingly fine.

Sancerre—the town

The town of Sancerre lies on a hill dominating the left bank of the river Loire. Its strategic importance has long been recognized, and some believe that it is the Cortona of Caesar's *Commentaries*. The town is much more lively than Pouilly and has several restaurants, cafés, and shops. There are fine views of the surrounding countryside and there are several important producers in the town such as Alphonse Mellot and Vacheron, who are worth visiting.

Three types of soil

There are three different types of soil in Sancerre: *chaillotes* (very thin, chalky soil), clay-lime-stone, and *silex* (flint). Wines from the *chaillotes* are very aromatic and are ready to drink young, while the other two soils produce wines that need more time to open up but age better. The main area of flinty soil is around Sancerre and Méné-tréol. The steeply sloping hills above the villages of Amigny, Bué, Champtin, and Chavignol are clay-limestone.

Most of the wine from Pouilly and Sancerre is made in modern stainless steel wineries. However, some of the top, or most expensive, wines are fermented and aged in new oak barrels.

A local cheese

The very steep Monts Damnés, one of the most famous vineyards, is split between the two villages of Verdigny and Chavignol. This latter village has also given its name to the second local gastronomic specialty: the goat's milk cheese called Crottin de Chavignol, which is protected by its own *appellation contrôlée*. My French dictionary politely translates *crottin* as droppings—the cheese is, after all, small in size! One of the best producers is SA Dubois-Boulay in the center of Chavignol (Tel: 02 48 54 15 69).

Vacheron
rue du Puits Poulton, Sancerre.
Tel: 02 48 54 09 93.
Email: vacheron.sa@ wanadoo.fr
TF; Open daily 10am–12pm and 2:30–6pm. WS. Museum visit (fee). Organic and biodynamic farming. E, G.

FOR FURTHER INFORMATION

Tourist Information Office of Pouilly-sur-Loire
61, rue Waldeck Rousseau, 58150 Pouilly-sur-Loire.
Tel: 03 86 39 03 75.
Email: pouillysurloire@ aol.com
www.ot-pouillysurloire.fr

Bureau du Centre
9, route de Chavignol, Sancerre.
Tel: 02 48 78 51 07.
Email: contact@ vins-centre-loire.com
www.vins-centre-loire.com

Tourist office
nouvelle place, Sancerre.
Tel: 02 48 54 08 21.
Email: ot.sancerre@ wanadoo.fr
www.sancerre.net/otsi

Other Central Appellations

Menetou-Salon

Of the other central appellations, Menetou-Salon is the most important and has the most attractive landscape. This appellation adjoins the western limit of Sancerre and produces broadly similar wines from Sauvignon Blanc and Pinot Noir. The area under vines has more than doubled over the past twenty years. The Menetou-Salon vineyards center around the two small towns of Morogues and Menetou-Salon.

Coteaux de Giennois

From Cosné northwards to Gien, which is famous for its porcelain, are the scattered vineyards of the Coteaux de Giennois, with wines made from Sauvignon Blanc, Gamay, and Pinot Noir. Around Orléans are the vestiges of the once important vineyards that used to supply Paris. Now only 100 hectares (242 acres) are left, growing Auvernat Blanc (Chardonnay), Auvernat Rouge (Pinot Noir), and Gris Meunier.

Orléans and vinegar

Orléans was once the port for wines that had come along the Loire and would be unloaded and sent to Paris. It was common for wines to go sour while being transported, so Orléans became famous for vinegar.

Quincy and Reuilly

West of the cathedral city of Bourges in the Cher valley are the small appellations of Quincy, with its crisp Sauvignon Blancs, and Reuilly, which makes wine in all three colors. The permitted varieties are Sauvignon Blanc, Pinot Gris, and Pinot Noir. Here the land is quite flat and the vines are planted on gravel beds. Well to the south of Bourges are the tiny vineyards of Château-meillant with its Gamay and Pinot Noir–based wines.

Where to stay and eat

Despite the popularity of the Central Loire area, there are few really good places to stay or eat.

Hotels

Coq Hardi Relais Fleuri
42, ave de la Tuilerie,
Pouilly-sur-Loire.
Tel: 03 86 39 12 99 (H/R).
Email: le-relais-fleuri-sarl@
wanadoo.fr
www.lerelaisfleuri.fr

Hotel de la Loire
2, quai de Loire, St-Satur.
Tel: 02 48 78 22 22 (H).
www.hotel-de-la-loire.com

Relais de Pouilly
quai de Loire, Pouilly-sur-Loire.
Tel: 03 86 39 03 00 (H/R).
www.relaisdepouilly.com

Hotel Panoramic
Remparts des Augustins, Sancerre
Tel: 02 48 54 22 44 (H/R).
www.panoramichotel.com

Restaurants

La Côtes de Monts Damnés
place de l'Orme, Chavignol.
Tel: 02 48 54 14 24 (R).
Small restaurant with good list of Sancerres especially from Chavignol.

La Tour
31, nouvelle place, Sancerre.
Tel: 02 48 54 00 81.
Email: info@la-tour-sancerre.fr
www.la-tour-sancerre.fr

MENETOU-SALON

Château de Chatenoy
Menetou-Salon.
Tel: 02 48 66 68 70.

Jacolin St-Céols.
Tel: 02 48 64 40 75.

QUINCY

Cave Romane de Brinay
Le Bourg, Brinay.
Tel: 02 48 51 09 45.

REUILLY

Claude Lafond
Le Bois St-Denis,
route de Gracay, Reuilly.
Tel: 02 54 49 22 17.
www.claudelafond.com

FOR FURTHER INFORMATION

Tourist offices
Menetou-Salon
23, rue de la Mairie
18510 Menetou-Salon.
Tel/Fax: 02 48 64 87 57.

Mehun-sur-Yèvre
place du 14 juillet
18500 Mehun-sur-Yèvre.
Tel: 02 48 57 35 51.
Fax: 02 48 57 13 40.

Reuilly
5, rue Rabelais
36260 Reuilly
Tél. : 02 54 49 24 94.
Email: otsireuilly@yahoo.fr
Fax: 02 54 49 39 26.
www.ot-reuilly.fr

Touraine

This is the heart of the Loire Valley. Here are many of the famous châteaux, such as Amboise, Azay-Le-Rideau, Chenonceau, Cheverny, Loches, Ussé (the inspiration for the castle in Sleeping Beauty) and Villandry, as well as a host of delightful but lesser-known châteaux. There is a little château or manor house around almost every corner! The châteaux are built using the local honey-colored limestone called *tuffeau*.

Château Chenonceau at twilight. Built across the River Cher, this is undoubtedly one of the Loire's most beautiful and enchanting châteaux. King François 1er planted vines on the estate. Image © Yan Kors/Dreamstime.com

The vineyards of Touraine stretch from the edge of the Sologne, a large area of forest and lakes, in the east to Chinon and St-Nicolas-de-Bourgueil in the west. However, the vines are by no means continuous. Apart from around Azay-le-Rideau, there are few vines between Vouvray and Chinon.

CHEVERNY

Jocelyne et Michel Gendrier
Les Huards, Cour-Cheverny.
Tel: 02 54 79 97 90.
Email: infos@gendrier.com
Fax: 02 54 79 26 82.
www.gendrier.com

TOURAINE

Henry Marionnet
La Charmoise,
41230 Soings-en-Sologne.
Tel: 02 54 98 70 73.
www.henry-marionnet.com

Confrérie des Vignerons de Oisly et Thesée le Bourg
41700 Oisly.
Tel: 02 54 79 75 20.

Domaine Sauvète
9, Chemin de la Bocagerie,
41400 Monthou-sur-Cher.
Tel: 02 54 71 48 68.
Email: domaine-sauvete@wanadoo.fr

JASNIÈRES

Joël and Ludovic Gigou
4, rue des Caves,
72340 La Chartre-sur-Loir.
Tel: 02 43 44 48 72.
Email: joel.gigou@liberty surf.fr

Eric Nicolas
Domaine de la Bellivière,
72340 Lhomme.
Tel: 02 43 44 59 97.
Email: info@belliviere.com
Fax: 02 43 79 18 33.
www.belliviere.com
TF; AN by phone. Open 9AM–7PM. WS. Wine museum in village. E, G.

Cheverny and Valençay

The imposing Château of Cheverny was built in 1634. The vineyards of Cheverny lie between the small eponymous town and Blois. The reds are made from Gamay and Pinot Noir and the whites largely from Sauvignon Blanc with a little Chardonnay.

Cour-Cheverny is a separate AC. It is reserved for whites made from Romorantin, a unique local grape variety. The resulting wine is pleasant enough, but the fact that no one has ever bothered to plant Romorantin elsewhere is a fair indicator of its potential.

Valençay's greatest claim to fame is that its château was the home of Talleyrand—one of the most flexible of politicians, who served in government before, during, and after the French Revolution without losing his head. Valençay's wines are of local interest.

Eastern Touraine

This is the transitional zone between the central vineyards and the rest of the Loire. Many of the vineyards are along the pretty Cher valley, especially between St Aignan and Bléré, and also up on the plateau between the Cher and the Loire, especially around Oisly.

A large number of grape varieties are grown including Cabernet Franc, Chenin Blanc, Gamay, Pinot Noir, and Sauvignon Blanc. Producers here tend to make up to a dozen different wines and have all three colors.

The basic Touraine appellation offers some of the best value in the Loire. Look for the easy-drinking, soft Gamays, crunchy Sauvignon Blancs, and Cabernets. In good years, the Cabernets can age remarkably well. The dark-colored Côt (known elsewhere as Malbec) is also worth trying.

Jasnières and the Loir Valley

The valley of the Loir is some 40 km (25 miles) north of the Loire. The Loir is a very pretty, pastoral valley with a few areas of vines. Jasnières, near to the attractive little town of La Chartre-sur-Loir, is the best known. With slopes facing due south, this is again pure Chenin Blanc territory. The wines are generally dry but some demi-sec and sweet (*moelleux*) wines are made in good years.

Surrounding Jasnières is the AC Coteaux du Loir. Here whites are made from Chenin and reds from Gamay and Pineau d'Aunis, a peppery local variety. Further east is the Coteaux du Vendômois. While in the Loir it is worth visiting Vendôme for its remarkable Gothic cathedral; Lavardin for its ruined fortress; the little market town of Montoire; and Trôo with its many troglodyte houses.

Vouvray and Montlouis

Close to Tours are the twin appellations of Vouvray and Montlouis, which face each other across the Loire, with the better-known Vouvray on the north bank and smaller Montlouis on the south. The sole variety here is Chenin Blanc, the great white grape of the Loire.

Chenin is remarkable in that it can be used to make still or sparkling wine. The still wines can range from bone dry to lusciously sweet. The grape's relatively high acidity means that these wines have a great potential to age: well-made wines from even moderate vintages can easily last for 50 years or more.

Driving through the center of Montlouis and Vouvray,

MONTLOUIS

Domaine des Liards (Berger Frères)
70, rue de Chenonceaux,
37270 St-Martin-le-Beau.
Tel: 02 47 50 67 36.

François Chidaine
5 Grande Rue
Tel: 02 47 45 19 14.

Domaine Taille aux Loups (Jacky Blot)
8, rue des Altres,
37270 Montlouis.
Tel: 02 47 45 11 11.
Email: la-taille-aux-loups@
wanadoo.fr
www.jackyblot.com

VOUVRAY

Catherine & Didier Champalou
7, rue du Grand Ormeau,
37210 Vouvray.
Tel: 02 47 52 64 49.
Email: champalou@wanadoo.fr
Fax: 02 47 52 67 99.

Bernard Fouquet
Domaine des Aubuisières,
37210 Vouvray.
Tel: 02 47 52 61 55.
Email: info@
vouvrayfouquet.com
Fax: 02 47 52 67 81.
www.vouvrayfouquet.com

Huet SA
11, rue de la Croix Buisée,
37210 Vouvray.
Tel: 02 47 52 78 87.
Email: contact@
huet.echansonne.com
Fax: 02 47 52 66 74.
www.huet-echansonne.com
Open Mon–Sat 9AM–12PM
and 2–6PM.

you will see no sign of vines, although there are signs offering wines for sale. Instead, the vines are grown along the top of the slopes overlooking the Loire and on the plateau.

Many growers have their cellars dug into the limestone hillsides. There are also troglodyte houses. The vineyards of Vouvray run from Rochecorbon in the west along to Vouvray, where they turn up the valley of the Brenne to Vernou and Chançay. The best wines tend to come from the south-facing vineyards of Rochecorbon and Vouvray. Across the river, most of the Montlouis vineyards lie to the east of the town of Montlouis, between the Loire and the small town of St-Martin-le-Beau in the Cher Valley. The appellation of Montlouis is a sixth of the size of its neighbor.

The wines of Vouvray and Montlouis are broadly similar. Depending on the year, they can cover the full range from dry white to sweet, still, and sparkling.

Tours
At the junction of the route from Paris to Bordeaux and the routes from the Atlantic to central France along the Loire and Cher valleys, is the

elegant, historic, and lively city of Tours, the largest conurbation in the center of the Loire Valley.

There is much to see in the center of Tours: the 13th-century St Gatien Cathedral, The Musée de Compagnonnage and the Musée des Beaux Arts, as well as the fine 19th-century central railway station. Vieux Tours around the Place Plumereaux is the liveliest part of the city, especially at night. In late July there is an annual basil and garlic fair in the nearby market area. Tours' size means that it is not the ideal base for visiting the vineyards. It is far more pleasant to find a hotel in the peaceful and gentle Touraine countryside.

FOR FURTHER INFORMATION

Interloire
12, rue Etienne Pallu,
37019 Tours.
Tel: 02 47 60 55 00.
Email: contact@
interloire.com
www.interloire.com
Information on Touraine,
Anjou-Saumur.

Chinon and Bourgueil

West of Tours there are few vineyards, apart from the little enclave around Azay-le-Rideau, until you reach the red wine appellations of Chinon and Bourgueil at the western end of Touraine. This is the start of the kingdom of Cabernet Franc.

In Bordeaux, with the exception of the wines of Cheval Blanc, Cabernet Franc has a minor role compared to its cousin Cabernet Sauvignon. But it is the other way around in the Loire. Cabernet Franc is undoubtedly the best red of the valley, while in most years Cabernet Sauvignon struggles to ripen properly. Chinon is the best place to start a tour of this area: approach the town from the south, which gives you a magnificent view of the ruined château and the river Vienne, with the medieval town squeezed between the two.

Apart from a small amount of white Chinon made from Chenin Blanc, these wines are essentially red— although a small amount of rosé is also made. The wines from Chinon are softer and more approachable than those from Bourgueil and St-Nicolas, which tend to be more tannic and need time in bottle to soften up. Chinon also has the great advantage of being easy to pronounce. The town is associated with Rabelais, who was born nearby at La Divinière, close to the village of Seuilly.

There are three types of soil in the area, giving three different types of wine. Around the confluence of the Vienne and Loire, the soil is sandy and the wines are light and often bottled early for drinking in the spring following the vintage. Gravel beds are widespread in all three appellations, especially in St-Nicolas-de-Bourgueil.

Rooftops in the old city of Chinon. Situated on the river Vienne, Chinon produces one of the best reds of the Loire Valley. Image © Sebastien Windal/Dreamstime.com

The wines from the gravel vineyards are more full-bodied and need a little more time before they are ready to drink. However, the wines that come from grapes grown on the limestone *coteaux* are the most structured and full-bodied and the most long-lived.

Bourgueil and St-Nicolas-de-Bourgueil

Although these are two appellations, it can be difficult to distinguish between a Bourgueil and St-Nicolas-de-Bourgueil. The soils and the sites are essentially the same, although more of St-Nicolas is on the gravel. St-Nicolas' separate existence is normally ascribed to having had a

CHINON

Cave Baudry-Dutour
12, Coteau De Sonnay
37500 Cravant Les Coteaux
Tel: 02 47 93 44 99.
Email: info@baudry-dutour.fr
www.baudry-dutour.com
Open Tues–Fri 10AM–12PM
and 2–6PM; Sat 9AM–1PM. WS.

Maison Couly Dutheil
12, rue Diderot, B.P. 234
37502 Chinon.
Tel: 02 47 97 20 20.
Fax: 02 47 97 20 25.
www.coulydutheil-chinon.com
Visit to cellar with tasting for
groups of 8–25 people; tours
of varying lengths.

SCEA Charles Joguet Sazilly
37220 l'Ile Bouchard.
Tel: 02 47 58 55 53.
Email: joguet@charlesjoguet.com
Fax: 02 47 58 52 22.
www.charlesjoguet.com
Open Mon–Fri 9AM–12:30PM
and 2–6PM; Sat by appointment.

forceful mayor when the appellation was created in 1937. He insisted that his village deserved its own appellation and must not be swallowed up by its larger neighbor, Bourgueil, three miles away.

Saumur

Saumur Champigny

The vineyards of Saumur start just beyond Candes St Martin where the Vienne joins the Loire. The main road along the south bank to Saumur passes through the small villages of Parnay and Souzay-Champigny. Just as at Vouvray, there are no signs of vines from the main road; the vineyards lie on the slopes above the old river cliffs.

These are the vineyards of Saumur-Champigny, one of the best reds of the Loire. Depending on the *cuvée* and the ambitions of the grower, they range in style from young, light summer quaffers to serious reds that need to be aged to show their best. Saumur-Champigny has long been fashionable in Paris and this is often reflected in the price.

Saumur—still wines

Outside the Saumur-Champigny zone, the reds are plain AC Saumur. These tend to be good value, early-drinking wines. Many of the best come from further south, from the area around Le Puy-Notre-Dame.

Whites are mainly made from Chenin Blanc. The overall quality has improved greatly over the past ten years.

Dry whites are appellation Saumur Blanc, while the delicate, local, but little-known, sweet wines are called AC Coteaux de Saumur. The whites of Saumur tend to be more delicate and citric than the more full-bodied Anjou Blancs.

Cave des Vignerons de St Cyr

One of the best-run cooperatives in France is on the outskirts of the small town of St Cyr, a few miles south of Saumur. There is an enormous cellar under the winery that is big enough to take trucks.

Sparkling Saumur

Saumur is the center of the production of sparkling wine in Loire. Ackerman-Laurance, the oldest house, was established in 1811. Because of the limestone soil, the local wines have a natural tendency to sparkle, and the limestone hillsides are ideally suited for constructing extensive cellars in which the bottles can be stacked up to mature. Chenin Blanc is the chief variety, along with Chardonnay and Cabernet Franc.

Most of the big Saumur houses have their premises in St-Hilaire-St-Florent, just to the west of Saumur. The exception is Gratien & Meyer, which is to the east of the town.

BOURGUEIL AND ST-NICOLAS-DE-BOURGUEIL

Maison Audebert et Fils
20, ave Jean Causeret,
37140 Bourgueil.
Tel: 02 47 97 70 06.
Email: maison@audebert.fr
Fax: 02 47 97 72 07.
www.audebert.fr

Francis Jamet
Domaine des Vallettes, 37140
St-Nicolas-de-Bourgueil.
Tel: 02 47 97 44 44.
Email: francis.jamet@
les-vallettes.com
Fax: 02 47 97 44 45.
www.les-vallettes.com
Open Mon–Sat 8AM–12PM
and 1:30–6:30PM.

Frederic Mabileau
5-6, rue du Pressoir, 37140
St-Nicolas-de-Bourgueil.
Tel: 02 47 97 79 58.
Email: mabileau.frederick@
wanadoo.fr
Fax: 02 47 97 45 19.
www.fredericmabileau.com

Taluau et Foltzenlogel
Chevrette, 37140
St-Nicolas-de-Bourgueil.
Tel: 02 47 97 78 79.
Email: joel.taluau@wanadoo.fr
Fax: 02 47 97 95 60.
www.vins-taluau
foltzenlogel.com
Open Mon–Fri 9AM–12PM
and 2–6PM; Sat AN.

SAUMUR AND SAUMUR–CHAMPIGNY ST–CYR–EN–BOURG

Caves des Vignerons de Saumur
49260 St-Cyr-en-Bourg.
Tel: 02 41 53 06 06.
Email: infos@
vignerons-de-saumur.com
Fax: 02 41 53 06 10.
www.vignerons-de-saumur.com
Open 9:30AM–12PM and
2:30–6PM.

Régis Neau Domaine de Nerleux
4, rue de la Paleine,
49260 St-Cyr-en-Bourg.
Tel: 02 41 51 61 04.
Email: contact@
domaine-de-nerleux.fr
Fax: 02 41 51 65 34.
www.domaine-de-nerleux.fr
Open Mon–Sat midday for
tours, tasting, and sales.
E, G.

Château de Villeneuve
3, rue Jean Brevet,
49400 Souzay-Champigny.
Tel: 02 41 51 14 04.
Email: jp-chevallier@
chateau-de-villeneuve.com
Fax: 02 41 50 58 24.
www.chateau-de-villeneuve.com
T. Open Mon–Sat 9AM–12PM
and 2–6PM. Closed holidays.
WS.

In addition to Saumur Mousseux, sparkling wines from Vouvray and Montlouis are well worth trying. In particular, look out for Vouvray or Montlouis Pétillant. This local specialty is a more delicate sparkler, having less pressure (2.5 atmospheres) than the more customary five atmospheres used in Champagne and other sparkling wines. In theory at least, Crémant de Loire is a higher-quality sparkling wine with stricter regulations, based on those used in Champagne. It can come from anywhere in Anjou-Saumur and Touraine.

Saumur

This is one of the most attractive Loire riverside towns. The small town, which has a number of attractive shops, is dominated by its imposing château. Saumur would make a good base from which to tour the region. As well as being handy for vineyard visits, places such as the historic Abbey of Fontrevaud and the pretty little towns of Candes St Martin, Montsoreau, and Montreuil-Bellay are within easy reach.

Haut-Poitou

Just to the north of Poiters are the vineyards of Haut-Poitou.

Some 500 hectares (1,235 acres) are planted with Cabernet Franc and Cabernet Sauvignon, Chardonnay, Gamay, and Sauvignon Blanc. Most growers belong to the Cave du Haut-Poitou. Worth a stop if you are in the area, but not a special journey.

Anjou

In Anjou the soil changes from the limestone and clay of the Paris basin to the hard, impervious rocks of the Brittany peninsula. This is an area of granite, schist, and slate. This change also affects the wines. The whites tend to be softer because they have less acidity, and the reds are often more tannic.

Most of the Anjou vineyards are south of the Loire, around the valleys of the Layon and the much smaller Aubance. Rosé, especially Rosé d'Anjou, remains by volume the most important wine made. But this semi-sweet wine is far from the most interesting.

Coteaux du Layon and Coteaux de l'Aubance

The longest-lived and most fascinating wines of Anjou are the sweet wines from these two valleys. At their best they are among the great sweet wines of the world. They have to be made

ST–HILAIRE–ST FLORENT

Bouvet Ladubay
rue de l'Abbaye, St-Hilaire-St-Florent, 49400 Saumur.
Tel: 02 41 83 83 83.
Email: contact@bouvet-ladubay.fr
Fax: 02 41 50 24 32.
www.bouvet-ladubay.fr
Free for groups of 12+. Open June 1–Sept 30, Mon–Fri 8:30AM–7PM, Sat 9AM–7PM, Sun 9:30AM–7PM. Open Oct 1–May 31, Mon–Fri 8:30AM–12:30PM and 2–6PM, Sat 9AM–12:30PM and 2–6PM, Sun 9:30AM–12:30PM and 2:30–6PM. Sparkling wines, audio-visual presentation, rock cellars, contemporary art center. WS.

SAUMUR

Gratien et Meyer
route de Montsoreau, 49400 Saumur.
Tel: 02 41 83 13 35.
Email: contact@gratienmeyer.com
Fax: 02 41 83 13 49.
www.gratienmeyer.com
Boutique open daily 9AM–6PM. AA off-season.

HAUT–POITOU

Cave de Haut-Poitou
32, rue Alphonse Plault, 86170 Neuville-du-Poitou.
Tel: 05 49 51 21 65.
Email: c-h.p@wanadoo.fr
Fax: 05 49 51 16 07.
www.cavehautpoitou.free.fr
AN for cellar visit; groups at 10PM, 2PM, and 6PM. Boutique open Mon–Sat 9AM–12PM and 4–7PM, Sun 9AM–12:30PM.

from Chenin Blanc. Although these wines can be very rich, they also have Chenin's acidity to balance them and stop them from being cloying.

The ideal conditions for making sweet wines are warm fall days that start with misty mornings. These conditions produce noble rot, or botrytis. Although this type of rot makes the outside of the grape look disgusting, it eats up the water content of the grape and so concentrates its sugars. Growers wait until the grapes are affected by botrytis and then pick selectively. Typically a vineyard will be picked over three or four times, taking only affected bunches.

Bonnezeaux and Quarts de Chaume

These are two small *grand cru* appellations in the Layon valley. They are two particularly favored sites and have special micro-climates very prone to autumnal noble rot. Travelling westward, the first is Bonnezeaux. Here the south-facing slopes become noticeably steeper.

Quarts de Chaume is further west. The vineyards are in an amphitheater facing due south. Quarts de Chaume have great concentration as well as delicacy and can last at least 50 years even in moderate vintages.

Savennières

This is the third *grand cru* of Anjou. Once again the grape is Chenin Blanc, but the wines are dry, although in hot years they may be *demi-sec* or even *moelleux*. The vineyards are on the north bank of the Loire just a few miles west of Angers.

Savennières tastes strongly of minerals, and, although it can be enjoyed young, it needs five or ten years to show its best. It is the ideal partner for a Loire classic: poached fish served with *beurre blanc*.

Anjou Villages

As the popularity of rosés declined in the late 1970s and early 1980s, vignerons increasingly turned to making red wines. In 1985 the AC Anjou Villages was created for red only. Cabernet Franc and Cabernet Sauvignon are the permitted varieties. These wines are generally best after three to five years.

A sea of vines—the Muscadet vineyards near Nantes.

ANJOU

Stéphane Branchereau
Domaine des Forges,
route de la Haie Longue,
49190 St-Aubin-de-Luigné.
Tel: 02 41 78 33 56.
Email: vitforge@wanadoo.fr
or forgescb@worldonline.fr
Fax: 02 41 78 67 51.

Philippe Cady
Valette, 49190
St-Aubin-de-Luigné.
Tel: 02 41 78 33 69.
Email: domainecady@yahoo.fr
Fax: 02 41 78 67 79.
www.domainecady.fr
Open daily AN.

Christophe Daviau
Domaine de Bablut,
49320 Brissac-Quincé.
Tel: 02 41 91 22 59.
Email: daviau.christophe@
wanadoo.fr
Fax: 02 41 91 24 77.

Vignobles Germain
Château de Fesles,
49380 Thouarcé.
Tel: 02 41 68 94 00.
Email: loire@vgas.com
Fax: 02 41 68 94 01.
www.vgas.com

Vincent Ogereau
44, rue de la Belle Angevine,
49750 St Lambert-du-Lattay.
Tel: 02 41 78 30 53.
Fax: 02 41 78 43 55.

Domaine Richou
Chauvigné,
49610 Mozé-sur-Louet.
Tel: 02 41 78 72 13.
Email: domaine.richou@
wanadoo.fr

Anjou Rouge and Anjou Blanc

As well as making Anjou Villages, most producers also make easy-drinking Anjou Rouge. This wine is designed to be light and to be ready as soon as it is put on the market, usually in the spring following the vintage. It can be served chilled. Anjou Blanc can be dry or *demi-sec* and a blend of Chenin with 20 percent Chardonnay or Sauvignon Blanc. Increasingly, the best growers are using only 100 percent Chenin Blanc in their product.

Muscadet

Muscadet is one of the great matches with fish and, in particular, shellfish. Fortunately for the visitor, Nantes is close to the sea, so there are plenty of *plateaux fruits de mers* available to wash down with a chilled bottle of Muscadet.

Muscadet is made from the Melon de Bourgogne, which as its name suggests originally came from Burgundy. As the Melon does not have a strong personality, the wine needs some contact with the lees to give it added yeasty flavor. Look out for the words *sur lie* on the bottle. This means that the wine was bottled straight off the fine lees. A *sur lie* should have a slight prickle of carbon dioxide at the back of the throat when you swallow.

In terms of volume, this is the most important vine-growing area of the Loire. There are three areas around Nantes. The Sèvre-et-Maine is reckoned to make the best Muscadet, but growers from Muscadet Coteaux de la Loire and the Côtes de Grandlieu would not agree. Muscadet Coteaux de Loire comes from around the town of Ancenis, east of Nantes and on the north bank of the Loire, while the Côtes de Grandlieu comes from vineyards around the lake of the same name.

The Sèvre-et-Maine is one of the most intensely planted vineyards of France. Much of the vineyard is quite flat, with short, steep slopes down into the valleys of the Sèvre and Maine and their tributaries.

Pays Nantais

Close to the Atlantic, early ripening vines are planted here because of the autumn rains. The wines are predominantly white.

Gros Plant

Even drier than Muscadet is the lemony Gros Plant. Poor versions can be unbearably and unbelievably acidic but good ones make you think of a dozen succulent oysters.

MUSCADET

Château de Chasseloir
44690 St-Fiacre-sur-Maine.
Tel: 02 40 54 81 15.
Email: contact@
chereau-carre.fr
Fax: 02 40 54 81 70.

Couillaud Frères
Château de la Ragotière,
44330 La Regrippière.
Tel: 02 40 33 60 56.
Email: frères.couillard@
wanadoo.fr
Fax: 02 40 33 61 89.
www.freres-couillaud.com

Donatien-Bahuaud
44330 La Chapelle-Heulin.
Tel: 02 40 06 70 05.
Email: dbahuaud@
donatien-bahuaud.fr
Fax: 02 40 06 77 11.
www.donatien-bahuaud.fr

Pierre Luneau
Domaine Pierre de la Grange,
44430 Le Landreau.
Tel: 02 40 06 45 27.
Email: domaineluneaupapin@
wanadoo.fr
Fax: 02 40 06 46 62.

**Les Domaines Louis
Métaireau la Févrie**
44690 Maison-sur-Sèvre.
Tel: 02 40 54 81 92.
Email: marielucemetaireau@
hotmail.com
Fax: 02 40 54 87 83.

Muscadet, continued

Sauvion
Château du Cléray,
44300 Vallet.
Tel: 02 40 36 22 55.
Email: sauvion@sauvion.fr
www.sauvion.fr
Open Mon–Fri 8:30AM–12PM
and 2–4:30PM; Sat, Sun, and
public holidays by app't. AN
for groups.

Les Vignerons de la Noelle
44150 Ancenis.
Tel: 02 40 98 92 72.
Email: vignerons-noelle@
cana.fr
Fax: 02 40 98 96 70.
www.vignerons-de-la-
noelle.com

FIEFS VENDÉENS

MJ Michon et Fils
11, rue des Vallées,
85470 Brem-sur-Mer.
Tel: 02 51 33 13 04.
Tel for Cave Michon:
02 51 90 55 74.
Email: contact@
domaine-saint-nicolas.com
Fax: 02 51 33 18 42.
www.domaine-saint-nicolas.com
Visits and tasting.

Gros Plant was originally planted in the area by the Dutch to turn into brandy, which is why it is also planted in Cognac—known there as Folle Blanche. Like Muscadet, look out for a *sur lie*, which will put a little flesh onto the thin bones of Gros Plant. It is also used as a base for sparkling wine.

Fiefs Vendéens

This is a small area of vines south of Nantes close to Les Sables d'Orlonne and well away from the Loire Valley. Cabernet Franc, Gamay, Negrette, and Pinot Noir are used for the rosés and reds. Rosés predominate and there is a small production of white made chiefly from Chenin Blanc plus some Chardonnay. Most of the wines are drunk young, although some merit a few years in bottle.

Food in the Loire

Because the Loire was the home of the French monarchy, the food of the region is largely that of classic French cuisine, which developed in the kitchens of the Royal Loire châteaux. There isn't a distinct region of cooking as there is in other parts of France, such Burgundy.

There are, however, a number of specialties, including freshwater fish such as pike-perch and shad served with a *beurre blanc* sauce. Eels are a specialty of Anjou-Saumur. Fish and, in particular, shellfish feature prominently in the Pays Nantais, close to the Atlantic. Nantes is also famous for its vegetables, particularly young, early ones, while the Sologne (south of Orléans) is known for its asparagus in the spring and game in the autumn.

When not used for wine, the limestone cellars of Saumur and Touraine also serve equally well for mushroom growing.

Touraine is one of the centers of goats'-milk cheese production, with some towns giving their names to particularly shaped cheeses. For example, St Maure is cylindrical, while Selles-sur-Cher is flat and round.

Other local specialties include *rillettes* and *rillons*, which are traditionally made from pork. Rillons are cubes of fat pork; *rillettes* are fat pork that has been shredded and are like potted meat. Vouvray is well known for its *Andoui-llettes*, a tripe sausage, *Geline de Touraine* is a recently reintroduced local species of chicken whose quality matches that of the famous *poulet de Bresse*.

An array of French cheeses. Image ©
Tomo Jesenicnik/Dreamstime.com

Where to stay and eat in Touraine

L'Aubinière
29, rue Jules-Gautier, St-Ouen-les-Vignes.
Tel: 02 47 30 15 29 (H/R).
Restaurant with rooms; northeast of Amboise.
Closed Sun, Mon, & Wed nights from May–Sept; closed
February. Final lunch order at 1:30PM, final dinner at 9:30PM.

Jean Bardet
Château Belmont, 57, rue Groison, Tours.
Tel: 02 47 41 41 11 (H/R).
Closed Sun night & Mon from Jan 1–Mar 31 & Nov 1–Dec 31.
Restaurant closed Sat lunch and Tues lunch; closed Mon lunch
and Tues night from April 1–Oct 31.

Bon Laboureur
6, rue du Dr-Bretonneau, Chenonceaux.
Tel: 02 47 23 90 02 (H/R).
Comfortable hotel run by the Jeudi family for 104 years; guests
have included writer Henry James. Fine cooking and good list
of Loire wines. Closed Tues lunch (high season); Wed and
Thurs (low season). Restaurant open 8–9AM and 12–1:30PM.

Hotel Diderot
7, rue Diderot, 37500 Chinon.
Tel: 02 47 93 18 87 (H).

Auberge du XII Siècle
1, rue du Château, 37190 Saché.
Tel: 02 47 26 88 77 (R).
Closed Sun night, Mon, and Tues lunch.
Closed 2 weeks in Jan, 1 week in June, Sept, and Nov.

Au Plaisir Gourmand
2, rue Parmentier, 37500 Chinon.
Tel: 02 47 93 47 (R).
Long-established restaurant in the center of Chinon. Closed
Sun night, Mon, and Tues lunch; all of Feb. Final lunch order
at 1:30pm, final dinner at 9pm. Dogs allowed.

Les Années 30
78, rue Voltaire, 37500 Chinon.
Tel: 02 47 93 97 18 (R).

La Promenade
11, rue du Savoureulx, Le Petit Pressigny.
Tel: 02 47 94 93 52 (R).

Where to stay and eat in Anjou and Saumur

Hôtel d'Anjou
1, blvd Foch, 49000 Angers.
Tel: 02 41 21 12 11 (H/R).

Anne d'Anjou
32-33 quai Mayaud, 49400 Saumur.
Tel: 02 41 67 30 30 (H).
Les Ménestrels (part of Anne d'Anjou)
11, rue Raspail, 49400 Saumur.
Tel: 02 41 67 71 10 (R).
Open Mon night–Sat night.

Loire Hôtel
rue du Vieux-Pont, 49400 Saumur.
Tel: 02 41 67 22 42 (H/R).

Hôtel du Mail
8, rue des Ursules, 49000 Angers.
Tel: 02 41 25 05 25 (H).
Closed Sun & public holidays 12–6:30PM.

Le Relais
9, rue de la Gare, 49000 Angers.
Tel: 02 41 88 42 51 (R).

Les Tonnelles
12, rue du Chevalier-Buhard, 49028 Behuard.
Tel: 02 41 72 21 50 (R).
Closed Sun night, Mon, & Wed night (off-season); Dec 20–Feb 20.

Where to stay and eat in Nantes

Domaine d'Orvault
Chemin des Marais-du-Cens, 44700 Orvault.
Tel: 02 40 76 84 02 (H/R).

La Bonne Auberge
1, rue Olivier de Clisson, 44190 Clisson.
Tel: 02 40 54 01 90 (R).
Closed Sun night, Mon, & Tues lunch.

Villa Mon Rêve
44115 Basse Goulaine.
Tel: 02 40 03 55 50 (R).
Open daily 12:15–2PM & 7:30–9:30PM.

Calvados
and Cider

CALVADOS AND CIDER

While there is nothing in the way of vineyards around the A13 motorway, which leads from the Channel ports of Caen, Le Havre, and Dieppe to Paris, there are the apple orchards of Normandy, which produce the only non-grape spirit of France to have its own *appellation contrôlée*: Calvados.

Like the finest vineyard regions, the area is split into a number of smaller areas, each producing its own style of spirit. In all there are some eleven different regional appellations of Calvados, but the finest comes from the Pays d'Auge, which lies on both sides of the river Touques. This river flows into the Channel at Deauville. The center of the region is Pont l'Evêque.

The Pays d'Auge Calvados is double distilled from cider in copper "pot" stills in exactly the same way Cognac is made from wine. The resultant spirit, which is approximately 70 percent pure alcohol, has a distinct roughness, which is smoothed out by many years' aging in oak casks. The strength is then reduced before bottling and sale.

A number of the cellars and distilleries are open to the public and for those with more time on their hands, there is the *Route du Cidre* circuit. This is best joined by taking the D49 south from the Cabourg exit on the A13, or at Cambremer, which is off the D50, west of Lisieux. Farms on the circuit have a Cru de Cambremer sign.

Pommeau is the local aperitif and is a blend of Calvados and apple juice and aged for at least 18 months in barrels.

Norman food

The food in Normandy is famously rich, traditionally based on cream and butter plentifully available from the region's rich pastures. Apples and Calvados also have an important place. Apples are used not only in desserts, especially apple tarts with a thin, delicate base, but also in chicken, game, and pork dishes. Calvados is used in sauces—*sole normande*, for instance, has a cream and Calvados

CALVADOS

Domaine Coeur de Lion
route Nationale 177,
Pont l'Evêque/Trouville,
14130 Coudray-Rabut.
Tel: 02 31 64 30 05.
Email: coudray@
normandnet.fr
Fax: 02 31 64 35 62.
www.coeur-de-lion.com/
francais
TF and free guided tour.
Open Mon–Sat 9AM–12PM
and 2–6PM. AN for Sun and
holidays. WS. Groups, school
groups welcome.

SA Calvados Boulard
Moulin de la Foulonnerie
route de Manerbe,
14130 Coquainvilliers.
Tel: 02 31 48 24 00.
Email: info@
calvados-boulard.com
Fax: 02 31 62 21 22.
www.calvados-boulard.com
Guided tours. WS. E, D, G.

Roger Groult, Clos de la
Hurvanière
14290 St-Cyr-du-Ronceray.
Tel: 02 31 63 71 53.
Email: calvados.roger.groult@
wanadoo.fr
Fax: 02 31 63 90 77.
www.calvados-roger-groult.com
Open Mon–Fri 9AM–12PM
and 1–4PM; AN for weekends
and holidays. WS.

sauce. It is also used as a digestif in the middle of the meal. A *trou normande* (a shot of Calvados) settles the stomach and clears a space for the courses still to come.

Fish is plentiful, especially along the coast. Dieppe is known for a fish casserole called *marmite dieppoise*, which can include sole, turbot, mussels, and Coquilles St Jacques. Caen is famous for its tripe—*à la mode de Caen*. This is cooked slowly with onions, leeks, calf trotters, and cider or Calvados. The region is also famous for its cows'-milk cheeses. Although Camembert is the best known, there are also Livarot, Pont l'Eveque, and, from near Dieppe, Neufchatel.

Image © Red2000/Dreamstime.com

Where to stay and eat

Hotel la Pommeraie/Le Manoir de Hastings
18, ave Côte de Nacre, 14970 Bénouville.
Tel: 02 31 44 62 43.

Le Dauphin
14130 Breuil-en-Auge.
Tel: 02 31 65 08 11.
Open 12–2PM and 7:15–9PM. Closed Mon and Sun night,
Nov 15–Dec 1, and mid-Feb.

La Bourride
15-17, rue du Vaugueux, 14000 Caen.
Tel: 02 31 93 50 76 (R).
Closes at 10PM.

Normandy Barrière
38, rue Jean-Mermoz, 14800 Deauville.
Tel: 02 31 98 66 22 (H/R).
Restaurant open 7–10AM, 12–2PM, and 7:30–10PM.

Royal Barrière
blvd Eugenie-Cornuché, 14800 Deauville.
Tel: 02 31 98 66 33 (H/R).

La Ferme Saint Siméon, Hôtel Relais & Châteaux
rue Adolphe Marais, 14600 Honfleur.
Tel: 02 31 81 78 00.
Closed Mon and Tues lunch, except holidays. Open all year.

Restaurant Au Caneton
32, rue Grande 14290 Orbec.
Tel: 02 31 32 73 32 (R).

Hostellerie du Moulin Fouret
27300 St-Aubin-le-Vertueux.
Tel: 02 32 43 19 95 (H/R).
Lunch ends at 2PM, dinner at 9PM. Closed Sun night and Mon,
except July–Aug and public holidays; also closed Tues lunch
Oct 1–Mar 31.

Websites

Below are a small selection of the vast numbers of sites about France and visiting the country.

www.autoroutes.fr
Gives details of journeys, timing, and tolls payable on French highways.

www.bienvenueauchateau.com
Bed & breakfast addresses in châteaux and manor houses in the west of France.

www.bison-fute.equipement.gouv.fr
French government site that gives advice on traffic conditions, road works, and weather forecasts.

www.thechaingang.co.uk
The Chain Gang organizes cycling holidays in France, including a number in wine regions such as Bordeaux, Burgundy, Loire, and Provence.

www.doucefrance.com/restaurants
Lists the 600 best restaurants in France by region.

www.franceafloat.com
Details of holidays on French canals, which often pass through wine regions.

www.franceguide.com
Maison de la France: the official Tourist Office website for France.

www.francetourism.com
The official website of the French Tourist Office.

www.french-at-a-touch.com
Gives a listing of a wide range of subjects: restaurants, hotels, wine producers, food, etc. Listings by region.

www.likhom.com/chambres_hotes.asp
List of chambres d'hôtes (bed & breakfast) with character throughout France. A number of owners of châteaux and other grand houses now offer bed & breakfasts, sometimes with the option of an evening meal. Chambre d'hôte is often an attractive alternative to staying in a hotel.

www.provenceweb.fr
Detailed tourist guide to Provence includes a section on the wines.

www.france-voyage.com
Details on travelling around France.

www.frenchwinesfood.com
Official government site for French wines and food.

www.Tourisme-en-Provence.com
Site that concentrates on the Vaucluse.

www.viamichelin.com
Michelin site that includes detailed route planning both in France and outside.

www.pagesjaunes.fr
Free search on the French telephone directory, both white and yellow pages.

www.sncf.com
French railways, possible to book and check train times online.

www.tourist-office.org
Lists all tourist offices and Syndicats d'Initiative in France along with their contact details.

Wine websites
These are in addition to those already listed earlier in the guide.

BORDEAUX

www.bordeaux-wine-office.com
Official site for the Bordeaux wine region.

www.lalande-pomerol.com
Syndicate of Lalande de Pomerol—includes lists of producers as well as maps to show where they are.

LANGUEDOC

www.aoc-corbieres.com
Site of the Syndicat de l'AOC Corbières.

www.languedoc-wines.com
Site for the Languedoc appellations. Gives details of wines, as well as addresses for where to find accommodation and something to eat.

LOIRE

www.ot-pouillysurloire.fr
Tourist office site includes section on the vineyards and producers from Pouilly-sur-Loire.

RHÔNE

www.vins-cotes-luberon.com
Site for the Côtes de Luberon, includes list of producers' addresses.

www.cotes-ventoux.com
Official site for the Ventoux appellation.

GRAPE VARIETIES

Whites

Chardonnay

Burgundian grape now planted all over the world for its soft, round fruit. Styles range from citric unoaked wines to tropical fruit, high alcohol, and toasty, vanilla oak.

NAMES/REGIONS: Chablis, Meursault, Montrachet, Limoux

FLAVOR HINTS: apple, melon, exotic fruit, butter, toast

Chenin Blanc

Native of the Loire, Chenin can produce some of the greatest and most varied whites in the world, but also some of the worst. Great vintages are almost immortal.

NAMES/REGIONS: Coteaux du Layon, Saumur, Vouvray

FLAVOR HINTS: lemon, quince, apricots, honey, minerals

Gewürztraminer

Alsace variety with a very distinctive intense floral perfume.

NAMES/REGIONS: Alsace

FLAVOR HINTS: intense floral and blossom aromas

Muscat

More of a family of grapes; one of the oldest varieties. Muscat à Petits Grains is the best quality. Sometimes vinified dry, but is often sweet and frequently fortified. One of the very few wines that actually can taste of grapes.

NAMES/REGIONS: Alsace, Muscat Beaumes de Venise, Muscat de Rivesaltes

FLAVOR HINTS: floral, grape, tangerine, orange

Pinot Gris

One grape variety but with two contrasting styles: Italian Pinot Grigio is lemony, easy-drinking and invariably dry, while Pinot Gris (often from Alsace) is spicy, weightier, generally more complex and varies from dry to markedly sweet.

REGIONS: Alsace, Italy

FLAVOR HINTS: honey, spice

Sauvignon Blanc

Grassy, aromatic grape has become extremely popular as wine drinkers look for an alternative to Chardonnay. Originally from Bordeaux, the classic style developed in the cooler climate of the Loire. Important role with Sémillon in Graves and Sauternes. Unripe versions can be aggressively vegetal.

REGIONS: Sancerre, Pouilly, Touraine, Bordeaux, Languedoc (*vin de pays*)

FLAVOR HINTS: grassy, gooseberry, asparagus, grapefruit

Sémillon

A crucial ingredient in white Graves and Sauternes.

NAMES/REGIONS: Barsac, Graves, Sauternes, and Bergerac

FLAVOR HINTS: honey

Viognier

Viognier used to be confined to Condrieu in the northern Rhône. Then it was planted in the Midi with mixed success. Usually dry, it needs to be opulent without being blowsy.

NAMES/REGIONS: Condrieu, Château Grillet, Vin de Pays d'Oc

FLAVOR HINTS: apricot, peach

Reds

Cabernet Franc

With Sauvignon Blanc, this is Cabernet Sauvignon's parent. Franc ripens earlier than its offspring. It has a leading role in Loire but in its native Bordeaux has a secondary role to Cabernet Sauvignon and Merlot.

NAMES/REGIONS: Bourgueil, Chinon, Saumur-Champigny

FLAVOR HINTS: blackberry, coal tar, raspberry, green pepper

Cabernet Sauvignon

Produces powerfully structured wines. Made its reputation in the Médoc and this, along with the fact that it is easy to grow, means it has been planted all over the world.

NAMES/REGIONS: Haut-Médoc, Pauillac

FLAVOR HINTS: Blackcurrant, cedar, and cigar boxes in older wines

Gamay

The grape of easy-drinking Beaujolais; often ready to be drunk as soon as it is bottled. Never a heavyweight.

NAMES/REGIONS: Beaujolais, Touraine Gamay

FLAVOR HINTS: brambly fruit, spice, bubble gum, and banana (not a positive)

Grenache

From the Mediterranean; the world's most planted red variety, especially in the south of France and Spain. Grenache has a wide range of flavors and tends to be high in alcohol. Often blended with other varieties.

NAMES/REGIONS: Banyuls, Châteauneuf-du-Pape

FLAVOR HINTS: tobacco, black cherry, strawberry, leather, coffee

Merlot

Provides softness to leaner, more structured Cabernet Sauvignon, especially on the right bank of Bordeaux. Pure Merlot is popular but it can be cloying.

NAMES/REGIONS: Pomerol, St-Émilion

FLAVOR HINTS: plum, damson, fig, soft tannin

Pinot Noir

Difficult to grow Burgundian grape, making it the "holy grail" for many winemakers. Top Pinot Noir has wonderful perfume and silky texture. Needs a cool climate.

NAMES/REGIONS: Vosne-Romanée, Pommard, Volnay

FLAVOR HINTS: strawberry, raspberry, undergrowth, and gamey with age

BIBLIOGRAPHY

Interlink Guidebooks to France

Café Life Paris: A Guide to the Cafés and Bars of the City of Light by
　　Christine and Dennis Graf; photography by Juliana Spear
France (Charming Small Hotel Guides) edited by Fiona
　　Duncan and Leonie Glass
Paris (Charming Small Hotel Guides) edited by Fiona Duncan
　　and Leonie Glass
Paris by Bistro by Christine Graf; photography by Dennis Graf
Paris by Metro: An Underground History by Arnold Delaney
Paris for Families by Larry Lain
Romantic Paris by Thirza Vallois; photography by Juliana Spear
A Traveller's History of France by Robert Cole
A Traveller's History of Paris by Robert Cole
*Walking in France: Exploring France's Greatest Towns and Finest Landscapes on
　　Foot* by Gillian and John Souter.

Maps and Guides

A good, detailed, up-to-date map covering the whole of France
is essential. The French have a considerable program of road
building and bypasses, so maps can soon be badly out of date.
The annual Michelin *Atlas Routier et Touristique* is highly
recommended and widely available.

Guide Michelin—The annual red Michelin Guide is an institution.
The first guide appeared in 1900. It covers hotels and
restaurants and includes maps for the larger towns. Top
restaurants are awarded stars from one to three.

Michelin Green Guides—These regional guides cover the geography
and history of the French regions, giving details of places of
interest to visit. Many have now been translated into English.

Gault Millau Annual Restaurant and Hotel Guide—This guide gives much
more of a commentary on its recommendations than the red
Michelin Guide, which is decidedly cryptic.

Books on Wine

Brook, Stephen. *Bordeau: Médoc & Graves*. London: Mitchell
Beazley Classic Wine Library, 2006.
Detailed study of the Médoc and Graves. This is the first of
two volumes on Bordeaux by Brook and replaces *The Wines of
Bordeaux*, a classic by David Peppercorn MW. Second
volume will cover the Right Bank and the sweet wines of
Bordeaux.

Clarke, Oz. *Bordeaux—The Wines, The Vineyards, The Winemakers*.
London: Websters/Time Warner Books.
One of the UK's most charismatic and outspoken wine
writers takes a fresh look at Bordeaux.

Coates, Clive, MW. *The Wines of Bordeaux: Vintages and Tasting Notes,
1952–2003*. London: Weidenfeld and Nicolson, 2004;
Berkeley: Univ. of California Press, 2004.
Coates covers the fine wines of Bordeaux in a much more
restrained style than Robert Parker.

Duijker, Hubert, and Michael Broadbent, MW. *The Bordeaux Atlas
and Encyclopedia of Châteaux*. London: Ebury Press, 1997.
Some 2,000 properties in Bordeaux are profiled.

Le Guide Hachette des vins. Paris: Hachette, 2007.
Well-respected guide to French producers based on a very
large annual tasting.

Friedrich, Jacqueline. *A Wine & Food Guide to the Loire*. London:
Mitchell Beazley, 1997; New York: Owl Books, 1998.
This is the best book on the Loire in English. However,
since it was published in 1997, it has become somewhat dated.

George, Rosemary, MW. *The Wines of the South of France: From Banyuls to
St. Raphael*. London: Mitchell Beazley Classic Wine Library,
2003.
Provides in-depth coverage of France's most dynamic wine
regions.

Jefford, Andrew. *The New France: A Complete Guide to Contemporary
French Wine*. London: Mitchell Beazley, 2002.
A well-written guide to who is making the best and most
interesting wine in France; includes pointers on what to
avoid. One of the best recently published books on French wine.

Johnson, Hugh. *Pocket Wine Book 2007*. London: Mitchell Beazley, 2006.
    The first of the annual pocket guides, it remains indispensable for quick reference.

Johnson, Hugh, and Jancis Robinson, MW. *The World Atlas of Wine*. 5th ed. London: Mitchell Beazley, 2001.
    This classic is now in its fifth edition and Robinson is now co-author with Johnson. First published in 1971, it showed the importance of place in the taste of a wine. Detailed maps of the major wine regions are particularly helpful.

Livingstone–Learmonth, John. *The Wines of the Northern Rhône*. Berkeley, Los Angeles: University of California Press, 2005.
    Passionate and detailed study on the Northern Rhône by the world's leading Rhône expert.

Peppercorn, David, MW. *Wines of Bordeaux*. London: Mitchell Beazley, 2004.
    This is a portable guide to Bordeaux, unlike the heavyweight editions from Coates and Parker.

Stevenson, Tom. *Christie's World Encyclopedia of Champagne and Sparkling Wine*. 2nd ed. London: Absolute Press, 2003.
    Detailed study of sparkling wines around the world, with extensive section on Champagne.

Strang, Paul. *Languedoc-Roussillon: The Wines and Winemakers*. London: Mitchell Beazley, 2002.

Sutcliffe, Serena, MW. *Wines of Burgundy*. London: Mitchell Beazley, 2005.
    Portable guide to Burgundy.

INDEX

Y